D1478464

Discard

PLATO AND THE
POST-SOCRATIC DIALOGUE

Plato's late dialogues have often been neglected because they lack the literary charm of his earlier masterpieces. Charles H. Kahn proposes a unified view of these diverse and difficult works, from the *Parmenides* and *Theaetetus* to the *Sophist* and *Timaeus*, showing how they gradually develop the framework for Plato's late metaphysics and cosmology. The *Parmenides*, with its attack on the theory of Forms and its baffling series of antinomies, has generally been treated apart from the rest of Plato's late work. Kahn shows that this perplexing dialogue is the curtain-raiser on Plato's last metaphysical enterprise: the step-by-step construction of a wider theory of Being that provides the background for the creation story of the *Timaeus*. This rich study, the natural successor to Kahn's earlier *Plato and the Socratic Dialogue*, will interest a wide range of readers in ancient philosophy and science.

CHARLES H. KAHN is Professor Emeritus of Philosophy in the University of Pennsylvania. His publications include *Anaximander and the Origins of Greek Cosmology* (3rd edn., 1994); *The Art and Thought of Heraclitus: A New Arrangement and Translation of the Fragments with Literary and Philosophical Commentary* (1979); *Plato and the Socratic Dialogue: The Philosophical Use of a Literary Form* (1997); *Pythagoras and the Pythagoreans: A Brief History* (2001).

PLATO AND THE POST-SOCRATIC DIALOGUE

The Return to the Philosophy of Nature

CHARLES H. KAHN

CAMBRIDGE
UNIVERSITY PRESS

CAMBRIDGE
UNIVERSITY PRESS

University Printing House, Cambridge CB2 8BS, United Kingdom

Cambridge University Press is part of the University of Cambridge.

It furthers the University's mission by disseminating knowledge in the pursuit of
education, learning and research at the highest international levels of excellence.

www.cambridge.org
Information on this title: www.cambridge.org/9781107576421

© Charles H. Kahn 2013

First published 2013
First paperback edition 2015

A catalogue record for this publication is available from the British Library

Library of Congress Cataloguing in Publication data
Kahn, Charles H.
Plato and the post-Socratic dialogue : the return to the philosophy of nature / Charles H. Kahn.
pages cm
ISBN 978-1-107-03145-6 (hardback)
1. Plato. I. Title.
B395.K235 2013
184–dc23
2013014286

ISBN 978-1-107-03145-6 Hardback
ISBN 978-1-107-57642-1 Paperback

For Edna always

Contents

Preface

I offer here a study of six late Platonic dialogues, from the *Parmenides* to the *Timaeus*. This is a sequel to *Plato and the Socratic Dialogue* (Cambridge University Press, 1998), in which I discussed Plato's earlier work, from the *Apology* to the *Phaedrus*. The current study represents an entirely new project. Although the author of these later dialogues is the same, the material is very different in both form and subject matter. Whereas Plato's earlier writing represents the finest literary achievement of ancient prose, with dramas such as the *Symposium* and the *Phaedo* designed to compete with the tragedies of Sophocles and Euripides, these later dialogues were scarcely designed for such artistic success. Instead of the brilliant conversational style of Plato's earlier work, the writing here is often difficult to the point of obscurity, and the reasoning more intricate, as if these dialogues were addressed to a less literary, more strictly professional audience. The philosophical content is even more surprising. There is nothing in Plato's earlier work to prepare us for his attack on the doctrine of Forms in the *Parmenides*, for the empiricist bias of the *Theaetetus*, or for the intricate conceptual analysis of the *Sophist*.

As a result, the interpreter of Plato's later work faces an entirely different task. To begin with, there are striking changes in literary form. We must take account of the replacement of Socrates as principal speaker, first by Parmenides, then by a visitor from Elea, and finally by the statesman-scientist Timaeus from another western Greek city. (In the *Laws* Plato himself will make a masked appearance in the person of an anonymous Stranger from Athens.) Even the Socrates who does return as chief speaker in the *Theaetetus* and *Philebus* is a less dramatic figure, less directly involved in the social life and conflicts of the Athenian *polis*.

To this eclipse of Socrates as a personality corresponds a new, more problematic treatment of the theory of Forms, the central philosophical doctrine of the preceding dialogues. We begin with the radical critique of this doctrine in the *Parmenides* (echoed by a reminder of similar problems in the *Philebus*), then a systematic avoidance of all reference to this theory in the *Theaetetus*, followed by its partial reappearance in the *Sophist* and *Philebus*, with a final, full-scale reformulation in the *Timaeus*. It will be our task to identify the underlying unity of Plato's intellectual project within the bewildering diversity of these six dialogues.

Formally considered, the dialogues discussed here, from the *Parmenides* to the *Timaeus*, are quite independent of one another (except for dramatic continuity between the *Sophist* and the *Statesman*); and they can be interpreted individually, without reference to the series as a whole. I claim, however, that as the work of a single philosopher, in the last decades of his long life, these dialogues are best seen as moments in a single project: namely, the coming to terms with natural philosophy on the basis of a system of thought (the Theory of Ideas) that had been worked out in earlier dialogues, with a different set of problems in view.

The classical theory was designed as a framework for Plato's original project: to develop the moral and intellectual legacy of Socrates in the context of Athenian political life. Thus. Plato's earlier work was addressed to a wider audience, the reading public of Greece, conceived as potential citizens in a reformed society. The dialogues to be considered here have a very different goal in view: to reshape the theoretical basis of Platonic philosophy in order to include the study of the natural world.

In the early tradition that stretches from Thales to Democritus, Greek philosophy had been primarily a philosophy of nature. Plato adopted the person of Socrates as his symbol for a deliberate turning away from this philosophical tradition and towards an investigation of the conditions for a good human life and a just society. Natural philosophy became, in this sense, pre-Socratic. What we have in these late dialogues is a new Platonic philosophy that can be seen as deliberately post-Socratic – an investigation in which Plato systematically returns to problems that were of primary concern for Socrates' predecessors: the nature of knowledge and the nature of the physical world. The symbol for this return is the replacement of Socrates by Parmenides as chief speaker, and by his sequel, the Stranger from Elea. Plato's return, then, is to a philosophical tradition that is independent of Socrates and directed towards the physical sciences, but founded now on the metaphysics of unchanging Being introduced by Parmenides. Thus, the project of these later dialogues is to reclaim the study of nature within the framework of a Platonic-Eleatic philosophy of intelligible Form.

Since the present work is designed as a sequel to *Plato and the Socratic Dialogue*, it may be appropriate to recall my principal claims in the earlier volume. One aim of that book was to oppose the then prevailing view of Plato's philosophical development before the *Republic* as divided into two distinct sections, one typically Socratic and the later, more fully Platonic, with some tension between the two. In reaction against this two-stage approach I denied the existence of any distinctively Socratic period in Plato's philosophy. I argued instead for a more unitarian view of these early-middle dialogues, from the *Apology* to the *Republic*. I introduced the hypothesis of deliberate withholding on Plato's part, specifically his withholding any full statement of the metaphysical notions that I found implicit in the dialogues of definition. I suggested that Plato will have had much of his theory of Forms in mind when, in dialogues such as the *Euthyphro* and *Meno*, he introduced the notion of essence as object of definition.

Today I would formulate my view more cautiously, to avoid the impression that Plato never changed his mind, or that he knew where he was going from the start. I would now rely less on the notion of prolepsis as suggesting such a plan in advance, for which there is no direct evidence. Although I still believe that we can detect proleptic intentions in many of the earlier dialogues (for example, in the *Lysis* and *Euthydemus*), I do not regard this as a thesis to be defended here. Instead, limiting my claims to what is explicit in the text, I would clarify my position by recognizing three stages in the sequence of dialogues that stretches from the *Apology* to the *Republic* and *Phaedrus*:

(1) the initial (pre-metaphysical) stage of Plato's writing, represented by the *Apology*, *Crito* and *Gorgias* (as well as by the *Ion* and *Hippias Minor*);
(2) the implicit theory of essences in the dialogues of definition (*Laches, Charmides, Euthyphro, Meno*);
(3) the explicit theory of Forms in the *Cratylus, Symposium, Phaedo, Republic* and *Phaedrus*.

(This division leaves out several dialogues that do not directly involve a search for definition, notably the *Protagoras, Lysis* and *Euthydemus*. I assume that these were written at roughly the same time as the dialogues listed under stage 2, and before the dialogues listed under stage 3.)

In my view, then, the dialogues of stage 1 represent the so-called Socratic period in Plato's writing, when he was fiercely loyal to the Socratic moral position but had not yet – even in the *Gorgias* – developed a metaphysical basis for this position. On the other hand, the beginnings of such a basis make their appearance in the conception of essences presented in dialogues such as the *Euthyphro* and *Meno*. Hence, without making any assumptions about Plato's unspoken intentions, we can recognize a clear progression from the Socratic moral position, as expressed in the *Gorgias*, to the search for a theoretical basis for this position, which we find in the dialogues of stage 2: namely, the notion of essences corresponding to the virtues. (It is no accident that, in all three stages, the argument appeals to what I call the normative trio – the just, the noble (*kalon*), and the good – as the conceptual basis for Socrates' pursuit of *aretē*.)

After the dialogues of definition we can recognize a further progression from an implicit ontology of essences to the explicit metaphysics of the Forms, beginning with the Beautiful (*kalon*) in the *Symposium* and culminating in the Good of the *Republic*. Hence the view which I previously described as unitarian can perhaps be more accurately formulated as the progressive working out of a theoretical basis for what was at first an essentially practical conception: the ideal of virtue modeled on the figure of Socrates.

This theoretical basis was provided by the metaphysics of Forms, as presented in the great "middle" dialogues (*Symposium, Phaedo* and *Republic*) and invoked also in the *Cratylus* and *Phaedrus*. The underlying ethical motivation for this theory is revealed in the central role of the normative trio – the Just, the Beautiful and the Good – even before the Good itself is identified as the supreme concept in the *Republic*. In the *Phaedo* the theory was expanded to include mathematical Forms (beginning with the Equal); and these will remain fundamental in all future versions of the doctrine. The *Cratylus* flirts with an extension to artifacts such as the spindle; and so we have the Form of Bed in *Republic* X. But this is an extension about which Plato may have had second thoughts, since such artifacts tend to disappear from later versions of the theory.

What is conspicuous by its absence in these earlier dialogues is any application of the theory of Forms to the realm of nature and to natural kinds. We recall that Socrates introduces this theory in the *Phaedo* as an alternative to – even an escape from – the natural philosophy pursued by his predecessors. But the application of the theory to such concepts as human being, fire or water remains a serious problem, as Parmenides will point out (*Parm.* 130c). A central theme of my present study will be Plato's systematic clarification and extension of the concept of Form in order to apply it to the domains of physics and biology, that is, to the territory explored by his predecessors the Presocratics.

From the *Parmenides* on, I suggest, Plato is preparing the basis for this long-postponed reunion with *peri phuseōs historia*. As a result, mathematics will begin to play a new role. Instead of leading upwards to the Forms and away from the visible world (as it is intended to do in the educational scheme of the *Republic*), geometry and number will now be directed downwards, to project a formal structure onto the realm of change, and thus to reveal a stable pattern underlying the flux of coming-to-be and passing-away. This new role for mathematics will involve some recognition of a middle ground between Being and Becoming, a revision of the sharp dualism between intelligible and sensible realms that is characteristic of the *Phaedo* and *Republic*. It is this ontological space between Forms and sensible particulars that will be opened up by the recognition of "beings that have come-to-be" in the *Philebus*, and by the mathematical structures imposed upon the Receptacle in the *Timaeus*. What we have, in effect, in Plato's later theory is a new notion of immanent form, conceived in mathematical terms. It is this gradual (and partial) emergence of a new theory of nature and change within the framework provided by a revised metaphysics of Form that will be the theme of this book.

Of course, Plato in his later years had not lost interest in issues of ethics and politics. That interest is reflected even in the titles of the *Sophist* and the *Statesman*; and the *Philebus* is primarily devoted to the place of pleasure in the good life. The long and unfinished project of the *Laws* testifies that Plato was to the end preoccupied with the philosophical reconstruction of life in the polis. These practical concerns are reflected in the introductory conversation of the *Timaeus*, with its echo of the *Republic*, as well as in the political myth that follows in the *Critias*. Instead of promising a third volume to deal with these topics, I offer here an Epilogue to take some account of Plato's concern with moral and political philosophy in his latest period.

In conclusion, let me record my sincere thanks to David Sedley, Verity Harte, and Leslie Brown for valuable comments on different parts of my text, and in particular to Leslie Brown for allowing me to make use of her excellent (and as yet unpublished) translation of the *Sophist*.

CHARLES H. KAHN

Note on Chronology

I take for granted the chronological division of the dialogues into three stylistically distinct groups, established in the nineteenth century by the studies of Campbell and Ritter. According to this division, the *Cratylus*, *Symposium* and *Phaedo* belong to the earliest Group 1 (together with the *Apology*, *Crito*, *Gorgias*, *Meno* and some nine other dialogues). Group 2 consists of the *Republic*, *Phaedrus*, *Parmenides*, and *Theaetetus*. The latest Group 3 includes the *Sophist-Statesman*, *Philebus*, *Timaeus*, and *Laws*. Although this chronological sequence is clearly marked by stylistic changes, it does not correspond to important stages of philosophical content. On the contrary, the so-called middle group of dialogues (*Symposium-Phaedo-Republic*), which is characterized by the classical doctrine of Forms, is divided between stylistic Groups 1 and 2; whereas the two last dialogues of Group 2 (*Parmenides* and *Theaetetus*) mark a sharp break with this classical doctrine. A new, more complex conception of Form will gradually emerge in the dialogues of Group 3, culminating in the *Timaeus*; while, on the other hand, a different kind of metaphysical restraint will later characterize the *Laws*. Although stylometry is our best guide for the chronological ordering of the dialogues, it tells us very little about the changes in philosophical content. For there is no simple story to be told of Plato's philosophical development corresponding to the chronological ordering of the dialogues.

For fuller discussion of the stylistic evidence, see Kahn (2002a) 93–127.

CHAPTER I

The Parmenides

The dialogue *Parmenides* has some claim to be the most problematic item in the Platonic corpus. We have from the beginning a radical change in dramatic framework and in the portrayal of Socrates. In contrast to his master role as exponent of fundamental doctrine in the *Phaedo* and *Republic*, Socrates appears here as a promising young man with a sketchy theory of Forms – a theory that will be exposed to withering criticism at the hands of Parmenides. The name of Parmenides had been barely mentioned in any previous dialogue; and his historical role belongs in fact to an earlier generation.[1]

The visit of Parmenides and Zeno to Athens, as represented in this dialogue, is clearly an invention of Plato, who is prepared here to ignore chronological possibilities. He has chosen Parmenides as the only philosopher deemed worthy to refute Socrates in dialectical exchange, but who, at the same time, will guarantee a fundamental commitment to a stable ontology. And such a commitment will be expressly reasserted here.

Nevertheless, the first part of the dialogue presents the singular spectacle of Plato, in the person of Parmenides, formulating a set of penetrating objections to his favorite theory, without any hint of how these objections are to be answered. The second, much longer part of the dialogue presents an object that is equally perplexing: a set of eight or nine deductions from a single hypothesis and its denial, with formally contradictory conclusions. Just as Part One leaves the reader without any response to the objections, so Part Two leaves us without any sign of how these apparent contradictions are to be resolved. The relation between the two parts of the dialogue is also mysterious. The deductions of Part Two are presented as a training exercise

---

[1] Contrast the isolated poetic quotation from Parmenides in *Symposium* 178b, with an echo at 195c. The exact dates of Parmenides are unknown, but his traditional "acme" (504–501 BC) is at least credible. Parmenides' influence is strongly marked on the following generation, represented by Anaxagoras and Empedocles in the middle of the fifth century. We note that in the *Phaedo* Socrates was not reported to have been in personal contact even with Anaxagoras, much less with Parmenides.

designed to prepare a philosopher like the Young Socrates to deal with
the criticisms formulated in Part One. But it is not immediately clear how
the arguments of Part Two are intended to bear on the problems raised in
Part One.

The absence here of any direct answer to the criticisms of Part One has
led some scholars to conclude that Plato was ready to abandon the theory of
Forms, or that he was uncertain how to proceed. (A "record of honest
perplexity" was Vlastos' diagnosis.)[2] But the text itself points in a more
positive direction. Parmenides, who formulates the objections, never suggests that the theory should be given up. On the contrary, if the theory is
reduced to its central thesis, the distinction between the changing objects of
sense perception and stable forms "that one can best grasp in *logos*,"
Parmenides indicates that giving up such forms would be equivalent to
giving up on philosophy itself. (Hence the pressing question at 135c5: "What
will you do about philosophy?") Without permanent, self-identical forms,
Parmenides says to Socrates, "you will have nowhere to turn your thought
to, . . . and you will utterly destroy the power of rational discourse (*dialegesthai*)."[3] What Socrates needs, according to Parmenides, is not so much a
different theory but more philosophical training, so that he will be able to
confront the problems raised in the objections. The second part of the
dialogue offers to provide the requisite training.

Part Two of the *Parmenides* is notoriously enigmatic. I suggest, however,
that the arguments of this Part will seem less bewildering if we consider
them not in isolation but in the larger context provided by the group of late
dialogues studied here, beginning with the *Theaetetus* and *Sophist* and
continuing with *Philebus* and *Timaeus*. Thus, I propose to regard the
Parmenides as a philosophical introduction to Plato's later work. Between
the *Theaetetus* and the *Sophist* there is a definite mark of literary continuity,
and both dialogues refer back to the fictional meeting between Socrates and
Parmenides that takes place only in the *Parmenides*.[4] Thus, there is a sense
in which the *Theaetetus* and *Sophist* are both presented as a sequel to the
Parmenides. The *Philebus* is linked to the *Parmenides* in a different way, by
allusion to several specific arguments, including an accurate summary of
Parmenides' objections to participation (*Philebus* 15b; cf. *Parm.* 131a–e).
Substantial portions of both the *Sophist* and *Philebus* can thus be seen as

---

[2] Vlastos (1954) 254.
[3] For the broad notion of "dialectic" here as the general method of rational inquiry, see *Phaedrus* 266b,
echoed at *Philebus* 16b5–c3. The basic contrast between the objects of sense perception and those of
λόγος is introduced at *Parmenides* 130a1 and repeated at 135e1–3.
[4] *Theaetetus* 183e7–184a1; *Sophist* 217c5–6.

responses to, or developments of, problems explored in the *Parmenides*. And the same will turn out to be true for the theories of flux and Receptacle in the *Timaeus*.

I propose, then, to see the *Parmenides* as the first, provocative step in Plato's enterprise of revising and expanding the doctrine of Forms in his later dialogues. This project will require him to clarify or correct some of the references to Forms in the *Phaedo* and *Republic*, passages that can lead to inconsistency or misunderstanding. And, it will turn out, there is above all a need to develop the theory to include an account of the natural world – an account that has been systematically neglected in earlier expositions, which focused on the moral and mathematical Forms. (The final argument of the *Phaedo* can be seen as a brief and unsuccessful attempt to extend the theory to notions like fire and fever.) Part One of the *Parmenides* has the function of raising difficulties and calling for clarification. Part Two responds with a constructive set of arguments, opening up new perspectives in preparation for a richer, more comprehensive theory. But the eight deductions by themselves raise more problems than they solve. For the development of a positive theory we must look to later dialogues, and above all to the *Sophist*, *Philebus* and *Timaeus*.

Since the arguments of the *Parmenides* raise many baffling problems, both for an analysis of the arguments and for the substantive interpretation of Plato's theory, I preface to each Part a summary of the problems raised and my proposed solutions. (For the summary of Part Two, see my comments below, pp. 18–21.) These summaries are designed to make it possible for a reader to pass on directly to the interpretation of the *Theaetetus* and the other dialogues, with the option of returning later to confront the nitty-gritty details of the *Parmenides*.

1.1 Part One: the six *aporias*

Socrates responds to Zeno's paradoxes by claiming that contrary properties, such as like and unlike, one and many, apply only to sensible things like sticks and stones and people, but not to the form of Similarity itself or to the One itself (129a). More generally, Socrates would be quite amazed if anyone could show that the Forms themselves (Similarity and Dissimilarity, One and Many, Rest and Motion and all such) "were capable of being mixed together in themselves and being divided apart (*diakrinesthai*)" (129e). What is ruled out, then, according to Socrates' exposition, is not only the Forms possessing contrary properties but also the division of a Form into parts and the combination of several Forms with one another. As every reader of the

Sophist knows, all three of these restrictions will be violated in Plato's later version of the theory.

Now it is not clear that such restrictions are actually implied in the *Phaedo* or *Republic*. But there are certainly passages that lend themselves to be so understood. Thus, the emphasis on the Forms as uniform (*monoeidēs*) and indivisible (*asuntheton, adialuton*) in the *Phaedo* (78c7, d5, 80b2), or on their being *one* rather than many, suggest a conception of Forms as simple and non-composite.[5] And the contrast with particulars as "rolling about" between opposites may seem to imply that Forms do not have contrary attributes (*Rep.* V, 479d). Whether or not such restrictions are intended in the earlier statements of the theory, they are clearly principles that Plato will renounce in his later dialogues. We may reasonably infer that, if these three restrictions are so explicitly emphasized in *Parmenides* 129a–e, it is because this text has been designed to flag them for rejection.[6]

A similar intention is evident in Parmenides' restatement of the theory in his interrogation of Socrates. The term *chōris*, "separately," plays no role in presentations of the theory of Forms in earlier dialogues.[7] In his exposition here Socrates had used the term just once, when he insists that one "distinguishes the Forms themselves by themselves separately" (*diairētai chōris auta kath' hauta* 129d7[8]). It is not clear whether Socrates means "separately from one another" or "separately from their participants," but Parmenides will take him in the latter sense. Furthermore, Parmenides seizes on this term; he uses *chōris* five times in the immediate sequel and several more in the text that follows. The first two occurrences echo and extend Socrates' own remark: not only are the Forms themselves separate; "separate also are the things that participate in them" (130b3). The next three uses of *chōris* are even more insidious: "And do you think there is Similarity itself apart from the similarity that we have? . . . And a Form of Human Being apart from us and from all those who are like us?" (130b4–c2). Socrates does not see the trap; he answers "Yes" to the first question and hesitates in the second case only because he is not sure whether he wants to attribute Forms to natural kinds. In the third case Socrates is disgusted by the examples of hair, mud and filth, and responds only with contempt to the question "Is there a

---

[5] For μονοειδής see also *Symposium* 211b1.

[6] This flagging is echoed in the account of the Dream Theory in the *Theaetetus*, in references to ἀμέριστον, ἀσύνθετον, and μονοειδής at 205c2–d2. See below, p. 84.

[7] Thus in the *Phaedo*, χωρίς is used for the separation of the soul from the body (64c5, 67a1) but not for the distinction between Forms and sensible participants. Contrast the quite different formulation at *Phaedo* 74a11, where the Equal itself is παρὰ ταῦτα πάντα ἕτερόν τι. Being other need not imply being separate.

[8] διαιρῆται χωρὶς αὐτὰ καθ' αὑτά.

separate Form for each of these, different from the things we are in contact with?" (130d1).[9]

By his focus here on the notion of separation, Parmenides opens up the gap between Forms and participants that will prove disastrous in the conception of two distinct worlds, as formulated in the final and "greatest" objection to the Forms (Aporia 6, below). The fatal step is the acceptance of "forms in us" distinct from the Forms themselves. (The phrase in question occurs repeatedly in the *Phaedo*.) Thus, despite the fact that the *Phaedo* explicitly suspends judgment on the nature of the relationship between Forms and participants (100d), it nevertheless implies the existence of immanent forms, as a version of the Form that is present "in us." This opens the way for the fatal separation between the Forms themselves and the forms-in-us that will be exploited in the final *aporia*.

Looking ahead, we may note that Plato will later hesitate to describe phenomenal properties as forms-in-us, distinct from the Forms themselves. As Aporia 6 will show, structures of this kind, immanent in the phenomenal world, tend to point in the direction of Aristotelian forms, and thus to make Plato's Forms superfluous. On the other hand, in later dialogues Plato will recognize a substitute for "forms-in-us" in formal structures corresponding to Aristotelian species-forms, structures described in the *Philebus* as "being-that-has-become" and which in the *Timaeus* will be conceived in the language of mathematics. But such conceptions lie in the future. Before the *Parmenides*, references to "forms in us" are limited to the *Phaedo*. In the *Republic* Plato is more careful to describe phenomenal properties only as images or appearances of Forms – not as "similarity in us" but only as an image or appearance of Similarity. We must wait until the *Timaeus* for this talk of images and imitation to receive a non-metaphorical interpretation. For a coherent ontology of images Plato will need the theory of the Receptacle, in which images are interpreted as mathematical modifications of the Receptacle, determined by their relation to a corresponding Form.

The first Aporia introduces us to the fundamental problem of applying the theory of Forms to the natural world: should we posit Forms for the elements, or for natural kinds like Human Being? But no solution is proposed here, and none will be forthcoming before the *Timaeus*. Aporia 2 shows that the metaphor of participation does not offer a coherent account of the relation between sensible homonyms and the

---

[9] In the following text, the term χωρίς occurs four more times, in different applications: 131a5, b1, b2, and b5.

corresponding Form. Aporia 3 is the notorious Third Man objection, which claims to show that (on any interpretation of the Form-homonym relation) the one-over-many principle that serves to posit a Form for a given homonymous many will generate an infinite regress. The regress follows if a new many can always be produced by adding the original Form to the previous homonymous group, and then applying the one-over-many principle once again. Plato's device for blocking this regress will be to distinguish two ways of *being F* (namely, *being F* for the Form F and *being F* for anything else), so that there is no uniform group of *things that are F* that includes both the Forms and its participants. This distinction (identified by Michael Frede as *is₁* and *is₂*, designated here as "being *per se*" and "being *per aliud*") will be introduced implicitly in Part Two, and explicitly later in the *Sophist*.

Aporia 4 is an attempt to block this regress by a psychological-conceptual interpretation of the Forms as thoughts (*noēmata*) in the soul. This proposal is equivalent to abandoning the theory as an account of objective reality, and it is not regarded by Plato as a serious alternative. By contrast, Aporia 5 results from taking the notion of likeness or imitation quite literally and showing that it implies similarity between Form and participant. But if two similar things must have a form in common, a regress will be generated just as in the Third Man argument, thus producing not a unique Form but an unlimited number of Forms. This regress can be blocked by showing that in a case of imitation the notion of similarity need not be reciprocal. But in any case the objection succeeds in exposing the limitations of the notion of image or imitation as an explanatory concept.

Aporia 6 presents the most serious problem of all, the separation between Forms and sensible phenomena. This separation is presented here by two parallel and independent pairings between knowledge and the objects known: on the one hand, the Form of Knowledge taking other Forms as its object; on the other hand, human knowledge taking sensible phenomena as its object. By insisting on a complete independence between these two pairings, the argument calls attention to the fact that no account has been given of the link connecting Forms to their sensible homonyms.

We consider now the six objections in detail. Our analysis will be two-fold, both formal and substantial. Formally, we try to see in each case how the objection might be blocked. The more important issue, however, is to identify the underlying problem to which Plato is calling our attention.

Aporia 1. *The population problem (130b–d)*

In this case there is no argument to be blocked, but rather a question to be answered: How far does the theory extend? How many kinds of things require Forms? The youthful Socrates is happy to acknowledge Forms for logico-mathematical concepts (one, many, similarity) and for the fundamental moral notions (the just, the noble and the good). The problem is to identify Forms corresponding to the structure and content of the natural world. Socrates hesitates to admit Forms for natural kinds such as human being, fire and water; and he indignantly rejects the suggestion of Forms for hair, mud and filth. (In Socrates' hesitation here there is a reminder of the *Phaedo* 96c and following, where Socrates reports abandoning natural philosophy because of a lack of talent for this subject.) Parmenides responds that Socrates' reluctance to generalize the theory is due to his youth and his unphilosophical fear of ridicule. The Socrates of other dialogues had been less inhibited. Thus, Socrates recognizes Forms for artifacts in the *Cratylus* (the shuttle) and again in *Republic* X (the bed). But only later, in the *Philebus* and *Timaeus*, will Plato undertake to apply his theory to the philosophy of nature.

Aporia 2. *The problem of participation (130e4–131e7)*

The *Phaedo* (100c–102b) made frequent use of the metaphor of participation (*metechein, metalambanein*) but left open how this relation was to be understood. The present objection takes participation literally as *possessing a share* of the Form in question, with the consequence that some aspect of the Form comes to be *present in* the participant. Some commentators assume that this physical interpretation of *metechein* preserves an archaic notion of participation as the sharing of elemental stuff, as illustrated in the fragments of Anaxagoras (e.g. DK 59B.6). On the other hand, the verb *metechein* (and to a lesser extent *metalambanein*) is frequently used metaphorically for possessing any quality or relationship, without the notion of physical sharing.[10] Hence it is possible (but certainly not necessary) to interpret Plato's use of *metechein* in the *Phaedo* in terms of literal sharing or having a part of, as is done in the present objection.

The argument divides into two subsections, depending on whether the Form is supposed to be present in its homonym as a whole or as a part. On

---

[10] See an example at *Symposium* 211a7: The Beautiful itself will not appear like a face or hands or like any other of "the things of which body has a share," ὧν σῶμα μετέχει.

the one hand, if the Form is present as a whole in many separate things, it will be separate from itself (131b1). (This objection, which Plato formulates again at *Philebus* 15b5–7, anticipates a problem that will reappear in the modern theory of universals: how can an item be one and the same and yet present in many places at the same time?) On the other hand, if each participant possesses only a fraction of a Form, other absurdities follow.

The consequence of these objections is to show that the metaphor of participation does not offer a coherent account of the homonym-Form relation. Hence (despite its popularity with Aristotle and later Platonists) *metechein* is rarely employed by Plato to express this relation in any dialogue other than the *Phaedo*. (The metaphor of sharing occurs once in the *Symposium* and once in the *Republic*, but frequently in the present context, and again in Aporia 6, 133d2.)[11]

The deeper consequence is that being F for a Form (designated as "the F itself") must be interpreted differently from being F for its homonyms. The Large itself is not another large thing. That is the point of the fundamental distinction between predication *per se* and *per aliud* (between being the Large itself and being something large), which will be introduced here in Part Two and developed in the *Sophist*. This distinction becomes more directly relevant to the following Aporia 3.

We note that in the *Sophist* the vocabulary of participation (*metechein, methexis, metalambanein*) will be transferred to a new use, to express a relation *between* Forms (251e9, 255b3, d4, e5, 256a1, a7, b1, b6, 256e3, 259a6–b1). The later use of *metechein* for a Form-Form relation will be anticipated here in Part Two (see 137e1, 138a6, and *passim* from 142b6, c1 ff).

Aporia 3. The Third Man (132a1–b2)

Since Gregory Vlastos' famous 1954 article, this is the most frequently discussed objection; and it was already much discussed in antiquity.[12] A single Form of Largeness is first posited by the one-over-many principle: "when many things seem to you to be large, there seems to be some one form, the same as you look at all of them." But the uniqueness of this Form is immediately threatened by a regress that generates an unlimited plurality of Forms of Largeness. If at every step we add the Form itself to the group of

---

[11] For μετέχειν in the thing-Form relation outside the *Phaedo* see *Symposium* 211b2 and *Republic* V, 476d1–2 (which might almost count as a quotation from the *Symposium*). By contrast, in the *Republic*, *Phaedrus*, and *Timaeus*, Plato prefers the terminology of image and likeness to express the homonym-Form relation.

[12] See references in Owen (1957) and Fine (1993) 203 ff.

many large things, the one-over-many principle will then introduce a new Form of Largeness at each step.

As Vlastos pointed out, this inference depends upon two unspoken assumptions, which he named Self-predication (SP) and Non-identity (NI). The assumption of self-predication, namely, that the Form Largeness is itself large, is needed for the Form to be included among the group of many large things; while non-identity (or some equivalent principle) is needed to guarantee that the Form generated by the *second* application of one-over-many is different from the first Form posited. Without some version of non-identity, no regress will follow; the one-over-many principle will, at each step, simply repeat the original introduction of a Form. As reconstructed by Vlastos, these two premises were mutually inconsistent, and hence, so formulated, they offered no prospect of a valid objection to the theory of Forms. But this inconsistency has often been regarded as a mere technicality. Alternative versions of Vlastos' NI were soon proposed that are compatible with SP and suffice to generate the regress.[13] We will return to the principle of non-identity, which may be regarded as a feature peculiar to this argument. Self-predication, on the other hand, represents a principle more deeply imbedded in Plato's theory.

It is essential to distinguish the formula for self-predication (*The Form Largeness is large* or *The Large itself is large*) from the interpretation given to this by Vlastos and others. There is no doubt that this formula represents a principle to which Plato is committed, for example in the *Phaedo* ("if anything is beautiful other than the Beautiful itself" 100c4), and much later in the *Sophist*: "just as the Large was large and the Beautiful was Beautiful. . ., so likewise the Not-Being was and is not-being" (258b10).[14]

Interpreting these claims as ordinary predications, Vlastos thought this principle could be defended only in special cases, where the predicate was a formal or categorial feature of all Forms, as in "the One is one" or "The Beautiful is beautiful." But in a case like "The Large is large," and hence for self-predication generally, Vlastos and others thought Plato was guilty of a logical confusion between being an attribute (largeness) and having that same attribute (being a large thing). Furthermore, as evidence that Plato's theory was committed to such a confusion, Vlastos claimed that Plato's

---

[13] The first proposal was by Colin Strang (1963) 193–94. For later versions, see the reference to Sandra Peterson and David Sedley, below.

[14] In this passage (*Sophist* 258b) the Eleatic Stranger is deliberately quoting (and reaffirming) self-predications both from the *Symposium-Phaedo* (the Beautiful) and also from the Third Man argument (the Large).

doctrine of love required the Form of Beauty to be beautiful in the same way as beautiful bodies and souls, only superlatively beautiful.

There are other interpretations of the self-predication formula that avoid this logical confusion by explaining how the Form of Beauty can be said to be beautiful without becoming another beautiful thing. Thus, Sandra Peterson proposed the notion of "Pauline predication" (named after Paul's *First Epistle to the Corinthians*), citing phrases like "Charity suffereth long and is kind" to illustrate the figure of speech in which statements about a property apply literally only to the things that possess this property.[15] On Peterson's account, "Justice is just" means (roughly) that participating in Justice is the reason why any act, person or institution is just: Justice itself is just because it is the source of, and the explanation for, whatever justice there is in the world. Peterson's proposal can be regarded as an explication of the passage at *Phaedo* 100c: if anything is beautiful other than the Beautiful itself, it can only be so by participating in this Form.

This notion of Pauline predication offers a non-trivial meaning for Plato's formula in *Phaedo* 100c and again in the *Sophist*. But a philosophically more significant interpretation of self-predication follows from the distinction between two kinds of predication that was introduced by Michael Frede and applied to the *Parmenides* by Constance Meinwald – the distinction that I refer to as predication *per se* and predication *per aliud*.[16] Self-predication can be seen as the default case of *per se* predications, predications that are true of the subject in virtue of its own nature. So understood, self-predication functions as a kind of shorthand substitute for a definition or statement of the nature, saying *what a thing is* in virtue of itself, as contrasted with *per aliud* predication, saying what attributes it has.

(Plato thus anticipates the Aristotelian distinction between essential and accidental predication. But the Platonic distinction applies only to Forms, whereas Aristotle will allow individual substances as subjects for both kinds of predication.)

This use of "is" (in "The Large itself is large," "the Form of Beauty is beautiful"), understood as the minimal statement of a nature, corresponds to the definitional "is" of the "what is X?" formula in earlier dialogues. It is

---

[15] Peterson (1973) 458.

[16] Frede identified the distinction in *Sophist* 255c12–13, expounding it first in his German dissertation (1967) 12–36, then, much later, in the English restatement (1992) 401–2. Meinwald used the distinction to ground her interpretation of the *Parmenides* (1991) and then applied these results specifically to the Third Man *aporia* (1992). An application to self-predication had been suggested also by Nehamas (1979 and 1982). The Frede distinction between "is$_1$" and "is$_2$" will be illustrated and discussed at length in section 2, below pp. 24–26.

precisely this "is" of *per se* predication that is represented in Plato's most technical expression for a Form: *to ho estin X*, "the what-is-X" or, in Aristotle's reformulation, "the what-it-is-to-be-X."[17]

It is clear that recognizing this distinction serves to block the Third Man argument. Since Largeness is not large in the same way as large sticks and stones (it is not large *per aliud*, by participating in Largeness), there is no basis for positing an expanded group of large things that includes the Large itself. But without such a group, the Third Man argument cannot get off the ground.[18] Even if we can find an acceptable version of the non-identity principle, no regress will follow if there is no legitimate group that includes Largeness itself in the class of large things. The one-over-many principle can introduce a new Form (F-ness$_1$) only for a group of F things that are logically homogeneous, that is, for things that are F *per aliud*, in virtue of something else. Since the Form itself is F in virtue of itself (*kath hauto* or *per se*), its F-ness does not require reference to anything else, and hence it does not fall under the one-over-many principle as applied to a uniform many. It seems that the ancient Platonists had clearly recognized this point. They maintained explicitly that the one-over-many principle applied only to groups that are logically homogeneous (*homogenēs*), and therefore not to a group consisting of a Form and its homonyms.[19]

Although the principle of non-identity becomes irrelevant if the argument is blocked before the regress begins, it will be useful to consider a proposed version of this principle that is designed to be compatible with self-predication, and thus to allow for a formally valid reading of the argument. Sandra Peterson has proposed to replace NI by a principle of non-self-explanation, namely, that nothing is self-explanatory, or nothing is F in virtue of itself.[20] But this principle is equivalent to a denial of *per se* predication. According to the Third Man argument, it was because the largeness common to many large things was *not* self-explanatory that the one-over-many principle was needed to introduce the Form of Largeness.

[17] I have borrowed from Nehamas (1979) this Aristotelian locution for Platonic self-predication. Aristotle has, of course, given his own twist to the Platonic distinction between essential and accidental predication, since for Aristotle (unlike Plato) there are individual essences.
[18] Hence Meinwald's title: "Good-bye to the Third Man" (1992).
[19] See the passages cited in Heinamen (1997) 369, with nn. 39–40, following Cherniss (1944) 298 ff., with n. 197. Heinamen points out that the principle was a commonplace for the Neoplatonists: e.g. Plotinus *Enneads* VI.1.1, 27: οὐκ ὄντος γένους κοινοῦ, ἐν οἷς τὸ πρότερον καὶ ὕστερον. This is the principle needed to block the Third Man, even in a formally valid version as reconstructed by Colin Strang or Sandra Peterson.
[20] Peterson (1973) 453, with n. 6. There is a partial parallel in David Sedley's reconstruction of NI as "No cause is identical with its own effect" (Sedley (1998) 131).

The Form itself needs no such explanation, being large *per se*. Peterson's revision of NI thus provides a formally valid argument only at the price of a non-Platonic premise.

Before leaving the Third Man argument, we need to take account of two passages in *Republic* Book X that seem to invoke the one-over-many principle in its unrestricted form. At 596a Socrates describes his "customary procedure" (*eiōthuias methodou*) as follows: "we are accustomed to posit some one Form for each case of many, to which <many> we apply the same name."[21] The last clause may be taken in two ways: either we posit a Form and then apply the name of the Form to the corresponding many (in what the *Phaedo* calls eponomy), or we posit a Form for each many that are already called by one name (e.g. the many large things). It is the latter reading that is presupposed in the Third Man argument. On either reading, the one-over-many principle is presented here as an habitual procedure, without any restriction to guard against those repeated applications of the principle that will generate the regress. Shortly later, at 597c–d, Socrates explains why the appropriate god produced only one Form of Bed (*ho estin klinē*): "If he were to make only two, there would appear again one bed of which both of these would have the form (*eidos*), and that would be the true Bed (*ho estin klinē*) and not the two." This argument from the *Republic* has in common with the Third Man argument the assumption that a plurality of Xs would require an additional X to ground their common nature, even if (*per impossibile*) the plurality includes a Form. This argument implies a disastrous version of non-identity, since it implies that the third Bed would be different from the hypothetical two, *even if these two were Forms*!

It may have been reflection on this peculiar reasoning from *Republic* X that suggested (either to Plato himself, or to a critic) that a similar argument could be constructed to produce the regress of the Third Man. Both passages just cited from *Republic* X imply an unrestricted use of the one-over-many principle. The second passage has the further defect of drawing a distinction (if only hypothetically and counterfactually) between a Form of Bed and its nature (*eidos*). Such a distinction suggests the notion of immanent forms, conceived as present in their homonyms – a conception that will prove disastrous in Aporia 6. Hence, both passages would need revision (and, in the second case, perhaps, elimination) in light of the Third Man.

This problem does not arise for the later and partially parallel argument for the uniqueness of the created world in *Timaeus* 31a. In that argument the

---

[21] εἶδος γάρ πού τι ἓν ἕκαστον εἰώθαμεν τίθεσθαι περὶ ἕκαστα τὰ πολλά, οἷς ταὐτὸν ὄνομα ἐπιφέρομεν.

singularity of the visible world follows directly from the uniqueness of its noetic model, and the latter is established not by the hypothesis of a shared common nature (as in the Third Bed argument of *Republic* X) but rather by the less problematic notion of a comprehensive whole containing a complete plurality of parts.

Aporia 4. Forms as thoughts (132b3–c11)

This is the first of two attempts by Socrates to evade the regress by reformulating his theory. But whereas the second attempt will point to an alternative version (Forms as paradigms, sensibles as images) that Plato has actually used in the *Republic* and will use again in the *Timaeus*, the present suggestion that Forms are thoughts (*noēmata*), located in souls, is in flat contradiction with a fundamental claim of the *Symposium* that the Form is not *in* anything: the Beautiful itself is not like "any discourse (*logos*) or knowledge, nor is it located somewhere, in something else, as in a living being or in earth or in heaven or in some other thing" (211a7). What is proposed here by Socrates is a fundamental change in the theory: to replace the transcendental Forms with a "conceptualist" account that might appeal to many philosophers both ancient and modern. Thus, some later Platonists were in fact willing to locate the Forms as "ideas" in the mind of God. But this is not Plato's version, and he disposes of it quickly.

How is this suggestion supposed to evade the regress? As David Sedley has pointed out, Plato had "planted" such an interpretation in the text of Parmenides' formulation of the Third Man, which emphasizes "looking with the soul" upon the new group formed by adding the Large itself to the many large things (132a7). The point of Socrates' new suggestion is that if the Form is located *in the soul*, it cannot be one of the external things looked upon *with* the soul, and hence no regress is generated.[22]

However, says Plato speaking with the voice of Parmenides, thought must have an independent object, some entity (*on ti* 132b11–c2), and if the thought is one, its object must be a unity. But if the object of this thought (e.g. of largeness) is one and the same for every case of largeness, this unitary object will itself be the Form, and we are back again with the regress. Furthermore, if the properties of all things are to be explained by sharing in the Form, and the Form is a thought, then all things are composed of

---

[22] Sedley writes: "The One over Many principle was designed to correlate a set of *objective* items accessed by the mind; if the Form proves instead to be *subjective*, it will cease to be one of the items taken in by the survey" (1998: 130), with original emphasis.

thoughts and all things will think. Or are these thoughts to be thoughtless (*anoēta*) after all? Parmenides' refutation ends here with a pun, and his inference from Forms as thoughts to participants in thinking does not seem compelling. One has the impression that Plato does not take this proposal seriously.[23] He mentions it, I suggest, because he is aware that others will find it attractive. But the doctrine of Forms was motivated not only by cognitive concerns, to explain our knowledge of the properties of things, but also by ontological issues, to explain how things possess properties in the first place. A theory of Forms as thoughts could explain the world only if the world consisted of thinking.

Aporia 5. Forms as paradigms, of which the many are images or likenesses (132d–133a)

Socrates' second proposal, that participation is to be understood as "being made like" (*eikasthēnai*), must be taken seriously, since it introduces the conception of Forms as models for imitation, originals for likenesses (*homoiōmata*), that represents Plato's standard formulation in the *Republic* and also in later dialogues. (Thus the Form-homonym relation is expressed in terms of likeness or resemblance in *Phaedrus* 250a–d, *Statesman* 300c–301a, as well as in the *Timaeus*.)

Parmenides' objection turns on the claim that the likeness conception entails a symmetrical relation of similarity: "If something resembles the Form, is it possible for the Form not to be similar to the thing that is made like it (*tōi eikasthenti*), to the extent that the latter has been made similar to it (*aphrōmoiōthē*)? Is there any way for the similar not to be similar to the similar?" (132d5). There is no doubt here concerning the reciprocal nature of similarity: If A is similar to B, B must be similar to A. The question is whether such reciprocal similarity is necessarily entailed by the likeness relation.

(I omit here an analysis of the argument by which Parmenides proves that if the relation between the Form and its homonym is one of similarity, a vicious regress will follow. The argument can be interpreted in two different ways, but each version entails the regress.)[24]

---

[23] As Myles Burnyeat points out, Plato is not inclined to take seriously "the idea that one might seek to explain the nature of the world by reference to the categories of our thought" (1982: 21). For criticism of Parmenides' argument here, see Gill (1996) 40–42.

[24] See the discussion in Gill (1996) 44 ff. and Allen (1997) 181 n. 28 who suggest that the ambiguity is deliberate.

As most commentators have seen, a refutation of the objection will refuse Parmenides' move in substituting the symmetrical relation of similarity for the asymmetric relation of imaging or representing by a likeness (*eikasthēnai*). This move is an easy one for Parmenides to make, since one of the Greek words for likeness (*homoiōma*) is derived from the adjective "similar to" (*homoios*), just as our word "likeness" is derived from "like." Nevertheless, this shift from imaging to similarity can be resisted. For it is not true, in general, that if a portrait resembles its subject, the person represented must therefore resemble his or her portrait. It was a joke when Picasso predicted that Gertrude Stein would come to look like his portrait of her. The resemblance between a thing and its image is not like a case of similarity between twins. Since they are different kinds of entities, a person and her portrait (like an animal and its photograph) need not have any property in common. The resemblance between a person and her portrait, if it exists at all, does not depend upon the portrait having a property which the person also has, but upon it somehow having "captured her likeness." The portrait is a good likeness, perhaps, because the person is thin and melancholy, and the portrait represents a thin and sad-looking person. But the painting itself is neither thin nor melancholy.[25]

Furthermore, if we look back at the argument in the *Phaedo* that introduces the notion of resemblance, we see that Plato is careful to point out that, although a pair of sticks or stone may *try* to resemble the Form of Equality, they will inevitably fall short (75b). Thus the image relation, by itself, does not introduce the notion of symmetry on which the objection depends.

Aporia 6. Separation as the last and greatest difficulty: two worlds with no causal or cognitive relation between them (133b–134e)

This is by far the longest and most elaborate objection, containing a passage on the concepts of Master and Slave that left a memorable mark on Hegelian dialectic. The point of the objection is to suggest, from an almost Aristotelian perspective, that the separate status of Forms as entities "themselves by themselves" (*auta kath' hauta*) makes them both unknowable to us and quite irrelevant for any account of things "among us." I see no reason to doubt Parmenides' claim that this is the greatest difficulty, since it raises the most profound problem for the theory – the problem signaled by

---

[25] I have benefited here from Richard Patterson's discussion (1985) esp. ch. 3, "Image and Reality."

Parmenides from the beginning in his emphasis on the language of separation (*chōris*).

We have already noticed the difficulty for Plato's theory to give a coherent account of immanence, that is, to explain how sensible homonyms depend upon, and are qualified by, their relation to the corresponding Form. This was recognized as a problem in the first general statement of the theory in the *Phaedo*, where Socrates claims that "nothing makes something beautiful except the presence or communion or connection, somehow or other, with the Beautiful itself – for I do not insist on this point, but only that it is by the Beautiful that all things are beautiful" (100d). The terminology of participation (*metechein*), familiar as a metaphor for something having an attribute or a feature, turns out to be only the place-holder for an explanation. As Aporia 2 has shown, this metaphor cannot bear any explanatory weight. In the preceding Aporia 5, Socrates proposed to replace participation by imaging or "being made like to," but he fell victim to a regress similar to that in Aporia 3. This concluding objection can therefore assume that no account has been given of participation. The fundamental influence of Forms on their sensible homonyms has been left as an unexplained fact, the presence "in us" of some property corresponding to a Form. Aporia 6 will divert attention from this unexplained vertical relation between Forms and homonyms to the two corresponding horizontal relations linking Forms to Forms and homonyms to homonyms.

The logic of this cunning argument has been carefully reconstructed by Sandra Peterson and others, and I refer to their discussions for a detailed account.[26] Since the argument is formally valid, we must identify one or more premises at work here to make the Forms unknowable and irrelevant to human beings. There are at least two points at which the argument can be challenged.

(1) Although it is reasonable to claim that the Form of Master is defined in relation to the Form of Slave, it does not follow that human masters and slaves are defined (as what they are) relative to one another. The human master is, as a matter of fact, master of a human slave, although he is by definition a master by satisfying the conditions specified in the Form of Mastery (i.e. in an answer to the question "what is a master?"). The argument relies on directing attention away from this vertical relation between a Form and its homonym by substituting the horizontal relation between two items "among us." What in fact links together masters and slaves "among us" is not a conceptual relation or a matter of definition but a power relation

---

[26] See Sandra Peterson (1981); also Mueller (1983) and Rickless (2007) 85–93.

of legal possession and physical intimidation. The fallacy comes from treating the relation of social power (*dynamis*) that connects human masters to their slaves as if it were a conceptual truth parallel to the relation between the corresponding Forms.[27]

(2) This misleading parallel between co-relative Forms and co-relative homonyms lends plausibility to the argument of Aporia 6, but it is not strictly necessary for the conclusion.[28] The more unavoidable fallacy in the argument is the parallel between the master-slave relation and the relation between knowledge and its object, where the latter is understood as truth or reality (and hence as Forms). For neither term in the master-slave case can be defined without reference to the other; whereas for Plato (and for realist philosophers generally), knowability is not part of the definition of truth, neither in the general case nor for definite subject matters. The fallacy is particularly clear for specific objects of knowledge. Thus, the definition of zoology requires a reference to animals, but not conversely.

These are formal imperfections in what is rightly presented as a very powerful objection. Its power comes from the prospect of separation between Forms and homonyms, where separation is understood as complete ontological and cognitive independence. We are left with two parallel levels of reality, with no account of how the properties identified in the sensible world are related to a Form in the eternal nature of things. The acceptance of such properties "in us" seems to point towards a different theory, one more like Aristotle's doctrine of immanent forms.[29] The recognition of such properties makes the positing of separate Forms "themselves by themselves" seem superfluous.

On the other hand, a commitment to such immanent properties is clearly implied by several passages in the *Phaedo* ("largeness in us") and assumed again in Parmenides' interrogation of Socrates. ("Similarity itself, separate from the similarity that we have," 130b4.) I take it that in Aporia 6 Plato is calling attention to this notion of properties in us, as items distinct both from Forms and from us as subjects, as a notion that must be either eliminated or radically reinterpreted in a satisfactory theory of Forms. Looking ahead, we can see that such properties will reappear as "being

---

[27] We might say that the argument of Aporia 6 equivocates on the term δύναμις in 133e5: "Things among us do not have their function (δύναμις) relative to the Forms, nor the Forms relative to us, but, as I say, the Forms are of themselves and relative to themselves, and things among us are likewise relative to themselves." In reference to Forms, δύναμις designates their nature or definition; between human masters and slaves it means simply power.

[28] For this and the following point I am indebted to comments by Uygar Abaci.

[29] For commentary on Aristotle's interpretation of and debt to Aporia 6, see Allen (1997) 198–202.

that has come-to-be" in the *Philebus* and as mathematical structures in the *Timaeus*. In the latter a full account will require the theory of the Receptacle as the field in which such images of the Forms can appear.

1.2   Part Two: the eight deductions

The second part of the dialogue consists of a labyrinth of arguments grouped under eight (or nine) separate deductions with contradictory conclusions. Many of these arguments are deductively valid; some are valid but with dubious premises, while others seem deliberately to exploit ambiguity and equivocation. (It has been claimed by some scholars that all the arguments are intended to be read as valid, but I do not find that claim credible.)[30] The whole enterprise is so strange that some friends of Plato have sought to protect his reputation by interpreting this long exercise in contradiction as an elaborate joke.[31] Scholars who look here for positive philosophical contributions have emphasized the links connecting these deductions to doctrines in the *Sophist* and *Philebus*, and also to conceptual analyses in Aristotle's *Physics*. But no single interpretation can capture all the goals and achievements of this bafflingly complex text. My own discussion will attempt to cast light on the philosophical content of Part Two in its close connections with the rest of Plato's work. I will suggest that these eight deductions can best be seen as an exercise in what the *Sophist* calls *sumplokē eidōn*, the weaving-together of forms with one another (in the four positive deductions), and in the corresponding futility of what we might call *chōrismos*, the separation or isolation of a single Form from everything else (in the four negative deductions).[32]

Two preliminary comments. (1) I will not follow the fashion of interpreting these deductions historically, either as critical response to Parmenides and Zeno, or as attacks on Megarian and Pythagorean philosophers about whom we know very little. Both here and elsewhere Plato treats Parmenides with something approaching awe, and he treats Zeno with considerable respect. (On the other hand, when in the *Sophist* Plato feels obliged to criticize a doctrine of Parmenides, he does not leave us in any doubt as to what he is doing.) Of course, some of the deductions do look like a parody

---

[30] For example, Meinwald (1991) 79, with 179 n. 1) and Peterson (1996) 170 n. 7.

[31] Notably, Cherniss (1932) and A.E. Taylor (1934) 8–9.

[32] The term χωρίς "separate" can mean what is either logically distinct, numerically distinct, or physically separate. However, the χωρισμός I have in mind here is something stronger, namely, the denial of any blending or connection between Forms, the negation of μετέχειν between Forms, indicated in the text by στέρεται (157c1 and *passim*) and by χωρίς in Deduction 4 (159b6, c4, c7).

of Zeno's style of argument, and there is an unmistakable comic streak in this dialogue, as in most of Plato's work. But I do not find any substantial insights to be obtained by reading these arguments as crypto-history, as polemical critique of one or more of Plato's predecessors.

(2) I think we should take at face value the indication in the text that this is a logical exercise designed to prepare the reader for constructive work in Platonic philosophy. Part of the training must be to detect fallacies in argument, of which there will be plenty. (The concept of formal validity was not thematized before Aristotle's work, but the familiar contrast with eristics was sufficient to acquaint Plato's readers with the notion of arguments aimed at deception.) However, the more constructive goal of this training is to recognize logical structures that represent connections, distinctions and mutual exclusions between objective concepts or Forms. One important innovation will be the distinction between two kinds of predication, a distinction that proves to be indispensable for any coherent statement of the theory of Forms. And a new goal that leads beyond these formal structures is to sketch the conceptual framework for an interpretation of the physical world, the world of coming-to-be and passing-away. Thus, one function of these eight deductions is to prepare the reader for constructive work in natural philosophy.

Fundamentally, then, the *Parmenides* can be seen as transitional, a transition symbolized in the replacement of Socrates by Parmenides. The *Parmenides* looks back critically at the metaphysical doctrine of the earlier dialogues, but it also looks forward towards a reconstruction of the theory designed for its application to the world of nature.

We turn now to a textual exegesis of Part Two. The subject for all these deductions is either "the one" or "the others than one." But what is the one? There are at least three possibilities: (1) the One itself as a Platonic Form; (2) the property of unity or being one; and (3) any entity whatsoever, anything that is one.[33] There is also a special case of (3) envisaged in Deduction 2, where the One takes on the properties of extension, time, and change, and hence can apparently be identified with the natural world.

By capitalizing "Form" I do not mean to prejudge the relation between interpretations (1) and (2). It is not at all clear that the metaphysical status of Forms in the classical theory (as criticized in Part One) is a topic under discussion in Part Two. There is no reference here to the participation of sensibles in transcendental Forms, no contrast between being in general and

---

[33] Compare Allen (1997) 247, who sees the subject of Deduction 2 as intentionally ambiguous: it "may be abstract, Unity or the property of being one, or it may be distributively generic, what(ever) is one."

the "true being" (*ontōs on*) of Forms. We are working in Part Two with a looser, less metaphysically charged notion of form (*eidos*). I use the terms "Form" and "concept" broadly here, for anything that can be called an *eidos* as distinct from an object of sense perception. The metaphysical notion of Form (from the classical theory) lies somewhere in the background, but it is not directly addressed in Part Two, despite the appearance of certain semi-technical expressions like *hoper estin hen* (139c1) and *auto to hen* (143a6). Perhaps the most basic ambiguity in the meaning of "the one" in Part Two is between subject and predicate syntax, that is to say, between the one as an entity possessing the attribute of unity (whatever is one) and the attribute itself (being one). The reference of terms like "one" seems to vary between these two construals from deduction to deduction, and even between arguments in the same group.

For clarity in reading I capitalize "One" and "Others" whenever these terms seem to refer to the subject of the hypothesis. This convention is designed to reflect the faint personification that adheres to the two principal characters in these dialectical dramas.

Although the range of reference for "one" as one entity (a subject possessing unity) is very wide, it is not, I think, unrestricted. The whole exercise seems to presuppose the condition, emphasized in earlier sections of the dialogue, that the discussion be "not about visible things but about those things that one might best grasp in *logos* and consider forms (*eidē*)" (135e, echoing 130a1–2). Although the One of Deduction 2 will have spatial and temporal properties and a share in becoming (and hence it is certainly not a Form), there is no mention here of any sensible properties such as color or smell, nor even of such qualities as hot and cold, wet and dry. The possibility of sense perception (*aisthēsis*) for the One of Deduction 2 is expressly affirmed at 155d6; and yet this One is never described in sensory terms. Deduction 2, and the other deductions insofar as they are constructive, provide a strictly conceptual framework for the spatio-temporal being of the natural world. Hence, the account of unity and plurality given in these deductions seems systematically to exclude sense qualities as such, the objects of the special senses. Although the One of Deduction 5 is (I suggest) clearly a non-Form, there is no hint, even in this case, of sensible qualities.

The first four deductions begin with the assumption *if the One is*: Deductions 1 and 2 consider what follows for the One; Deductions 3 and 4 consider consequences for the Others, that is for a plurality. The next four deductions begin with the negative hypothesis *if the One is not*, again with two deductions concerning the One (numbers 5 and 6) and two concerning the Others (7 and 8).

Four of these deductions reach only negative results. Thus, Deduction 1 argues that, since the One is not a many, it can have no attributes, not even Being. (Hence the One of Deduction 1 *is not* after all, and is not even one.) Deduction 4 concludes that if the Others are entirely separate (*chōris*) from and have no share in the One, they can have no unity and no properties whatsoever. Deduction 6 argues that if the One is not in any way, nothing can be said or known about it. (This One prefigures the absolute Not-Being of the *Sophist*.) Deduction 8 argues that if the One is not at all, there is not even an appearance of the Others. Thus, the scheme of deductions finds its conclusion in the darkness of nonentity.

It is less easy to summarize the claims of the four constructive deductions. As noted, Deduction 2 presents the conceptual outlines for a full theory of the natural world. Deduction 3 explores the notion of plurality represented by the Others, and thus prefigures the concept of the Unlimited to be developed in the *Philebus*, as well as in the indefinite Dyad of the "unwritten doctrines." Deduction 5 pursues the constructive notion of Not-Being that will be more fully analyzed in the *Sophist*, including both the theme of negative predication and the veridical sense of *einai* as being-the-case. Finally, Deduction 7 presents the weakest form of plurality as mere appearance, in the condition of the Others where no unity is to be provided by the One.

Within this system of eight deductions, we must recognize the exceptional position of Deduction 2. Taken together with its appendix on the instant of change, Deduction 2 is as long (15 Stephanus pages) as the seven other deductions combined. Although all the deductions make some positive contribution, Deduction 2 presents philosophical thought on an entirely different scale, as an outline theory of the conceptual properties required for spatio-temporal being and becoming. So I postpone discussion of Deduction 2 until we have surveyed the system as a whole.

I take the other seven in order, before returning to Deduction 2.

Deduction 1

Deduction 1 presents the hypothesis of the One in a slightly different form: "if it is one" (*ei hen estin*) instead of "if one is" or "if there is one" (*hen ei estin*), which is the version we find in the other three affirmative hypotheses. There is no logical distinction between the two formulae, but there is a clear rhetorical contrast. (Logically, both formulae can be read as partial versions of the self-predication *The one is one*, with existence implied for the subject.) The difference is that the formula in the other three deductions, by placing "one" (*hen*) before the if-clause, identifies the One as subject and shifts attention to the predicate "is" (*estin*). By contrast, the word order in Deduction 1 encourages us to construe "is one" as a predicate with no subject specified. Hence, one way to understand Deduction 1 is to see it as positing *being one* as an attribute alone, without connection to any subject or any other attribute. (Implicitly, of course, the One will also be its own subject.)

Now, if there is no connection between the One and anything else, the consequences must be systematically negative. (This is the fatal consequence of what we can recognize as *chōrismos*, the separation of one Form or concept from everything else, denounced in the *Sophist* as the folly of the Late-learners.) Formally speaking, the sequence of negative results (denying parts, shape, place, motion, etc. to the One) all follow in Deduction 1 from the assumption that the concepts *one* and *many* are simple contraries that exclude one another. Hence, if the One, or whatever is truly one, cannot be many, it cannot have any attributes other than being one. The only possible predication is self-predication: the One is one. (Even this will finally be denied.) The One cannot be self-identical and different from other things, because having identity or difference would make it plural. "If it had any attributes besides being one, the One would have the attribute of being more than one, and that is impossible."[34] If, as we learn in Deduction 2, Being and One are distinct, then the One cannot even share in Being, that is, it cannot even *be*, without incurring plurality. But it is a law of Platonic ontology that *X is F* implies *X is*. True predication implies existence for the subject. Hence, if the One cannot have being, it cannot even be *one* (141e9–142a1), and for the conclusion of Deduction 1 we are left with a flat contradiction of our initial hypothesis.[35]

What has gone wrong? At a minimum, we must recognize that being one and being many do not necessarily exclude one another. That will be one of the lessons taught against the Late-learners in the *Sophist*: a single subject can have many attributes (251a5 ff.). As the very first inference to be drawn from the assumption "if it is one" in Deduction 1, the proposition "the one is not many" (at 137c4) is flagged for rejection as the ultimate consequence

---

[34] 140a1–3: Ἀλλὰ μὴν εἴ τι πέπονθε χωρὶς τοῦ ἓν εἶναι τὸ ἕν, πλείω ἂν εἶναι πεπόνθοι ἢ ἕν, τοῦτο δέ ἀδύνατον.

[35] I am assuming now that the hypothesis of Deduction 1 did assert something, that is, that it did not posit being one as an attribute alone, with no subject understood. The understood subject was, of course, the One. To serve as premise for the deduction, the hypothesis must imply a predication, and in this case a self-predication.

of this *reductio*. (It was flagged even earlier in Socrates' presentation of the Forms; see 129b7, e2.)

As just described, the self-contradiction of Deduction 1 depends on a premise that is not formulated until Deduction 2, namely, the non-identity of Being and One (142b–c). Instead, the *reductio* of Deduction 1 actually relies on a premise that a Platonist might reasonably reject, namely, that all being is temporal. Thus, the proof that the One is not depends on a proof that the One is not in time (141d–e). The claim that all being is in time recurs in Deduction 2 (151e7), and is nowhere denied in this dialogue. Since it is denied elsewhere in Plato's work (explicitly in the *Timaeus* and implicitly whenever the Forms are described as eternally unchanging), we must take note of this as a point that calls for explanation.[36] If this claim that all being is in time is accepted throughout Part Two, it confirms our impression that the Forms of the classical theory are not under consideration here.

For the moment we notice only that a commentator who wishes to salvage Deduction 1 from self-contradiction might choose to deny the premise that all being is temporal. The contradictory conclusion of Deduction 1 would then be formally valid but unsound, because it follows from a false premise. This might seem to support the claim of those interpreters who wish to read all the arguments of Part Two as formally valid. But, as we have seen, the same devastating conclusion could be reached by an obviously true premise, namely, that being and one are distinct. The real culprit in Deduction 1 is the assumption that the same subject cannot be both one and many. The falsity of this assumption will be taken for granted in Deduction 2.

We are left, then, with a view of Deduction 1 as an argument that destroys itself by finally denying its premise, that the One is, or has being. Since the One outlined in Deduction 1 is not a coherent entity, it cannot be the object of naming, statement, or cognition (142a). And if it cannot be the object of *logos* or *doxa*, it cannot even be the object of false statement or false belief.[37] But why was it constructed in the first place, and what is the philosophical moral? At a minimum, as I have suggested, the point is to show that *being*

---

[36] I take it that *Timaeus* 37d–38b states that the eternal paradigm is not in time; time came into being together with the heavens (38b6). For Plato and Aristotle the notion of time is inseparable from the notion of motion or change. So to say that the Forms are eternally unchanging is equivalent to saying that they are not in time.

[37] For interesting parallels between Deduction 1 and Gorgias' treatise *On Nature or on Not-Being*, see Palmer (1999) 111–17. As Palmer suggests, Gorgias' treatise may have been Plato's inspiration for the form of the Deductions.

one does not necessarily exclude *being many*. But the point to be developed against the Late-learners in the *Sophist*, and implicit here, is more general. Concepts like *being one* cannot function in isolation. The lifeblood of predication, and hence of language, depends on the connection between subjects and attributes or, more generally, between concepts. As the Eleatic Stranger puts it, "*logos* is given to us by the weaving-together of Forms with one another" (259e). Deduction 1 contradicts itself by attempting to assert a One that is in no way many, a Form that does not blend with any other Form. The fundamental requirement of blending between Forms, which will be positively asserted in the *Sophist*, is here expressed in negative terms, in the failure of this attempt to define a unity with no plurality. And the final denial of unity to the One points to a more specific version of this lesson. As we have seen, for Plato a subject must have the attribute of being in order to have any attributes at all. (Being is, as the *Sophist* will say, the indispensable vowel Form.) If the One does not have being, it cannot even be one (141e10).

But this negative lesson is not the whole story. Deduction 1 leads us down a path of concepts (or Forms) that we will revisit with more profit in Deduction 2: part/whole, location, motion/rest, same/different, like/unlike, equal/unequal, older/younger. Thus we are introduced, by means of a negative image, to the outline of a positive theory that will be provided in the second deduction. We are also introduced (and again by way of denial) to the radically new notion of participation (*metechein*) as a connection between Forms or concepts. This notion, to be systematically developed in the *Sophist*, is here silently presupposed in the denials that the One partic-ipates in shape or time or being (137e1, 138a6 and *passim*). Deduction 2 will make positive use of this notion of predication as a connection between Forms. But in Deduction 1 we already have, at least implicitly, the crucial distinction between the two types of predication that I will call predications *per se* and *per aliud*. (This is the distinction that Michael Frede identified in the *Sophist* as is_1 and is_2, and that Constance Meinwald has described in the *Parmenides* as predication *pros heauto* and *pros ta alla*.)[38] Beginning here in the *Parmenides* and continuing in the *Sophist*, Plato carefully distinguishes between what is true of a Form in virtue of its own nature (*phusis* or *ousia*) and what is true of it in virtue of its link to another Form. This latter mode of *per aliud* predication is identified here by the concept of participation (*metechein*), in a new use of the old term for sharing in a Form. The

---

[38] References above, n. 16. Frede's recognition of this distinction is one of the most important contributions to Plato scholarship in the last generation.

contrasting notion of *per se* predication is first presented inconspicuously in the proof that the One is not different from anything else:

> It won't be different from another, as long as it is one; for it does not belong (*prosēkein*) to one to be different from something, but it belongs only to the different (to be different) from another, and to nothing else. . . So in virtue of being one (*tōi hen einai*), it will not be different. (139c3–6)

We have here an implicit contrast between what is true of a Form in virtue of its own nature and what depends upon its sharing in another Form.

A few lines later the idea of a nature corresponding to a Form is again emphasized: "The nature of one is not the nature of the same (139d2) . . . The same is separate (*chōris*) from the one in nature" (139e9).[39] It is of course because of such separation, taken as a denial of blending (*metechein*) with any other Form, that the One of Deduction 1 has no properties, not even the property of being one.

This distinction between the two kinds of predication is drawn again repeatedly, and even more obviously, in Deduction 2: "Necessarily, the being of the One is different from the One, since the One is not being, but as one it shared (*meteschen*) in being" (143b1–3; cf. 142b7–c2). Here "The One is not being" provides a negative example of *per se* predication: it is not in virtue of its own nature that the One has being. On the other hand, the being of the initial hypothesis "if the One is" is identified as an example of *metechein*, and thus of *per aliud* predication. Such clear examples of the contrast can be multiplied (see below, p. 27 n. 43). Following Meinwald, I have called attention to the less obvious distinction between the two modes of being in Deduction 1 in order to demonstrate the care and subtlety with which Plato has composed Part Two, silently introducing here notions that will be thematized only in the *Sophist*, where the two modes of being are expressly distinguished (255c12–e6). Notice that in its negative form ("the One is not being"), *per se* predication seems to coincide with our notion of the *is* of identity; and the corresponding negatives at *Sophist* 258b–c have sometimes been so interpreted. But that interpretation is both anachronistic and inaccurate. Negative examples of the *is* of identity will not be *per se* predications at all, but will involve sharing in the Different. Even true statements of identity for Plato will not be predications *per se* but will involve sharing (*metechein*) in the Same.

---

[39] Compare Meinwald's discussion of this passage (1991) 64–67.

We can understand the importance of this *per se/per aliud* distinction in the *Parmenides* if we bear in mind the problems associated with self-predication and with the regress argument of the Third Man. Plato has often been accused of a confusion between the notions of having a property and being a property, as if a self-predication of the form *The F itself is F* assigned the property of *being F* to the Form in the same way that sensible things are F; as if the Beautiful itself was simply the most beautiful thing in the world, or Largeness itself the largest. As we have seen, the regress of the Third Man relies upon forming a class of *things that are F* which includes the Form. But the distinction between predications *per se* and *per aliud* is designed precisely to guarantee that the Form F will never be F in the same way as anything else. As Frede and Meinwald have shown, self-predication is simply the default case of the *is* of definition, the expression of a definite nature or what-it-is-to-be-F.[40] *Per se* predication is thus the ancestor of the Aristotelian notion of essential predication; but it is not the same notion. The difference between Plato's *per se* predication and essential predication in Aristotle reflects a metaphysical difference between the two conceptions of sensible individuals. For Plato, only Forms can be the subject of *per se* predication, because only Forms have (more precisely, are) definite natures.

Deduction 1 has been interpreted here as a *reductio* argument against the possibility of a unity without plurality. One might object to this view of Deduction 1 on the grounds that Part Two contains several references to a One without parts as "truly one" or "completely one." Thus, in Deduction 3 we read "If they (the Others than the One) did not have parts they would be completely (*pantelōs*) one" (157c3). Similarly, in Deduction 4 it is denied that "the truly one" (*to hōs alēthōs hen*) has parts (159c5). This notion of a true unity with no plurality, and hence no parts, seems to be confirmed in the *Sophist* 245a8, in a context that refers to the unity of "the one itself" (*auto to hen*): "According to the correct *logos*, the truly One should, I suppose, be completely partless." Being without parts means being without plurality. But this is precisely the claim that has been shown to be indefensible on our reading of Deduction 1.

I think the conflict here is only apparent. The assertion at *Sophist* 245a8 is part of a dialectical critique of the unrestricted monism that claims to define a unity with no plurality. As Deduction 2 points out, a *One that is*, by sharing in Being, is already a many (143a5). Hence, in order to explore the notion of a unity without plurality, Deduction 2 resorts to a thought

---

[40] Frede (1992) 402; Meinwald (1991) 69, (1992) 380. See also Nehamas (1982) 204–5, with n. 20.

experiment that separates the One itself from the being that it has (143a6–9). This moment of abstraction allows us to count One and Being separately, as a pair, and thus to introduce the number two. (By recognizing their difference, we add Difference to compose a trio, and so introduce the number three.) It is for this purpose, in the brief section on numbers (143a–144a), that Deduction 2 distinguishes in thought the One itself from the One-that-is (*to on hen*). But Plato makes clear that this One without plurality is only a dialectical maneuver, an item of thought with no foothold in being. For the rest of Deduction 2, the subject under discussion is a real unity with parts, a One-that-is.[41]

Deduction 3

Postponing the discussion of Deduction 2 with its appendix, we pass on to Deduction 3, which directs attention to the Others: "What attributes will belong to the Others if the One is?" (157b6–8). The first inference to be drawn from the otherness of the Others is a new application of the *per se/per aliud* distinction. On the one hand, "the Others are not one"; on the other hand, "the Others are not altogether deprived of the One but share (*metechei*) in it somehow" (157b9–c2).[42] The contrast is formulated even more explicitly in what follows. The Others share in the One by being one whole of many parts. But each part must also share in the One, "while being something other than the One. Otherwise it [the part] would not share but would itself be one. But as it is, it is surely impossible for anything except the One itself (*auto to hen*) to be one" (158a 3–6, translation after Gill-Ryan). The kind of being one that belongs exclusively to the One itself is precisely the being of *per se* predication: what belongs to the subject in virtue of its nature, because of what it is. This distinction, first presented in Deduction 1, becomes a persistent theme throughout Part Two.[43]

By turning from the consideration of the One to that of the Others, Deduction 3 focuses our attention on plurality. Deduction 3 is at first concerned with the structure of unity in a whole composed of parts

---

[41] On the other hand, in the expanded scheme reported later, which stretches from the One above to the Indeterminate Dyad below, there is a more positive role for the notion of a One without plurality. See below, p. 28.

[42] The link between the two statements is expressed grammatically by the balance between οὔτε at 157b9 and οὐδὲ μήν at c1.

[43] I count five or six occurrences of the distinctions in the *Parmenides*, of which this (158a) is the last. The others are 139c–d, 142b–c, 143b, 157b–c.

(157c–158a).[44] Parmenides then explores the concept of plurality itself. Plurality had always been a concern of the classical theory, where a Form is often "the one over the many" (*Rep.* V, 476a; VI, 507b; X, 596a). So in the *Parmenides* Socrates begins by referring to "me and you and the others that we call 'many'" (129a2). This theme returns in Deduction 2, where the One is a whole of parts, characterized by several forms of unlimited plurality (*apeiron plēthos*). What is new in Deduction 3 is a concern with plurality as such, as a principle contrasting with definite form. The unlimited multitudes of Deduction 2 were determined with mathematical precision, either by a systematic division into two parts modeled on Zenonian bisection (142d–143a) or by a process of addition and multiplication introducing the natural numbers, starting with doubles and triples of one (143c–144a). There is nothing indefinite about such pluralities; they are only unlimited in number. Deduction 3, by contrast, introduces the notion of plurality as a principle of formlessness, a multiplicity deprived of intrinsic structure, without definiteness or limitation (*peras*).

Commentators since Cornford have recognized in this *apeiron* of Deduction 3 a kinship with the Indefinite Dyad reported as the principle of plurality in the so-called Unwritten Doctrines.[45] The relation described between the One and the Others in Deduction 3 seems to parallel the metaphysical relation between the One and the Indefinite Dyad (or the Great and the Small) in the oral doctrine of first principles reported by Aristotle. Unfortunately, those unwritten doctrines are inaccessible to us; Aristotle's polemical report gives only a vague outline. What we do have, however, is three parallel passages in the dialogues that allow us to form some conception of what Plato had in mind. The first text is the one before us, the discussion of the Others as *apeiron plēthos* in Deduction 3. The second text is the description of the Others as *apparent* plurality, again "unlimited in multitude," in Deduction 7. The third and fullest text concerns the principle of the *apeiron* in the cosmological scheme of the *Philebus*. We briefly survey all three.

The topic begins here with a thought experiment, echoing the experiment of Deduction 2 in which the One itself was conceived in separation from the being that it has (143a). Here we are asked to grasp in imagination ("let's see as follows" (*hōde idōmen*) at 158b8) the unlimited multitude of

---

[44] Verity Harte (2002) esp. ch. 3, "A New Model of Composition") has shown that Plato is here escaping from the grip of a conception of the whole as identical with its parts, a conception presented in the *Theaetetus* as the source of paradox and puzzles.
[45] Cornford (1939) 155–57, 208–10. More fully Sayre (1996) 276–83.

"things that share in the one as a part and in the one as a whole," at the moment when they are acquiring a share of the One (*metalambanei*) but do not *yet* participate in the One (*oude metechontai*). They then represent "multitudes in which there is no one" (158c1):

> Now, if we are willing to subtract in thought the very least we can from such multitudes (*plēthē*), must not that which is subtracted be also a multitude and not one, if it doesn't share in the One? . . . So always, as we examine in this way its nature, itself by itself, different from the form (*eidos*), won't as much of it as we ever see be unlimited in multitude? (158c2–7, trans. after Gill-Ryan)

We are asked to conceive the Others as a pure many, a plurality that has not been organized into any unity whatsoever. The reference to the One as form (*eidos*) suggests that plurality is conceived here as a sort of unstructured, pre-Aristotelian matter awaiting form. The repeated mention of vision (*idōmen, horōmen*) may indicate only the recourse here to visual imagination; but it may also suggest a connection between this principle of plurality and the world as perceived by the senses:

> Furthermore, whenever each part comes to be one part, the parts then have a limit (*peras*) in relation to each other and to the whole, and the whole has a limit in relation to the parts . . . It follows for things other than the One that from the One and themselves gaining communion (*koinōnēsantōn*) with each other, as it seems, something different comes to be in them, which provides a limit for them in relation to each other; but their own nature, by themselves, provides unlimitedness (*apeirian*). (158c7–d6, trans. after Gill-Ryan)

Here the term "limit" (*peras*) denotes the unifying structure, over and above the sum of the parts, that makes a whole out of the parts, a one out of many.[46]

The structure of the world, as a whole of parts, is thus the product of a mixture (*koinōnia*) of two principles: the One and the nature of the Others, a nature which is responsible for plurality and indefiniteness (*apeiria*). The same nature of indefinite plurality returns in a more blurred form in Deduction 7, where, since by hypothesis there is no One to combine with, there is no possibility of a creative blend that might introduce any sort of unity. Under these circumstances the principle of plurality can provide no real structure but only the appearance of such. In the absence of any unit, there is not even any genuine plurality in Deduction 7, but only the vague appearance of masses or bulks (*onkoi*). "Each mass of them, as it

---

[46] For commentary on this passage, see Harte (2002) 137–38, following Gill (1996) 90–91.

seems, is unlimited in multitude (*apeiros plēthei*), and if you take what seems to be smallest, suddenly, just as in a dream, instead of seeming to be one, it appears many, and instead of very small, immense in relation to the bits chopped (*kermatizomena*) from it" (164c8–d4, trans. after Gill-Ryan). What is missing here is the structure (*peras*) that makes a whole out of many parts, something of definite size out of fluctuating relations of greater and smaller. In imagining a world completely deprived of unity, Plato thus resorts to a dream experience like that in *Alice in Wonderland*, where absorbing the contents of a bottle labeled "Drink me" produces a sudden transformation of size.

Deduction 7 continues with this fantastic description of the apparent properties of a world without structure. The masses seem to have a beginning and an end, but "whenever you grasp any bit of them in thought as being a beginning, middle or end, before the beginning another beginning always appears, and after the end another end remains . . . So all being that you grasp in thought (*dianoia*) must, I take it, be chopped up and dispersed, because surely, it would always be grasped as a mass (*onkos*) without the One . . . So must not such a thing appear one to a person who sees dimly from far off; but to a person conceiving (*noounti*) it sharply from up close, must not each one appear unlimited in multitude, since it is deprived of the One which is not?" (165a7–c3, trans. after Gill-Ryan).

The reliance on vision in the thought experiment suggests again that this indefiniteness is related to the world of sense perception, whose deceptiveness is only partially overcome by conceptual thought (*noein*). The whole picture of a world whose structure is only apparent is presented here in a highly comic spirit. (The last two deductions, in which the Others are abandoned by a non-existent One, are probably the most ridiculous moments in this "laborious play," the *pragmateiōdēs paidia* promised by Parmenides at 137b20.) The serious contribution of Deduction 7 is an implicit view of the One as the indispensable source of all unity, a principle without which the world would have no structure whatsoever. Perhaps the Neoplatonists might have been better advised to recognize their transcendental One in the missing principle of Deduction 7 rather than in the unsuccessful unity of Deduction 1.

The positive account of plurality, on the other hand, is given in Deduction 3, in the concept of the *apeiron* that combines with the One to form a *peras* that organizes a structured plurality, and hence makes the world into a unified whole of parts. Deduction 3 thus introduces the Limit-Unlimited scheme that Plato will develop more fully in the four-fold cosmology of the *Philebus*. Here we have only the bare sketch of such a scheme. There is nothing in the *Parmenides* to prepare us for the fourth principle of the *Philebus*, the teleological cause or cosmic Reason that brings Limit and Unlimited together into harmonious blends. (There is also no hint in the *Parmenides* of the mixture of Being and Becoming that emerges in the *Philebus*.) The *Philebus* gives a richer account of the principle of Limit in terms of mathematical ratios, and of the Unlimited as pairs of opposed qualities like the hot and the cold, admitting unlimited degrees of more and less.

The *Philebus* was probably written much later, and there is no reason to suppose that Plato had this whole theory in mind when he composed the *Parmenides*. Nevertheless, there is a striking degree of continuity here between the two dialogues. In the *Philebus* Plato again presents the doctrine of Limit and Unlimited in the context of a discussion of One and Many, where the notion that unity excludes plurality is mentioned only as a toy for playing logical games. Instead, the paradoxical connection between the two (that the one is many, and the many one) is said to be an "immortal and unaging property of *logoi*" (15d). Everything that is ever said *to be* is described as "beings (derived) from one and many" and therefore as "having limit and unlimited in them by nature" (16c9–10). This is essentially the doctrine of Deduction 3, where the Others, as the many, provide *apeiria* by their own nature, whereas *peras* is produced by their union with the One. Since the indefinite multitude (*apeiron plēthos*) is represented in Deduction 3 by the Others alone, without the One, it does not have the mathematical infinities of Deduction 2, derived from a One-that-is (see below, pp. 39–42). We can only guess how this one-many or *peras-apeiron* scheme may have been elaborated in oral speculation, once the many Others came to be represented by the Indeterminate Dyad. We may reasonably suppose that mathematical conceptions will have played a more prominent role in the later theory, as suggested in the *Philebus* by the account of *peras* in terms of ratios. What we can see in Deduction 3 is only an initial sketch of this pattern of thought, to be developed later in the *Philebus* and in the oral teaching.

Deduction 4

Because they participate in the One, the Others of Deduction 3 constitute a genuine many, in effect the plural version of the One of Deduction 2. This continuity with the immediately preceding One is reflected in the conclusion to Deduction 3, where the Others are said to be "the same as and different from one another, and both in motion and at rest, and having all the opposite properties," thus echoing the results of Deduction 2. (Compare 159a6 with 147b7.) By contrast Deduction 4 begins by assuming that One and Others are separate (*chōris*) from each other (159b6), where "separate" means not distinct but incompatible. Unlike the Others of Deduction 3, these Others are totally deprived of any share in the One.[47]

Just as the first Deduction showed (by negation) that it is necessary for a subject to share in Being in order to share in anything else, so Parmenides will now show that it is necessary to share in the One in order to have any properties at all. In effect, both One and Being are presented as vowel Forms in the sense to be indicated at *Sophist* 253a: for a subject to have any nature at all, it must participate in both Being and One.[48]

The argument in Deduction 4 infers, then, that these Others do not constitute a plurality ("are not many" 159d4), since they have no unit. As a consequence, they can have no share in two or three or number generally, since the numbers are groups of units. They cannot have pairs of opposite properties (*eidē*) because "they cannot have even one" (159e7). There may be an equivocation here on "being one." (Having one property is not the same as having a unit for counting.) The deep point is that something must be one thing – must possess a unity of some kind – in order to be anything at all.[49]

By being entirely separate from any form of unity, the many of Deduction 4 are thus deprived of all attributes. The vocabulary of Deduction 4 is noteworthy, because the term *eidos* is here used twice for the properties of likeness and unlikeness (159e5, 160a1). Similarly, in Deduction 3 we had the term *idea* for the structure that makes a whole out of parts (157d8).[50]

This is familiar terminology, used in Part One for the Forms of the classical theory. In Part Two (beginning here in Deductions 3 and 4) we find these terms (*eidos*, *idea*, *genos*) used more freely, as later in the *Sophist* and *Philebus*, for abstract structures and kinds of things, without any definite metaphysical connotation. But if there is no commitment here to the full ontology of the classical theory, this terminology will nevertheless preserve the fundamental contrast, established at the beginning of the dialogue, between visible things and those entities "that we grasp in *logos* and think to be *eidē*."

---

[47] See 159e1, 160b1; contrast 157c1.
[48] We may be reminded here of the passage in *Metaphysics* Zeta where Aristotle shows that being and unity are convertible attributes (1030b10).
[49] Compare *Sophist* 237d.   [50] See also *eidos* in Deduction 3, 158c6.

Deductions 5 and 6

Deductions 5 and 6 form a pair, concerning what happens to the One "if the One is not." We get two alternative interpretations of Not-Being, prefiguring the full discussion of this topic in the *Sophist*. The One of Deduction 6 corresponds to the absolute Not-Being that is rejected in the *Sophist* as "unthinkable, unspeakable, and irrational," since it *is* in no way at all (*Sophist* 238c10). The One of Deduction 5, on the other hand, is a definite subject for negative predication, a subject that turns out to have some share in being (*ousia*) after all. Deduction 5 looks like a preliminary study for the positive analysis of Not-Being to be given in the *Sophist*. But there is as yet no hint of the account of Not-Being in terms of being-other that will be presented in the later dialogue. What Deduction 5 has to offer is a positive conception of Not-Being that includes the notion of negative predication.

We may take Deduction 6 first, since there is so little to be said about it. The "is not" of Deduction 6 means a total absence of being; it "signifies that what-is-not (*to mē on*) is not in any way whatsoever and has no share at all in being (*ousia*)" (163c). Here we have the strong notion of separation (*chōrismos*), without the word. Hence this Not-Being cannot admit coming-to-be (since becoming means acquiring being) nor perishing (losing being), nor can it undergo change or motion or rest. It has no properties and no relations and is in no state or condition. Like the One of Deduction 1, which also finally *is not*, this One-that-is-not cannot be the subject of any name, statement or cognition (164b1, echoing 142a3–4). It is only here in Deduction 6, in the case of absolute Not-Being, that Parmenides repeats from Deduction 1 the concluding denial of any possibility for language and thought in regard to such a subject. Deduction 6 thus reinforces the fundamental lesson of the first deduction: that a subject that does not share in being cannot be anything at all, and hence cannot even be the subject of a coherent statement or denial.

The Not-Being of Deduction 5 is the subject of a much more convoluted tale. This is the fullest of the four negative hypotheses, corresponding to the positive being of Deduction 2. It is the only negative hypothesis in which the One represents a definite subject for predication. I suggest that these positive predications will all be *per aliud*, whereas the being denied in this hypothesis ("if the One is not") is best understood as being *per se*. It is only only this distinction between two kinds of predication that can account for the sharp contrast drawn in the paradoxical assertion of 160e7: "Being (*einai*) is not possible for the One, *since it is not*; but nothing prevents it from sharing (*metechein*) in many things." "Sharing" here can only mean being *per aliud*. As this text goes on to say, the One will necessarily share in many things, have many attributes, if it is a definite subject. If it is a specific one – this one and not another – that is posited as subject (*hupokeitai*) for not-being, then "it will necessarily have a share (*meteinai*) in the *that* and in many other things" (161a4).

Since we have here a positive subject for which *per se* being is denied, this one cannot be a Form and hence does not have an intelligible nature. But it is nonetheless a definite entity, an individual object or sensible particular, to which attributes can be assigned or denied (160c8). As a subject selected for description, this one is recognizable (*gnōston*) as different from others, and hence there will be some knowledge of it (160d5). Note that *epistēmē* is used here very broadly for cognition in general, including, in this case, the minimal capacity to pick out an object for reference. If we know what we are talking about, we must be able to tell it apart from other things. Otherwise it is not worthwhile even trying to say anything (*oude phthenges-thai dei ouden*, 161a3). Identifying a definite item for reference is the necessary basis for significant speech, as well as for cognition.

Parmenides goes on to specify the requirements for this minimum subject of discourse. As an item recognized and spoken about, this one must share not only in the *that* but also in the *this* and in the *something* (*ti*), to which other things can be related. Although being (in a specific sense) has been denied to this one, it is still available as a subject for general (*per aliud)* predication. Thus the One of Deduction 5 is a something (*ti*) distinct from others, a definite item or individual, but not an essence or Form. In the language of *Republic* V, this is a one that-is-and-is-not.

The argument proceeds to assign pairs of contrary properties to this One by a series of dubious inferences: like and unlike, unequal and equal, large and small. A later passage will also assign motion and rest together with other pairs of contradictory attributes: being altered and not being altered, coming-to-be and perishing, and not coming-to-be and not perishing. There is a formal parallel here to the attribution of contrary properties to the One of Deduction 2, together with its Appendix on attributes of change. The denial of equality is of particular interest, because it restates the lesson of Deduction 1 (to be repeated in Deduction 6) that a thing must have being in some sense in order to have any properties at all. We may call this the first law of Platonic ontology: that *X is Y* entails *X is*. "Furthermore, it [the one] is not even equal to the others. For if it were equal, it would already *be*, and also be like the others in regard to equality. Both of these [cases of being] are impossible, if the one is not" (161c3–5). The inference is surprising here, since it seems to ignore the distinction between being *per se* and *per aliud*; it seems to interpret the negation of *is* in the hypothesis of Deduction 5 as a denial of all being whatsoever. But in that case the one could have no properties at all, and Deduction 5 would collapse into the absolute non-entity of Deduction 6.

Parmenides' argument makes use here of a subtle formal device to avoid this consequence of denying all attributes to the One. He manages to ascribe attributes without ascribing being and thus to avoid a formal violation of the first law. Instead of the usual ascription of an attribute by means of the copula *is* with the One as subject, Parmenides in Deduction 5 resorts cunningly to the possessive construction of *einai* with a reference to the One in the dative case. In this construction, the grammatical subject of *to be* turns out to be the attribute, not the One. For example: "And inequality belongs to it [the One] in relation to the others."[51] Literally, then, it is Inequality rather than the One that is said to be.[52]

Up to a point, then, Deduction 5 manages to describe the One without assigning being to it and thus without formally violating the law. Ultimately, however, the argument must find a way to assert that this Not-Being also has being (and thus to anticipate Plato's correction of Parmenides in the *Sophist*). It does so by introducing the veridical *is* associated with the notion of truth, a meta-sentential use of *einai* that is not covered by the *per se/per aliud* dichotomy. This second-order use of *is* is first expressed by an alternative idiom for denoting what is the case without using the verb *to be*: *echein houtōs* "being so." This idiom provides Plato with a subtle device for introducing the veridical notion without a use of *einai*:

> And yet it must somehow share in being (*ousia*) . . . It must *be* (*echein houtōs*) as we say it is. For if it is not this way (*mē houtōs*), we would not be speaking the truth when we say *that the one is not*. For if <what we say> is true, we are clearly saying *what is the case* (*onta auta*, "things that are so"). (161e3–6)

These final words introduce the veridical use of *einai* for "being the case." This is the idiom employed in the traditional formula for truth, from Protagoras to Aristotle, as "saying of what-is that it is." This veridical use of *einai* is not covered by the division of predication into *per se* and *per aliud*, since it is syntactically of higher order. (It takes as its subject not things but propositional contents or states-of-affairs.) In formal terms, the veridical *einai* is a sentence-operator, applying the notion of truth to the object sentence in which *einai* serves as the copula.[53] (In some cases, both the

---

[51] καὶ ἀνομοιότης ἄρα ἐστὶν αὐτῷ πρός τὰ ἄλλα (161a6).
[52] There is a formal parallel here to inverse predication in the *Sophist*.
[53] See Kahn (1981).

veridical notion and the predicative function will be expressed by a single occurrence of the verb.) This dual function of *to be*, as the sign both for predication and for truth value, is carefully worked out here in section 161e–162b. The One must *share in being* in the veridical sense in order to be *truly* a not-being – in order for the hypothesis "the One is not" to be true. Parmenides' reasoning will be clearer if we translate the initial being/not-being of the hypothesis as "existent/non-existent."

"As it seems, the One must *be* non-existent (*ouk on*). For if it will not *be* not-existent but will somehow slide from [veridical] being to [veridical] not-being, it will straightway be an existent (*on*)" (162a 1–3). The emphasis falls here not on the double negative but rather on the truth value of the basic negation (The One is not), together with something like the law of excluded middle. If it is false that X is not Y, then it is true that X is Y. Thus, if it is false that One is not an existent, then the One is an existent. The *einai* in question is the veridical link (*desmos*) between a subject and a true predicate, as the following sentence makes clear:

> So it must have as a link of its not existing (*tou mē einai*) the *being* a non-existent (*to einai mē on*), if it is not to exist (*ei mellei mē einai*), just as the existent (*to on*) must have the (veridical) not-being non-existent (*to mē on*), in order to be completely. Thus the existent (*to on*) will definitely exist, and the non-existent will not exist, since the existent shares in the [veridical] being of being existent (*ousias tou einai on*) and in the [veridical] not-being of not being non-existent (*mē ousias tou {mē} einai mē on*), if it is going to be completely; whereas the non-existent (*to mē on*) will share in the [veridical] not-being of not being existent (*on*), but in the [veridical] being of being non-existent, if the non-existent is also to be perfectly not-existent. (162a4–b3)

I have translated Burnet's text here, but with Shorey's corrections.[54] It is understandable that a copyist might be confused by these repeated negations. Once corrected, however, the text offers no confusion and no fear of a regress of levels of being. We need simply distinguish between (1) the substantive being of *to on* and *to mē on* (translated here as "existent/non-existent") as the predicate denied in the hypothesis; (2) the ordinary syntactic copula (*einai* three times in 162a4, 6, 8 and twice in b2); and (3) the semantic or meta-sentential copula of veridical *einai*, which is introduced in this argument. It is in this third, veridical sense of "being" that the One-that-is-not must have a share in *ousia* after all, in order to have any attributes at all, and specifically in order *truly to be* a not-being, that is, truly

---

[54] By contrast, the manuscript readings are followed in Gill-Ryan (1996) 170.

to not-be (or "not exist") in the sense of the hypothesis in Deduction 5 (*eis to mē einai*, 162b5).[55]

The argument concludes that both being and not-being belong to the One-that-is-not (162b6–7). As we have seen, this conclusion serves to introduce a series of contradictory properties concerning change and becoming, with close parallels to the Appendix for Deduction 2. This parallelism suggests that, as an individual thing without a definite nature, this One-that-is-and-is-not of Deduction 5 is a pale copy of the One-that-is of Deduction 2, just as homonyms in general represent pale copies of the corresponding Form.

Deductions 7 and 8

If the One is not, what is the condition of the Others? The distinctive feature of Deduction 7 is the claim that the Others *are*, and *are others*, despite the fact that the One *is not* (164b6–7, 165e1). But what kind of plurality can there be without a unit, and what kind of being without any One? The answer is: only the *appearance* of being and of being many. Deduction 7 thus offers the sketch of a world of appearance only, without a stable basis in being. In Deduction 8 even the appearance of plurality is denied, since there is no connection (*koinōnia*) between the Others and anything else. Thus, Deduction 8, which ends with the assertion that "nothing is" (*ouden estin*, literally "there is not even one"), completes the series of negative arguments (Deductions 1, 4, and 6) by representing pure *chōrismos*. Deduction 7, on the other hand, presents the final and weakest (because merely apparent) version of the positive account of unity and plurality that was given in Deductions 2 and 3.

Deduction 7 begins with a clarification of the term "other" as referring to the same thing as the term "different" (164b). Both terms are incomplete (and also reflexive): anything that is different must be different from something else (which is also different from it). Incompleteness is the inseparable feature of the concept Different that serves to distinguish it from Being in the *Sophist* (255c12–d7), where Being is said to be both complete (*auta kath' hauta*) and also relative to another (*pros alla*). This contrast has sometimes been interpreted as syntactic only, between the absolute and predicative constructions of *is*. But (following Michael Frede) we can recognize this

---

[55] I extend here my earlier analysis (1981) 115–17. Gill (1996) 95–99 construes this argument differently, taking the analysis of participation (sharing) to entail a regress. She does not distinguish between the syntactic and the semantic roles of the copula.

distinction between two kinds of being as properly semantic or ontological, as a distinction between the attribution of Being alone and the attribution of Being together with another Form or concept. This distinction may sometimes coincide with the syntactic dichotomy between the absolute ("complete") and copulative ("incomplete") construction, but it need not do so. In a self-predication of the form *The F itself is F*, the syntax of the verb is copulative but the being attributed to F is *per se*, since no Form other than Being is attributed to the subject F. In *The F is one*, on the other hand, the Form One is attributed to F, together with Being.

Because Difference is an incomplete attribute, the Others must be different from something. Deprived as they are of the One, the Others of Deduction 7 can be different only from themselves, that is, from one another. But this is unsatisfactory, since there is no one among them, no unit, and hence no true plurality. The negative consequences of a lack of unity have been drawn in the blank non-entity of Deduction 6. Here in Deduction 7 we derive more positive conclusions from the *appearance* of plurality that is given by a many with no definite unit. The dreamlike fantasy of "masses" without stable structure has been described above, in connection with the account of true plurality in Deduction 3 (p. 29). These Others only appear one "to a person who sees dimly from afar; but to someone conceiving it (*noounti*) sharply from up close, each one will appear unlimited in multitude" (165c1). They are both like and unlike one another, because they have no stable character. Their reality is that of an optical illusion: "just as, to someone standing at a distance, all things in a painting appear as distinct unities," the representation of men and women, gods and goddesses; but, as the viewer comes closer to the painting, these apparent unities dissolve into blotches of color (165c–d). The plurality of Deduction 7 is no more than a set of shifting images, like the deceptive, temporary specificity of things in the phenomenal world.

Concerning the Others of Deduction 8, there is even less to be said. For these Others, the plural version of the absolute Not-Being of Deduction 6, there are no true statements, not even in the language of appearance. Our conclusion here is mere negation: "if the One is not, nothing is" (166c1). We thus conclude the eight deductions by returning, in effect, to the purely negative result of the first hypothesis.

Deduction 2

This is the centerpiece of Part Two, the constructive theory of a One that is taken as subject for an outline sketch of being in space and time. All of the attributes denied of the One in Deduction 1 are presented here in positive form. As a result, the One is described by a series of apparently incompatible attributes: one and many, whole and part, limited and unlimited, in itself and in another, in motion and at rest, same and different, like and unlike, equal and unequal, larger and smaller, older and younger. In many cases the incompatibility is only apparent. Thus, this subject is coherently both one and many because it is one whole composed of many parts. The parts in turn are unlimited in number, but they are also limited by being united in the whole. Similarly with regard to location: the One is *in itself* as parts contained in a whole, but *in another* as a whole contained in something else (145e). In the latter case the apparent contradiction is explicitly resolved by a *qua* distinction between two different descriptions of the subject (*hē men, hē de*). In other cases a genuine contradiction seems difficult to avoid, and the supporting reasoning is correspondingly problematic. Particularly noteworthy are the claims that the One is different from itself but the same as other things (146b–147b), while also unlike itself but like other things (147c–148b). In such cases, as one commentator has observed, an implausible conclusion seems to be supported by even more implausible arguments.[56] On the other hand, a thesis that might be accepted as self-evident, for example, that the One is the same as itself, is "proved" by a systematic elimination of the less promising alternatives (146b–c). In such passages, where the inference seems to be playful or fallacious, it is natural to suppose that the student of dialectic is being challenged to find his or her way through a thicket of treacherous arguments.

Carried along in this torrent stream of arguments good, bad, and ingenious, is a rich flotsam of philosophical insights. Many of these have been identified by other commentators.[57] I will add a few details. But first we must try to characterize Deduction 2 as a whole.

Deduction 2 is Plato's most extended use of the method of hypothesis, which was borrowed from the mathematicians (as he tells us in the *Meno*). The hypothetical method is, of course, a method of deductive inference, but it is more than that. In the *Phaedo* Socrates describes it as a procedure in which "I begin by laying down (*hupothemenos*) in each case the *logos* that I judge to be the soundest. And whatever seems to accord (*sumphōnein*) with this I posit as true ... and whatever does not, I posit as not true" (100a).

---

[56] The phrase is borrowed from Richard Patterson (in his unpublished commentary on the *Parmenides*, p. 285). Notice that the "proof" at 148a that all things are similar to all things (because they all have the common property of being different) is a stellar example of the form of argument cited in *Philebus* 13c–d as the mark of the lowest and most immature practitioners of λόγοι.

[57] See e.g. Owen (1970) and Allen (1997) 246–312.

There has been much scholarly debate as to the logical force here of the metaphor of accord or agreement. It is reasonable to reject whatever contradicts your premise, but it is not reasonable to accept whatever is logically compatible with it. In an earlier discussion of this passage in the *Phaedo*, I argued that what Plato means here by *sumphōnein* must be stronger than logical consistency but weaker than logical entailment.[58] Thus, Socrates speaks of the consequences not as what follows logically (*sumbainein*) from the hypothesis but as "what has moved forward" from it (*ta hormēthenta*, 101d4. The hypothesis is what has been laid down as a foundation (*hupothesthai*) to build upon. My suggestion is to understand the corresponding method as a form of constructive theory building, where a proposal will "accord" with the hypothesis if it makes a coherent contribution, like notes in a melody or voices singing together. This is not strictly a form of logical inference, although it is controlled by the logical requirement of avoiding contradiction. It is rather a flexible method of developing a consistent structure on a clearly defined basis, like theory construction in mathematics or physics.

This constructive view of the hypothetical method will explain some of the features of Deduction 2. The initial steps in the argument can be interpreted as a logical analysis of the assumption *that the One is* or has being. But the first conclusion, that the One is a whole of parts, follows from this premise only if the initial One-that-is (*to on hen*) is construed as a conjunction, with One and Being as its logical parts.[59] This conclusion is then generalized: "So whatever is one is a whole and has parts" (142d8). Each of these parts is again interpreted as a conjunction of the same type, as a being that is one and as a one that has being. This move will then be repeated for the parts of the parts, in a reasoning modeled on Zeno's iterated bisection of a line. ("To say it once is to say it always" DK 29B.1). This process of repeated reduplication leads to the first paradoxical conclusion, that the One-that-is is not only one but also unlimited in multitude (*apeiron to plēthos*, 143a2).

Together with a few implicit premises (that every being is a one, and that every one is a being, nearly explicit at 142e7), the reasoning thus far can be construed as deductive inference.[60] But that is no longer the case when the

---

[58] Kahn (1996) 315; compare Robinson (1953) 126–36.
[59] This notion of μέρος or μόριον as the logical part of a conceptual whole is familiar from other dialogues. Thus, the *Meno* uses the whole-part terminology to express a genus-species relation: virtue is the whole of which justice and piety are parts (78e1, 79a3). In Deduction 2 all the numbers will be recognized as parts of number (144a8).
[60] Thus Parmenides begins by asking what follows (συμβαίνειν) from the hypothesis at 142b3, c3, 8.

One is said to share in shape (schēma), "either straight or round or some mixture of the two" (145b3). Instead of a whole of logical parts, the One is now presented as an extended entity with spatial parts. This new, spatial conception of the One is then developed by considering the attributes of location, contact, size, and motion. The shift here from deduction to innovation was recognized by Cornford, who interpreted the statement that the One will have shape to mean "that the attribute of extension can, without any illogicality, be added . . . I understand these sections as describing a sort of evolution by process of thought, starting simply from the 'One Entity'. . . [and then adding] further attributes, successively, until we reach the conception of a physical body situated in space and capable of motion and rest."[61] If we see this development as the progressive construction of a theory, by adding new attributes that are compatible with the starting point but not derived from it, we have an example of the hypothetical method as I have interpreted it. What remains exceptional in Deduction 2 is, on the one hand, the intricate arguments that support each claim, and, on the other hand, the systematic assertion of (at least apparently) contradictory properties. Plato is deliberately developing all possible relations between the One and the attributes in question. As a result, the One of Deduction 2 is finally presented not as a definite entity (and certainly not as an eternal Form) but as the subject for possible combinations of (often incompatible) pairs of attributes, ranging from the basic plurality of the part-whole relation to different forms of motion, change, and becoming. The result is an outline or conceptual grid for the whole range of basic properties for a being in space and time — as it were, the conceptual outline for a theory of nature, with the details to be determined by further argument or perhaps by observation.

We can see this systematic structure of Deduction 2 from another point of view if we think of it as a step-by-step vertical descent from unity into plurality, spatial extension, and change. We begin at the top with an entirely abstract One, of which we know only that it participates in being. We end, at the bottom, in the Appendix, with an extended entity that not only exists in space and time but undergoes every kind of change and becoming. But before descending into the spatial level of shape and location, the One first divides into an unlimited number of logical parts, including the numbers. When it does acquire shape, this is described in geometric terms: "either straight or round." Next come the spatial attributes of a physical entity: location, contact, and motion. Finally we reach temporal attributes, including change and coming-to-be, with an analysis of the moment of change in

---

[61] Cornford (1939) 146.

the Appendix. If we interpret this pattern in the terms provided by the Unwritten Doctrines (as suggested in Deductions 3 and 7 above, we can construe Deduction 2 as a hierarchy of levels, beginning with an overarching principle of unity comparable to the One of the oral teaching, immediately paired with plurality in the form of the part-whole relation. The next level down is characterized by the mathematical properties, first of number and then of geometric figure. The argument then descends gradually into spatial being (as presented in solid geometry), and then into motion (as in astronomy) and finally to all forms of change and becoming. (There is some parallel here to the order of mathematical studies in *Republic* VII.) Some Forms appear at or immediately below the highest level, in the figures of One, Being, and Different (at 143b). Below the Forms come what Aristotle calls "the mathematicals" – arithmetic first and then geometry. The lowest level is marked by the temporal change and becoming of the natural world. But even at this latest level there is a striking absence of any reference to sense qualities, despite the fact that the One of Deduction 2 is explicitly identified as an object for sense perception (155d6). There is also no reference to body as such, but only to spatial location, contact, and movement. We have, as it were, the *a priori* conditions for natural science, recognizing alternative, incompatible possibilities, with no basis for deciding between them. That decision will need to be made empirically, by observation and sense perception. But such data lie outside the dialectical exercise of the *Parmenides*. What we have here is, in effect, the schematic outline for an essentially mathematical account of the natural world, an account of the sort that will eventually be given in the *Timaeus*. But what is given here is only a set of abstract conditions, in the form of a quasi-logical deduction from general principles.[62] However, because this One-that-is (*to on hen*) is in some sense to be identified with the natural world of becoming (or at least with its mathematical structure), Deduction 2 can, like Deduction 1, accordingly assume that all being is being in time (151e7–152a3).

I conclude this discussion of Deduction 2 with a comment on particular points of philosophical interest.

(i) We have already noted the distinction between being *per se* and being *per aliud*, introduced in the first deduction but more fully developed here.

---

[62] After writing this, I see that Luc Brisson has come to a similar conclusion about Part Two as a whole (but without referring to the One-Dyad background): "the eight series of deductions form the conceptual structure of a cosmology ... The *Parmenides* provides the 'tool box' required for the construction of a cosmological model" (2002) 18.

Thus, in the discussion of equality between the One and the Others, neither is said to be larger or smaller "by their own essences (*ousiai*)," "by the One being one or the Others being other than the One" (149e1–4). They may be large or small, but not in virtue of their own nature. On the other hand, "to whichever form (*eidos*) largeness is added, it will be larger, and to whatever smallness, it will be smaller."[63] This defines being large or small *per aliud*, in virtue of the largeness or smallness that is present to a subject. (We have here an echo, and even a parody, of a problematic passage in the *Phaedo*, as we shall see in a moment.) Now this expression for largeness "being added" to the subject (*proseinai*) is ambiguous. It can mean either spatial proximity or logical conjunction. The sequel here will exploit the spatial reading, and show that it leads to absurdity. For the argument goes on to infer that smallness cannot be present in any being, neither in a part nor in the whole. By taking participation as physical presence, the argument provides a *reductio* for this physical interpretation of *per aliud* predication, being small by participating in smallness. Therefore, the argument concludes, if anything is small, it can only be something that is small *per se*: "Nothing will be small except smallness itself" (150b6).[64] Since (on this interpretation) participation is impossible, there is no such thing as predication *per aliud*. The only true predication is self-predication.

(ii) The misinterpretation of participation as physical presence is exploited again in the proof that the One must be equal in size to the Others, since neither smallness nor largeness can be present in it (150a–d). As Cornford and others have pointed out, this passage presents an implicit correction of a doctrine in the *Phaedo*.[65] In illustrating the notion of participation in that dialogue, Socrates had referred to the largeness and smallness "in Simmias" to explain why Simmias is taller than Socrates but shorter than Phaedo (*Phaedo* 102b). He had there spoken of "the largeness in us" as not admitting its opposite but "withdrawing or perishing" when smallness approaches (102d). It is not obvious that this spatial language was intended to be taken literally in the *Phaedo*. Shortly before (at 100d) Socrates had expressed doubt as to whether local presence, *parousia*, was the correct understanding of participation. But in the argument that follows

---

[63] 149e7–8. In this context, the term εἶδος refers to both largeness and smallness, as well as to One and Others.

[64] There is a parallel conclusion in Deduction 3: "it is impossible for anything to be one except the One itself," 158a5. The logic implies that "largeness itself will be larger than nothing other than smallness itself, and smallness itself will be smaller than nothing other than largeness itself" (150c4–6). These claims echo what Sandra Peterson has called the principle of definitional isolation in the final *aporia* of Part One: Mastery itself rules over Slavery itself but not over human slaves.

[65] Cornford (1939) 172–75.

in the *Phaedo* the notion of properties approaching and withdrawing plays a central role. (See e.g. 103d.) Whatever Plato had in mind in these passages of the *Phaedo*, he now makes clear in Deduction 2 that if such language of immanence is interpreted literally, in spatial terms, it leads to unacceptable conclusions:

> If smallness comes to be present in the One, it must be present in the whole or in part of the One ... What if it comes to be in the whole? Won't it be in the One by being equally spread (*tetamenē*) throughout the whole of it or by containing it? ... Then if smallness were in the One equally throughout, wouldn't it be equal, but if it contained the One, larger? ... So is it possible that smallness be equal to or larger than something, and do the work of largeness and equality but not its own? ... Therefore smallness will not be in One as a whole, but, if at all, in a part ... But not in the whole part. Otherwise it will do the same as it did with the whole: it will be equal to or greater than whatever part it is in ... Then smallness will never be present in any of the beings, since it comes to be neither in the part nor in the whole. Nor will anything be small except smallness itself. (150a1–b7, trans. after Gill-Ryan)

This bizarre argument seems not so much to refute as to make ridiculous the doctrine of the *Phaedo* according to which Socrates is smaller than Simmias by the smallness that is *in him*. It achieves this result by taking for granted the distinction between two different ways of being small, and then eliminating the possibility of being small *per aliud* that corresponds to participation. The deep point will be to remind us that smallness, whose work is to make things small, is not itself a small thing – because, once more, being F for F-ness is not the same as being F for anything else. Plato seems deliberately to be reminding us here, by an obviously false conclusion, of this fundamental distinction between two ways of being F – a distinction whose absence from the *Phaedo* accounts for at least one dubious conclusion.

(iii) I conclude with a logical contribution from another perverse argument in Deduction 2. At 147c1–148a6, Parmenides proves that the One and the Others are like one another in being different from one another (and, by an obvious corollary, that everything is like everything else for the same reason). He derives this result from a curious semantic argument that comes close to anticipating the Fregean distinction between sense and reference. The argument makes use of the archaic conception of meaning as naming (still utilized in the *Cratylus*) in order to insist that repeated utterances of the term "different" (*heteron*) will continue to predicate or name the same nature (*phusis*, 147e5). It follows that by being different from one another the One and the Others share the same attribute (*tauton peponthos einai*), namely, being different. Thus, they satisfy the definition of "being alike" (*homoion einai*) provided earlier, namely, having an attribute in common (in Deduction 1, 139e8). This virtuoso performance in eristics is then doubled by showing that the One and the Others are not only alike in being different but unlike in being the same (148c1–2).[66]

The argument for similarity trades here on the fact that "different" is a co-relative term, or as the *Sophist* says, "whatever is different is necessarily what it is *from something different*" (255d6). Hence, although the intrinsic meaning or *phusis* of the Different remains the same throughout repeated utterances of the word (and this stability is what makes language possible), the full meaning of the term in any particular case depends upon what it differentiates its referent *from*. The fallacy succeeds, then, in deliberately eliding the distinction between these two kinds of meaning, one of which is the stable concept or sense of the term "different." The meaning that changes from case to case does not exactly correspond to the Fregean notion of reference. But the argument does show Plato deliberately playing here with the ambiguity of word-thing connections, just as a famous passage in the *Sophist* shows his acute awareness of the use-mention distinction (257b9–c3).[67]

Concluding comment on Part Two

We have recognized four constructive deductions, including two with an affirmative hypothesis ("if the One is," D2 and 3) and two with a negative hypothesis ("if the One is not," D5 and 7). Among these D2 stands apart, as a survey of all positive properties in an abstract theory of the natural world, including spatial and temporal properties, but excluding sensory qualities. D3 explores an even more general structure of unity and plurality as a blend of limit and the unlimited. D5 develops a positive account of Not-Being understood as negative predication, for a subject that is not a being in the fullest sense, i.e. not a Form. Finally, D7 gives a brief sketch of a world in which plurality would be only apparent, since it lacks any stable principle of

---

[66] For Plato's own comment on this argument form see *Philebus* 13d, cited above, n. 56.

[67] For another Platonic anticipation of the sense-reference distinction see *Cratylus* 439d9: it is impossible to describe an object in perpetual flux, because it is impossible to say "first, that it is this (*ekeino*), and then that it is such (*toiouton*)," because, even as we speak, "it is immediately departing and no longer in the same condition (*mēketi houtōs*)." There is an even sharper contrast between reference (*touto*, "this") and description (*toiouton*, "such") in the flux passage of the *Timaeus* 49e1. See the discussion of these texts below, in Chapter 6.

unity. Thus, each of these constructive deductions explores a different aspect of plurality, in the context of a possible account of the natural world.

By contrast, the other four deductions are all negative in content, including two with an affirmative hypothesis (D1 and D4: "if the One is. . ."), two with a negative hypothesis (D6 and 8: "if the One is not"). Each of these destructive deductions illustrates a mode of *chōrismos* or total separation of a proposed subject (the One) from Being, and so from any other Form, an isolation that excludes all predication and all propositional content.

Thus, Part Two of the *Parmenides* presents us with a catalog of conceptual space, a wide range of possible structures of unity and plurality, limit and the unlimited, form and formlessness. Among these alternatives, the One of Deduction 2 stands out as bearing a definite relation to the natural world: it not only undergoes motion and rest as well as coming-to-be and passing-away, but it is actually the object of sense perception, together with knowledge and opinion (155d). In short, Deduction 2 presents an abstract range of possible properties for the world of nature. But there is nothing in these deductions to tell us which properties are actually realized in the world. For this we would need information from sense perception. Although some relation to perception is recognized here, no discussion of sensory qualities is included. The methodical exercise of the *Parmenides* may be seen as a preparation for physics, but by itself it cannot provide the basis for natural science. For that we would need some empirical data, in other words, information from the senses and from perceptual judgment (*doxa*). So we turn to the *Theaetetus* for a critique of these two faculties.

CHAPTER 2

The Theaetetus *in the context of the later Dialogues*

Passing from the *Parmenides* to the *Theaetetus*, we move from an exercise in abstract ontology to something more like empiricist epistemology. The transition is abrupt. But this sequence is, I suggest, indicated by a formal clue: both the *Theaetetus* and the *Sophist* contain retrospective references to the meeting with Parmenides reported in the dialogue named after him.[1] In literary terms, both *Theaetetus* and *Sophist* are thus presented as sequels to the *Parmenides*. (And the *Sophist* in turn contains a backward reference to the *Theaetetus*, confirming this sequence.)

Why should Plato want to present the *Theaetetus* as in some sense a continuation of the *Parmenides*? Clearly, the critique of Part One serves to establish a methodological distance from the doctrine of Forms. On the other hand, the absence of any reference to empirical data in Part Two may point to the need for reflection on the role of sense perception in any full account of knowledge. This concern for a link between abstract metaphysics and empirical knowledge may explain why Plato should want to present the *Theaetetus* as in some sense a follow-up to the *Parmenides*. After a radical critique of the metaphysics of Forms, we turn to an account of knowledge from which such metaphysical concerns are systematically eliminated.

2.1   The hermeneutical problem: how to read the *Theaetetus*

The *Theaetetus* is an extraordinary dialogue from every point of view. Read as a self-standing work on epistemology, it offers us a series of brilliant arguments on a surprising number of themes that have become the focus of attention in modern philosophy, from Descartes' dream to the logical atomism of the twentieth century. On the other hand, if the dialogue is read in the context of Plato's other writings, we are confronted with surprises of a different sort. Socrates seems to be a familiar figure, and the

---

[1] *Theaet.* 183e; *Soph.* 217c.

role of intellectual midwife that he assigns to himself here has become paradigmatic for our view of Socrates in the earlier dialogues. But the philosophy that we think of as distinctively Platonic is not to be found in the *Theaetetus*. It is as if Plato had returned to the aporetic mode of those earlier works. Indeed, the formal structure of the *Theaetetus* is modeled on that of the dialogues of definition, like the *Euthyphro* and *Meno*. The *Theaetetus* might claim to be the conceptual sequel to the *Meno*. The *Meno* asks the question "What is virtue?" and discusses the Socratic answer that virtue is a form of knowledge. The follow-up question might well be "What is knowledge?" However, when that question is actually posed in the *Theaetetus*, the philosophical landscape is entirely different. By introducing the theme of recollection and the method of hypothesis, the *Meno* points towards the conception of knowledge that will be developed in the *Phaedo* and *Republic*. But when in the *Theaetetus* we actually try to answer the question "What is knowledge?" there is no mention either of recollection or of the method of hypothesis. Above all, there is no reference to the metaphysical doctrine of Forms, which dominates the conception of knowledge in the *Phaedo* and *Republic*. Although (as we shall see) several passages in the *Theaetetus* can be read as indirect allusions to the notion of Forms, these are hints from the author to the knowing reader, as it were over the heads of the persons in the dialogue. Like his namesake in the *Meno*, Socrates in the *Theaetetus* seems never to have heard of a theory that he presents in the *Parmenides* as his own juvenile invention. It is as if the critique of the Forms in the *Parmenides* had wiped the slate clean.

The ignorance of Socrates here is surprising, since in this same dialogue Socrates actually refers to his earlier meeting with Parmenides (which, we may be sure, never occurred outside that dialogue). His apparent ignorance will seem even more puzzling if we bear in mind that in the *Philebus*, when we meet Socrates again (as principal speaker for the last time), he is quite familiar with a doctrine of monads reminiscent of the classical theory, and familiar also with problems of participation that were addressed to him in the *Parmenides* (*Phil.* 15b, *Parm.* 131a–e). Thus among the middle-to-late dialogues, from the *Parmenides* to the *Philebus*, the metaphysical ignorance of Socrates in the *Theaetetus* is strikingly isolated, and it calls for some explanation.

This problem of a Socrates "almost entirely innocent of Platonic metaphysics" was treated recently by David Sedley, who suggests that Plato is deliberately returning in the *Theaetetus* to the figure of Socrates as portrayed in the aporetic dialogues.[2] Thus, Socrates is represented here only as "the

---

[2] Sedley (2004) 7, 17.

midwife of Platonism," the historical and philosophical antecedent for the mature Platonism represented in the *Phaedo* and *Republic*. As in the aporetic dialogues, Socrates himself is barren of positive doctrine.

I agree with Sedley that Plato is deliberately distancing Socrates here from his own philosophical position, and I agree also that the dialogue gives us oblique hints of that position. But why has Plato selected a metaphysically barren Socrates to carry out this elaborate discussion of knowledge? The conception of Socrates as midwife does not account for the close relationship between the *Theaetetus* and the *Parmenides*, on the one hand, and, on the other hand, its immediate sequel in the *Sophist*. As I see it, the central challenge for any interpretation of the *Theaetetus* is to relate its overtly non-Platonic, even anti-Platonic metaphysical perspective to the rest of Plato's philosophy as articulated in these neighboring dialogues.

In the *Parmenides* the classical theory of Forms, as presented in the *Republic* and *Phaedrus*, comes under attack. This theory then disappears from view in the *Theaetetus* and reappears in the *Sophist* only as the object of a critical examination, the doctrine of the Friends of Forms. In the *Sophist* the visitor from Elea will present a new way of seeing Forms, as members of a connected network. But the relationship between Forms and sensibles – the core of the classical theory – is presented in the *Sophist* only as the view of the Friends of Forms.

How are we to understand the silence of the *Theaetetus* and the critical distance of the *Sophist*? Some scholars have inferred that Plato had given up on metaphysical Forms. But, as we have seen in Chapter 1, such a total rejection of Platonic metaphysics is confirmed neither by the *Parmenides* nor by the later dialogues. It is essential here to draw a sharp distinction between the classical theory and Plato's basic metaphysics. On the one hand, the classical notion of participation between Forms and their sensible homonyms was attacked in the *Parmenides* and it remains problematic in the *Philebus* (15b). On the other hand, the basic contrast between changing objects of sense perception and stable forms "that one can best grasp in *logos*," is reaffirmed by Parmenides and presupposed in all the later dialogues, with the sole exception of the *Theaetetus*. Even in the *Sophist* the protagonist is after all an Eleatic, who is firmly committed to the requirement of unchanging objects for knowledge (248b–d). The *Theaetetus* is the only text among Plato's later works to discuss the question of knowledge at length without even considering this Eleatic claim that cognition requires stable being as its object. As we shall see, the refutation of the flux theory clearly implies the need for stability in any object of knowledge. But that positive conclusion is never explicitly drawn. On the contrary, the discussion of knowledge in this dialogue is systematically designed to avoid the consideration of any theory of unchanging Being, whether Platonic or Eleatic.[3]

It is natural to connect these unusual features of the *Theaetetus* and the *Sophist* with Plato's attack on the classical theory of Forms in the *Parmenides*. Both the *Theaetetus* and the *Sophist* stand as it were in the shadow of the *Parmenides*. That is why both dialogues are deliberately neutral with regard to the theory under attack. They leave us in genuine doubt as to how much of the classical theory can survive the Parmenidean critique. Of course, the basic metaphysical contrast between Being and Becoming will reappear in the *Philebus* and *Timaeus*, with a reminder in the *Statesman* and a remote allusion in the *Sophist*. In the meantime, however, both in the *Sophist* and in the *Theaetetus*, the entire theory is put between brackets – neither rejected nor presupposed, but ignored in the latter and subject to critical review in the former.

Limiting ourselves now to the *Theaetetus*, we need to ask: What is going on here? Why has Plato temporarily abandoned metaphysics in order to discuss the concept of knowledge from what is essentially an empiricist perspective, seeking to define knowledge first in terms of sense perception and then in terms of *doxa* or belief, but in both cases without a stable ontology – without any reference to the need for unchanging objects of cognition? This is not a question that can be directly answered from the text. We need some hermeneutical hypothesis to account for this basic disparity between the epistemology of the *Theaetetus* and the rest of Plato's work.

I take my clue here from a passage in the *Parmenides*, which insists that the method of dialectic requires us to consider not only the consequence of our own thesis but also what follows from its denial (136a). This principle of method can, I suggest, account for the doctrinal peculiarity of the *Theaetetus*. The Platonic thesis in question is the claim that knowledge and understanding (*nous*) require an object that is stable and unchanging. (This is essentially the Eleatic thesis formulated in *Republic* V and reasserted in *Sophist* 249b–c.) From Plato's point of view, an attempt to define knowledge on the basis of *aisthēsis* and *doxa* implies a denial of this thesis. Thus, the logical connection between an epistemology of sense perception and an ontology of universal flux is made explicit in the first part of the *Theaetetus*. The link between *doxa* and a similar ontology is left implicit in the second part, but it is obliquely indicated by the refusal to discuss

---

[3] At 183d–e the dialogue mentions but refuses to discuss the extreme Eleatic thesis that everything in the world is stationary.

Parmenides' doctrine of Being (184a). As the *Republic* explains (and as the *Timaeus* will reassert), *doxa* is essentially linked with sense perception in the cognition of objects that undergo change.[4] (This conception of *doxa* as tied to change is, of course, the Parmenidean counterpart to the thesis that knowledge takes stable Being as its object.) Hence, for Plato as a Parmenidean, neither perception nor *doxa* can provide the basis for a definition of knowledge, because neither one establishes contact with the kind of being that is exempt from change. Read as an exercise in dialectic, the double *reductio* here of attempts to define knowledge, first in terms of *aisthēsis* and then in terms of *doxa*, will provide indirect support for the Eleatic thesis, that an ontology of stable Being is required as the object for knowledge. In the light of this two-fold *reductio*, the *Theaetetus* as a whole can be seen as repeating on a broader scale the argument against an ontology of flux (181c–183b). Reliable cognition and truthful discourse (*logos*) both require stability in the object, some element of Being rather than unmitigated Becoming. I take it that the failure here of all the proposed definitions is to be explained by this implicit assumption, that neither sense perception nor *doxa* can guarantee contact with stable Being. Hence, neither can provide the basis for an adequate account of knowledge.

Thus the positive conclusion, implied by the negative outcome of the entire dialogue and established more directly by the refutation of unrestricted flux, is that *some* element of unchanging Being is required as an object for knowledge. But of course this conclusion does not imply support for the specific ontology of the *Phaedo* or *Republic*. Cornford has overstated the positive interpretation of our dialogue by assuming that it defends the classical theory of Forms.[5] On the contrary, the double *reductio* points to a claim more general and more Parmenidean. An adequate account of knowledge will require an ontology that provides a definite object for thought and language, by positing a fixed structure for things in the world. Hence the positive sequel to the negative outcome of our dialogue will be assigned not to Socrates, Plato's spokesman for the classical theory, but to a sympathetic visitor from Elea.

Since this constructive reading of the *Theaetetus* goes beyond anything in the text of the dialogue, let me add a word about the strategy of interpretation. I am relying here on an unspoken complicity between the author and his readers. As readers we have access to the presentation of Plato's

---

[4] *Rep.* 478a–480a; *Tim.* 28a. Cf. *Phil.* 59a1.
[5] Cornford (1934/1957) 161 ff. For partial parallels to Cornford's interpretation, see the references to Cherniss, Shorey, and Ross cited by Burnyeat (1990) 238, n. 133.

philosophy in earlier and later dialogues. Hence we are in a position to draw conclusions that the metaphysically barren Socrates of the *Theaetetus* will not draw for us. For example, we can (but Socrates does not) recognize in the long ethical Digression (172c–177b) several distinct echoes of the moral doctrine of the *Gorgias* and *Republic*. Similarly, we can suspect an indirect allusion to the concept of Forms in those two "paradigms established in Being" (*paradeigmatōn en tōi onti hestōtōn*) that a person comes to resemble by a life either of justice or of injustice (176e).[6] And we may again be reminded of the Forms in the later reference to the *koina* or common objects of thought, cognized not through the body but by the soul itself (184b–186). These texts in the *Theaetetus* do not directly present Plato's metaphysical views, but they are clearly designed to recall such views to an informed reader.

It is on the basis of this author-reader complicity that Plato can imply the indirect conclusion suggested above, a conclusion that we must draw but that Socrates will not draw for us. It is because we are familiar with the theory of the *Phaedo* and the *Republic* that our suspicions will be raised from the start by the proposal to define knowledge in terms of sense perception. These suspicions will be further confirmed by the alternative attempt to define knowledge in terms of opinion (*doxa*). For we recognize that both proposals directly contradict Plato's usual assumptions. It is this recognition that alerts us to the possibility that the entire dialogue is intended as a dialectical enterprise. This enterprise has to be understood in terms of an implied communication between Plato and his reader, not in terms of the overt conversation between Socrates and Theaetetus. It is only from this external point of view – the point of view of the informed reader – that we can identify the content of the *Theaetetus* as a *reductio* argument against any attempt to define knowledge without an adequate ontological basis.

2.2 Part One: knowledge as sense perception

The initial definition of knowledge in terms of sense perception, proposed by Theaetetus at 151e, has no parallel in Plato's work. Sense and rational cognition are normally contrasted with each other (for example in *Phaedo* 64b–66a; *Republic* VI, 508c). Theaetetus' proposal is all the more unexpected, coming as it does after repeated references to the mathematical quadrivium taught by Theodorus, and after the report of Theaetetus' work on irrational quantities in geometry (145a, c–d2, 147d–148b2). How is it

---

[6] See Appendix 2 on the Digression.

possible, in a conversation with two distinguished mathematicians, for the search for knowledge to begin with the notion of sense perception? By highlighting from the outset the role of mathematics as an epistemic model, Plato the arch-rationalist has deliberately marked in advance this sharp contrast with the empiricist approach that will be introduced by Theaetetus' definition. The initial emphasis on mathematics draws attention to the fact that this search for a definition of knowledge will begin from a standpoint as remote as possible from Plato's usual perspective.

The implications of Theaetetus' proposed definition are developed with the aid of two doctrines familiar from the *Cratylus*: (1) the Protagorean thesis of subjective relativism – the doctrine that things are as they appear to a given subject; and (2) the Secret Doctrine of universal flux, claiming that all things change and nothing stands still (ascribed in the *Cratylus* first to Protagoras at 152c10 and later to Heraclitus).

The link between (1) and (2) is established by (3) a theory of sensation as the joint product or offspring of two agencies, conceived as two slow motions, one internal and one external, that produce twin qualities, one projected onto the percipient subject and the other onto the external object or cause of sensation (156a ff.). This theory of sensation is clearly Plato's own invention, a more subtle version of the mechanistic accounts of perception proposed by Empedocles and Democritus. Since the twin theory is never directly refuted, scholarly opinion has been divided as to whether it represents Plato's own view. On any interpretation, this theory offers a brilliant account of the phenomenology of perception. Thus, on the one hand, it allows for a private sensory experience of the perceived quality as projected inwards onto the subject, while, on the other hand, the twin quality that is projected outwards onto the object will account for useful information about the world. With appropriate modifications, this theory can be made compatible with Plato's own mechanistic account of perception theory to be offered in the *Timaeus*.[7] In its present context, the twin theory offers a plausible account of the mechanism underlying sensory experience, on the basis of an assumed doctrine of flux.

2.3 The ontology of flux

The ontology of flux itself is a different story. This is not simply a component in the theory of perception; it is the direct denial of Plato's own Eleatic insistence on a stable object for knowledge. As foundation for

---

[7] For a fuller discussion of the twin theory of sensation, see Appendix 3.

the Protagorean identity between reality and appearance, the theory of flux in the *Theaetetus* provides the centerpiece for the Secret Doctrine supporting the identification of knowledge with sense perception. As in the *Cratylus*, the doctrine of flux is linked here with Protagorean relativism to represent the worldview most directly opposed to Plato's own conception of a stable and objective (not observer-relative) structure of reality.[8]

Was the doctrine of flux ever accepted by Plato himself as an account of the sensible world? So claims Aristotle. In *Metaphysics* A.6 he tells us that Plato "in his youth had become acquainted with Cratylus and the Heraclitean doctrine that sensible things are always in flux and there is no knowledge of them; and this is what he believed also later."[9] On this point Aristotle has been followed by many modern scholars, who see Plato as conceiving sensible phenomena as a realm of ceaseless change. And this interpretation can find some support in a passage from the *Phaedo*. While Forms are said to be free from every kind of change, their sensible homonyms are "so to speak never in any way in the same state, neither with themselves nor with one another" (78e3). We might claim to find the same view of sensibles in *Republic* V, where it is asserted that all the many beautiful objects will also appear ugly, and the many just actions also unjust, so that sensible things generally are seen to be "rolling about (*kulindeitai*) between what is not and what purely is" (479a, d4).

It is true, then, that Plato presents the realm of the sensible "many" as a realm of change and becoming, in contrast to the changeless being of the Forms. To this extent Plato's persistent concern with the theory of flux does reflect his own conception of the natural world as subject to change. But it does not follow that the doctrine of flux as presented in the *Cratylus* and *Theaetetus* represents Plato's own view. On the contrary, in both dialogues this doctrine is rejected as incoherent. What both dialogues show – and what has been surprisingly neglected, under the influence of Aristotle's text – is that we must draw a sharp distinction between Plato's view of becoming and the doctrine of universal flux. Although Aristotle may be right to claim that for Plato there is no knowledge (*epistēmē*) of sensible things, if knowledge is taken in a strong sense, it is nevertheless clear that,

---

[8] This connection between the view of Protagoras, cited at the beginning of the *Cratylus*, and the doctrine of flux expounded later in that work, is established in their joint denial: (we do not each have our private reality but) "things themselves have their own stable being (οὐσία τις βέβαιος), not relative to us and not dragged up and down by the way things appear to us (τῷ ἡμετέρῳ φαντάσματι)," *Crat.* 386e.

[9] *Met.* 987a32. By "also later" (καὶ ὕστερον) I take Aristotle to mean not only in the *Cratylus* but also in the *Theaetetus*.

even for Plato, we do have some kind of cognition for persons, horses, and cloaks. On the contrary, there can be no cognition at all of a world in universal, unrestricted flux. Plato is fascinated by the theme of incessant change, not because he is an extreme Heraclitean in the style of Cratylus, but because his own contrast between Being and Becoming reflects a view of the natural world for which the Heraclitean river might properly serve as a symbol.[10] The arguments of the *Cratylus* and *Theaetetus* are there to show that such a world must *also* contain essential elements of stability. And on this point Heraclitus need not disagree. After all, for him too the river remains the same, even though its waters are ever new. What is specifically Platonic is not the requirement of stability but the hypothesis of an absolutely changeless Being as source for the durable structure of Becoming. This is the underlying view clearly hinted at in the *Cratylus* but never mentioned in the *Theaetetus*.

It seems that Socrates was exaggerating in the *Phaedo* when he described beautiful human beings and horses and cloaks as not being the same "in any way" (*oudamōs*) (78e4). He means only that they are not permanently and invariably beautiful.[11] We may, if we wish, think of the rejection of unrestricted flux in the *Cratylus* as a deliberate correction of this passage in the *Phaedo*, if the latter is taken too literally. But in any case it would be a mistake to follow Aristotle in identifying the doctrine of unrestricted (Cratylean) flux as Plato's considered view of sensible reality. The flux of the *Theaetetus*, like the flux of the *Cratylus*, represents a doctrine to be rejected, not to be accepted as Plato's account of the sensible world.

Of course, the flux doctrine does capture something essential for Plato's own view of the contrast between Forms and their sensible homonyms. This is the point more carefully expressed in the formula of *Republic* V: for any Form F, the many sensible Fs both are and are not F (479b9, echoing the contrast between the Beautiful itself and the many beautiful things at *Symposium* 211a2–5). Or, in an alternative formulation of the same point,

---

[10] Plato may be a Heraclitean, but (*pace* Aristotle) he can scarcely have been a follower of Cratylus. Aristotle's picture of Cratylus as reduced to hissing and wagging his finger is derived from a lost dialogue of Aeschines. *Rhetoric* 1417b1 mentions only hand-waving (τοῖν χειροῖν διασείων), not wagging the finger (*Met.* 1010a13); but it is unlikely that these two portraits of Cratylus come from separate dialogues. (Aristotle's memory is not infallible on such matters.) In that work Cratylus must have been represented as an even more ridiculous figure than in Plato's dialogue, where he is stubbornly resistant to argument.

[11] This rhetorical exaggeration at *Phaedo* 78e4 is softened by "so to speak" (ὡς ἔπος εἰπεῖν). It is provoked by a symmetrical contrast with the preceding denial of any change whatsoever for the Forms: (οὐδέποτε οὐδαμῇ οὐδαμῶς ἀλλοίωσιν οὐδεμίαν) at 78d6. The exaggerated οὐδαμῶς for the many beautiful ("not the same in any way") is eliminated in the parallel statements of the contrast at *Philebus* 59b1–2 and *Timaeus* 28a.

the homonyms *appear* to be Fs but they are not truly F, because they are not eternally and invariably F. Appearing to be F is thus equivalent to the notion of both being and not being F.[12]

Unlike the immanent forms of Aristotelian nature, Plato's sensibles do not have stable essences as their own intrinsic natures; all their stability is derivative from the unchanging Form.[13] That is why the problem of participation is so fundamental. Plato returns again and again to the theme of flux, not only because of its popularity among his predecessors (he is probably exaggerating when he attributes it to all of them except Parmenides), but because it expresses this fundamental ontological deficiency of the natural world. Thus, he will appropriate the notion of flux for an account of the Receptacle of the Forms in his own cosmology.[14]

The distinctive features of this refutation of flux in *Theaetetus* 181c–183b will emerge more clearly if we compare it with the argument against a similar doctrine at the end of the *Cratylus*. Both arguments aim to refute the doctrine of universal, unrestricted flux (*panta aei kineitai*). And both arguments emphasize the claim that things are changing "even as we speak" (*hama hēmōn legontōn* at *Crat.* 439d10; *aei legontos hupexerchetai* at *Theaet.* 182d7), because both are concerned with the problem of correctly describing things in the process of change.[15] Thus, both arguments conclude that no coherent account can be given if things are always changing in every respect. But the differences are instructive.

The issue of a description in language is central for the argument of the *Theaetetus*, which concludes that the thesis of unrestricted flux would require a new dialect (*phōnē*), since we do not have expressions (*rēmata*) that can formulate the doctrine without bringing things to a halt (183a7–b 4). That is why the thesis of total flux is self-refuting. Like the doctrine of the Late-learners in the *Sophist*, it cannot be formulated without

---

[12] For appearing-F as distinctive of non-Forms, see φανήσεται, φανῆναι, φαίνεται at *Rep.* 479a7–b4; φαντασθήσεται *Symp.* 211a5; φαίνεται, ἐφάνη, φαίνεται in *Phaedo* 74b8–d5. In the *Phaedo*, appearing-opposite is directly connected with deficiency (ἐνδεῖν, ἐνδεέστερα, φαυλότερα, 74d6–75b8).

[13] This is true at any rate for the classical theory of the *Phaedo* and *Republic*. As we shall see, Plato's doctrine is more complex in the *Philebus* where he introduces the notion of γεγενημένη οὐσία, a nature or essence that has come into being (27b 8). Similarly, in the *Timaeus* the mathematical structure of the elements provides an intrinsic basis for stability within the world of change.

[14] *Timaeus* 49–52. Hence in terms of Burnyeat's commentary neither Reading A nor Reading B is quite the right story for flux in the *Theaetetus*. (See Burnyeat (1990) 8–9, 45–52.) Since the theory of total flux is shown to be unacceptable, it cannot be Plato's own account of the natural world. But because of its affinity to Plato's view of becoming, it represents more than a mere moment in the *reductio* argument.

[15] *Crat.* 439d8 προσειπεῖν ὀρθῶς; *Theaet.* 181e5 ὀρθῶς ἕξει εἰπεῖν; 182c10 εἴχομεν ἄν που εἰπεῖν; d4 οἷόν τέ τι προσειπεῖν... ὥστε καὶ ὀρθῶς προσαγορεύειν; e3 προσρητέον, etc.

presupposing its own denial. In effect, the argument of the *Theaetetus* shows that we cannot have a descriptive language – a language that applies to the world – without points of fixity at both ends, without some things and some concepts that remain unchanged. The consequence of radical flux is that "language is emptied of all positive meaning."[16]

There is some disagreement among commentators as to how this devastating conclusion is reached. How do changes in the world deprive our words of meaning? The point is not about language considered in isolation but about language as descriptive – about the fit between language and the world. If everything is changing "even as we speak," there will be no definite objects for words to refer to. But without definite objects, words themselves cannot have definite meanings. To this extent, words are like names: their meaning is fundamentally referential.

A modern thinker might suppose there could be fixed concepts in language, or in the mind, even if there were no stable structures in an objective world. Plato, however, is a realist about concepts. For a thought to be definite it must be a thought about *something* definite. (Hence the inference at *Parmenides* 132b–c that any *noēma* must be the thought of something that is, and is one: *on ti hen*. It is because of this realism about conceptual content that the problems about Not-Being and falsity loom so large for Plato, as we will see in the next chapter.) For Plato there is no realm of mental concepts whose meaning could be entirely independent of their application to objects in the world, whether sensible or intelligible.

According to the argument of the *Theaetetus*, if there is nothing definite in the world, there will also be nothing definite in human thought. Definite meanings require definite objects. That is the idea behind the claim that in a realm of total flux "one should not call anything 'seeing' rather than 'not seeing', or any other perception rather than not" (182e). It would be misleading to suppose that words like "white" and "seeing" could have a fixed meaning, even if there were nothing for them to be true of. For if such meanings were fixed, at least some negative claims might still be true in the absence of any stable reality. But at 183b–1 Socrates seems to doubt whether even the sheerly negative conclusion "not even so" (*oud' houtōs*) is indefinite enough to avoid attributing stability.

The conclusion here that language cannot coherently represent a world in total flux corresponds to the warning of Parmenides in his own dialogue

---

[16] Burnyeat (1990) 45. Sedley (2004) 93 reminds us that the alleged Heracliteans of the Secret Doctrine have consciously rejected the terms of ordinary language that imply stability (152d, 157b). What they do not realize is that they will have no vocabulary left in which to formulate their thesis.

that, without stable forms (*eidos, idea*), we would have no object for thought (*dianoia*) and no capacity for rational discourse (*dialegesthai*) (*Parm.* 135b–c). What is required is not necessarily the transcendent Forms of the classical theory but at least some stable structure or fixed reality.

There is a certain parallel between the refutation of unrestricted flux in the *Cratylus* and *Theaetetus* and the rejection of unrestricted Not-Being in the *Sophist*. In neither case is it possible to give a coherent formulation for the concept to be rejected. But in both cases it is not only possible but necessary to salvage a restricted version of this concept by a more careful formulation. That is achieved for the concept of Not-Being in the *Sophist*. For the doctrine of flux the salvage operation is still more complex, and it will require the elaborate theory of the Receptacle in the *Timaeus*.

To return now to the earlier argument in the *Cratylus*. It begins with a reference to this problem of a descriptive language for things in continuous flux – things that change "even as we speak" (439d10) –, but it immediately shifts to the question of knowability. Taking cognition very widely to include recognition (*gnōsis*), it argues that any object of cognition must be a thing or fact that is definite, and hence minimally stable. "How could there be something that is never in the same state? . . . Furthermore, it could never be cognized (*gnōstheiē*) by anyone" (439e7). Thus, there cannot *be* an object that is totally indefinite. And even if there were such a thing, it could provide no information about the world to a percipient subject. Thus, the rejection of flux in the *Cratylus* is both ontological and epistemic: such an indefinite object cannot be, and it could not be known or even accurately identified.

This concern in the *Cratylus* with the possibility of cognition is an element that disappears from the corresponding argument in the *Theaetetus*. As a point of good method, the *Theaetetus* avoids the issue of knowability for flux, since the concept of knowledge is itself in question here. A second, major difference is the presence of Forms in the *Cratylus* context. The *Cratylus* is less concerned to deny the flux theory in general than to deny its application to a range of entities designated as "beings" (*ta onta*). In contrast to the doctrine of flux, Socrates introduces (as in a dream, 439c–7) the doctrine of stable Forms that do not change: "the beautiful itself, the good, and each one of the things that are beings in this way (*ta onta houtō*)" (439c8–d5). The *Cratylus* leaves open the possibility that sensible homonyms of *ta onta* (beautiful faces, and the like) might actually be in flux. But they could not be in *total* flux: "How could there be something that is never in the same state? For if it is sometimes in the same state, in that time it clearly does not change" (439e–2). Thus, the argument of the *Cratylus* allows the possibility of partial or temporary change. But it begins and ends with a reference to "the beautiful, the good, and each one of *ta onta*" as completely exempt from flux (440b–6). The *Cratylus* does not argue for the *existence* of Forms; their presence has been assumed from the beginning of the dialogue (389b). It insists only that they must be unchanging.

By omitting any reference to Forms, and by limiting the question to linguistic expression rather than cognition, the *Theaetetus* provides a tighter, more sharply focused argument. It also distinguishes two different kinds of change (locomotion and alteration) and thus makes clear that the thesis applies to *every* kind of change. This distinction is new, and it calls for a new terminology. (The word *poiotēs* for "quality" is recognized as a fresh coinage at 182a–8.) But the thesis of flux was from the beginning a thesis of total flux.[17] The Secret Doctrine of *Theaetetus* 152d and 157b is essentially the same as the general Heracliteanism of the *Cratylus*.[18]

Unlike the parallel passage in the *Cratylus*, however, the new refutation of flux makes no reference to Forms. This is to be expected, since the *Theaetetus* generally avoids all discussion of things that do not change. On the other hand, if it is not the case that everything always changes in every way (and if there is anything at all), then there must be something that sometimes remains the same in some way. This positive conclusion is not drawn, but it is silently implied when the refutation is completed at 183b. Where should we look for such stability? Is there any basis for stability short of the unchanging Forms? What follows in the next section of the dialogue is the introduction of the *koina*, the common objects or concepts that the soul apprehends "itself through itself," not through the organs of the body (185b–e). Nothing is said about the ontology of these *koina*, nor that they are free of change. They are distinguished only epistemically, as objects of incorporeal cognition. This is as close as the *Theaetetus* comes to recognizing Forms. Or, looking forward to the mathematical structures of the *Timaeus* and the "Being that has come to be" of the *Philebus*, are the *koina* to be seen here rather as intermediate between Forms and sensibles? The author of the *Theaetetus* may not have made up his mind on this question of intermediates. In the parallel argument of the *Cratylus* it is the Forms themselves that are presented as the unchanging objects of cognition. On either reading of

---

[17] See *Crat.* 402a8: πάντα χωρεῖ καὶ οὐδὲν μένει; cf. 401d5. Qualitative change was included in the flux of the *Cratylus*, even without the new terminology: ἄλλο καὶ ἀλλοῖον γίγνεσθαι . . . μηδαμῶς ἔχειν (440a1–4).

[18] For a different reading of this argument see McDowell (1973) 180–84.

ta koina, we may regard these common features here as the unspoken beneficiaries of the rejection of universal flux.

The implicit connection between *koina* and Forms lies outside the text of the dialogue. There is a more internal link between the denial of universal flux and the twin theory of sensation, where slow movements in organ and object beget fast movements in the act of sensory perception. For this bilateral schema for perception must itself be exempt from change. Plato's rejection of absolute flux will also have important consequences for physics, for example in the theory of elementary triangles. But it is not the role of the *Theaetetus* to explore such consequences. The author of this dialogue has left physical theory for the *Philebus* and *Timaeus*, and eventually for *Laws* X.[19] Within the present discussion of knowledge, it is only the common concepts or *koina* that offer a pale reflection of the stable system of Forms.

2.4   The *koina* as the object of thought (*dianoia*)

The final refutation of Theaetetus' definition of knowledge as sense perception is prepared by a careful distinction between two levels of cognition, only one of which can claim to count as knowledge. This distinction is important in many ways, of which I examine only one.[20] This text marks a decisive step towards the classical conception of reason or intellect as a distinct capacity of the mind.

In principle, the distinction is not new. Democritus had already drawn a line between sense perception (*aisthēsis*), as defined by the five bodily sense modalities, and a higher form of cognition that we might recognize as reason.[21] Democritus imagined a picturesque wrestling match between these two faculties. "Poor mind (*phrēn*)," say the senses, "do you overthrow us, although you take your conviction from us? Our overthrow is your fall" (fr. 125). In Democritus' context, now lost, the original disagreement between these two powers probably concerned the existence of atoms and the void, posited by reason but inaccessible to the senses. Now generalized, this distinction between two cognitive powers – together with the notion of a conflict between them – is adopted by Plato in the *Phaedo*, where the

---

[19] In the *Theaetetus* itself there is one hint of a quasi-atomic physical theory. Something of this sort must lie behind the reference to a "collection" (ἄθροισμα) of slow motions corresponding to a human being, animal or stone at 157b9.

[20] For the general recognition here of a unified subject of cognitive experience, see the discussion in Burnyeat (1976) 29–51 and (1990) 58–62.

[21] Democritus fr. 11 DK distinguishes two modes of cognition (γνώμη), the genuine (γνησίη) and the dark or shadowy (σκοτίη). Dark cognition includes seeing, hearing, smelling, tasting, and perceiving (αἰσθάνεσθαι) by touch.

rational principle is identified as *psuchē* and sensory cognition is assigned to the body. Like Democritus, Plato insists that it is by reasoning or calculation (*logizesthai*), not by bodily sense perception, that the soul grasps truth (*Phaedo* 65b–c). (This will be again the central claim of the *Theaetetus*, in the final argument against the definition of knowledge as sense perception.) Plato's conception of the soul in the *Phaedo* is profoundly new, since it is now linked to eternal Forms by way of recollection. But Plato's new conception is situated within a scheme of soul-body dualism that he has taken over from Democritus.[22]

A new, entirely Platonic scheme is introduced with the tripartite psychology of the *Republic*. Reason is again represented by the principle of calculation, the *logistikon*, but the senses have now dropped out of sight. The concerns of this tripartite theory are motivational rather than epistemic. Hence the principle distinct from and potentially opposed to reason is represented in this theory not by sense perception but by the emotions: spirit and appetite. When Plato turns to the epistemic critique of art in Book X, he does expand this new conception of the non-rational soul to include perceptual judgment (602c–603a). However, these two theories are not smoothly blended; in the third part of the psyche, the relation between *aisthēsis* and the emotions remains obscure. The situation is not much clearer in the later version of tripartition in the *Timaeus*. Here again "irrational sense-perception" (*aisthēsis alogos*) is simply "mixed together" with the emotions, including pleasure and pain, in the non-rational part of the soul (69d).

It seems that Plato never fully integrated the properly cognitive contrast between reason and sense perception, inherited from Democritus, with his own tripartite psychology, designed for moral psychology and action theory rather than epistemology. On the one hand, the dichotomy between the two cognitive faculties dominates the central books of the *Republic*, where the *noēta* or objects of rational cognition are systematically distinguished from the *horōmena*, the objects of sight and sense. On the other hand, in the tripartite theory of Books IV and VIII–IX the contrast with reason is provided not by perception but by bad judgment under the influence of passion and desire. Plato is not prepared to recognize an Aristotelian distinction between practical and theoretical reason. The principle designated in the *Republic* as "calculating" (*logistikon*) and "lover of learning"

---

[22] For details see Kahn (1985) 1–31. Democritus has no fixed term for reason, but (like Plato) he sometimes employs the word for calculation, λογισμός; see fr. 187. Cf. also his use of the cognate term εὐλόγιστος for "reasonable, good at calculation" in fr. 236.

(*philomathes*) is destined both to rule the soul and to study the Forms. By introducing the contrast between theory and practice, the Aristotelian account of *nous* manages to unify these two originally independent traditions, entailing two different conceptions of reason: on the one hand, a practical notion of good judgment and reasonable conduct going back to Homer; on the other hand, a theoretical distinction between cognitive powers first dramatized in Democritus' combat between reason and the senses and elaborated by Plato in the *nous-aisthēsis* opposition of the central books. In the *Republic* as later in the *Timaeus*, we find the two traditions side by side, never fully united in a general theory of the mind.

In an important passage of the *Phaedrus*, as in our text in the *Theaetetus*, Plato returns to the more strictly epistemic concept of reason, without reference to the emotions and their impact on action. The doctrine of recollection is invoked here as the source of our capacity to interpret experience in rational terms. "For a human being must understand what is said by reference to a form, passing from many sense perceptions to a unity gathered together by reason (*logismos*). This is a recollection of those things which our soul once saw, travelling with a god and looking beyond the things we now call real and gaining access to what is really real (*to on ontōs*)" (*Phaedrus* 249b6–c4). Recollection thus signifies for Plato our human access to the realm of concepts.

This *Phaedrus* passage provides the immediate background for our passage on the *koina* or common concepts. In the *Phaedrus* text two points have been added to the traditional, Democritean distinction between reason and sense. (1) The one-many, Form-homonym contrast introduced by the doctrine of Forms is presented here as a cognitive achievement, advancing from many perceptions to a unified concept. (2) This ability to form general concepts is, in addition, identified with the capacity for language: "to understand what is said according to a form." The phrase "said according to a form" (*kat' eidos legomenon*) applies ambiguously both to what is spoken and also to what is understood. Thus, both active and passive linguistic competence is here said to depend upon the grasp of forms or concepts. This connection with the doctrine of Forms will necessarily disappear from the *Theaetetus*. The *Phaedrus* passage presents that doctrine in strictly epistemic terms, as a range of linguistic concepts required for the rational interpretation of sensory experience – a nice anticipation of the Kantian *a priori*. The stage is set for the *koina* of the *Theaetetus*.

In this, his final argument against Theaetetus' definition of knowledge, Plato returns to the Democritean distinction between the sense modalities on the one hand, defined by their relation to a bodily organ, and a higher cognition belonging to the mind alone. Relying now on this connection with the bodily organ of sense, Plato prepares the ground for a careful distinction, probably for the first time, between sensation or sense perception narrowly construed, on the one hand, and perceptual judgment taken generally. Perception in this broader sense introduces the higher level of cognition that Plato calls "thought" (*dianoia*) or "opinion" (*doxa*). In what follows, thinking will be analyzed as a para-linguistic activity, a silent discourse (*logos*) of the soul speaking to itself (189e–190a). As in the *Phaedrus* so in the *Theaetetus*, rational cognition is modeled on linguistic competence. The concepts required for language and thought are introduced here as *koina*, the common properties not directly accessible to the individual sense modalities, and hence not perceived "through the body." Higher cognition, or thinking, is thus distinguished in two ways: both by taking as its object more than one sense modality and also by its quasi-linguistic structure. In contrast to Aristotle's notion of "common sensibles" (motion, number, shape, and size), properties defined as the direct object of more than one sense, Plato's *koina* are essentially language-dependent and reflexive, not properly the objects of sense perception as such. Plato's common properties *apply to* the objects of the individual senses, but (unlike Aristotle's common sensibles) they are not themselves the object of any bodily sense.[23]

The list of *koina* begins with three items that will reappear in the *Sophist* as the first three of the "greatest kinds": being, same, and different (185a). It ends with terms familiar from the classical theory of the *Republic*: beautiful and ugly, good and bad (186a8).[24] The list includes negation, similarity, dissimilarity, opposition, and number, together with mathematical terms such as odd and even. We are here in the conceptual domain covered in other dialogues by a doctrine of Forms. (Compare, for example, the list at *Parmenides* 130b.) Given the ontological constraints of the *Theaetetus*, such forms will appear here only as objects of thought and concepts of language,

---

[23] See *De Anima* 418a for Aristotle's contrasting notion of common sensibles. In the present context Plato does not discuss motion or shape, but these are treated in the *Parmenides* as concepts of reason rather than sensory qualia. Plato explicitly denies that number and unity can be perceived "through the bodily organ" (*Theaet.* 185d1–e2). The dissenting view in Aristotle probably reflects the latter's greater interest in animal perception. On this disagreement between the two psychologies see also below, n. 28.

[24] The mention here of the negative terms ("ugly" and "bad") next to the positive terms ("beautiful" and "good") is rare in statements of the theory of Forms, but not unprecedented. For a parallel see *Rep.* V, 476.

not as full-scale beings (*onta*). What remains distinctive, nevertheless, of
Platonic realism is that the relevant cognitive capacity is defined by its
object, and not conversely. What we might call the faculty of reason is
specified here by its distinctive content, namely, by the set of concepts
corresponding to a doctrine of Forms. Thus, even in the *Theaetetus* epistemology is dependent upon ontology, although the notion of ontology
appears here in its thinnest form, reduced to a list of properties.

What is decisive for the refutation of Theaetetus' definition is the
presence in this list of the notion of being, a notion required for any truth
claim and hence for any claim to knowledge. No knowledge without truth,
and no truth without being (*ousia*): that is the premise of the argument at
186c. For the purposes of this argument it is essential that *aisthēsis* be defined
narrowly, in terms of the sense modalities, and hence limited to sensory
experience (*pathēmata*) obtained "through the body." It is sense perception
so strictly defined that can have no access to being.[25]

Sense perception proper is thus carefully distinguished from perceptual
judgment. Plato was not always so careful. In the *Phaedo* and *Republic* the
usage of the term *aisthēsis* is looser, and often includes elements that are here
assigned to judgment (*doxa*). For example, in the famous passage on
concepts that summon the soul to intellectual thought in *Republic* VII,
the senses are said to make judgments (*krinein*) and to report (*parangellein*)
to the soul about opposite qualities, including whether something is hard or
soft (523e6, 524a3–8); and these sensory judgments are not distinguished
from quantitative judgments about number or size.[26] In earlier passages in
the *Theaetetus* itself, *aisthēsis* was understood broadly to include perceptual
judgment – for example, when it is taken as equivalent to appearance
(*phainesthai*; 152a–c and *passim*). By returning here to the sense modalities,
with the bodily organs of sense as a criterion, Plato is able to redraw the
distinction between sense and intellect more strictly than he or Democritus
had ever done before.

---

[25] For this notion of sense perception conceived as a movement "through the body to the soul" (*Theaet.*
186c1), compare *Philebus* 33d–34a, *Timaeus* 43c4. There is a parallel in *Rep.* 584c4 for the sensation of
pleasure.

[26] The distinction in *Rep.* VII, 523–24 turns only on whether or not the property in question is perceived
together with its opposite, not whether these properties are matters of sensation alone. The judgment
"this is a finger" goes well beyond sensory qualia but (according to this passage) provokes no call to
reason because it is not accompanied by an opposite judgment, unlike the judgment "this is soft" or
"this is large." It may be with this passage from *Rep.* VII in mind that Plato again introduces "hard"
and "soft" as subjects of perceptual judgment in *Theat.* 186b. But the distinction is now drawn more
carefully.

In the context of this distinction, sensation "through the body" is conceived narrowly as the sensory event (*pathēma*) of seeing color or hearing sound, but not as an explicit identification of experience as "this is red" or "this is a loud noise." Such a descriptive labeling of sensation will introduce the conceptual equivalent of the word "red," a unifying notion that applies to different occurrences of seeing the same color. The notion of red in this sense is precisely what the *Phaedrus* passage calls a "form" or "structure" (*eidos*), the grasp of which permits one to pass "from many sense perceptions to a unity gathered together by reason (*logismos*)." Only in such quasi-linguistic cognition does the soul have access to the word "red," or to the equivalent concept, in its silent dialogue with itself.[27] To label a color experience "red" implies (as the *Phaedrus* passage makes clear) a generalizing judgment of sameness over a plurality of items deposited in memory. Such labeling belongs to what the *Theaetetus* calls judgment or opinion (*doxa*) and thought (*dianoia*), not to sensation strictly understood. For this labeling represents a quasi-linguistic mode of cognition in which the soul acts not through the body but "itself by itself."[28]

In depriving the sensory experience or *pathēma* of any conceptual content, Plato has laid the basis for a radical attack against empiricist epistemology that will find an interesting parallel in modern criticism of the "myth of the given." What is given in sensation, according to our text, is only the sensory event itself, the fact of seeing or hearing. Since it reaches "through the body to the soul," this event becomes a matter of feeling or awareness, such as an animal might have. But without the conceptual resources of language, this mere feeling (and its behavioral consequences) does not have the cognitive content to serve as the basis for a truth claim. In order to be either true or false, this sensory content needs to be articulated in a perceptual judgment (*doxa*), the psychological equivalent of a proposition, which (on Plato's view) the body cannot provide but the soul must formulate from its own resources.

---

[27] For a different view of the *Theaetetus* distinction see Cooper (1970) 130–34, 141, reprinted in Cooper (1999).

[28] Notice that this distinction between sensation and quasi-linguistic perceptual judgment leaves us without any account of the intermediate powers of perception by which non-linguistic animals are able to unify their sensory input and gain information about the world. Animals must somehow generalize their sensory input without language. But Plato is interested here only in isolating sensation proper from perceptual judgment and higher human cognition, not in defining the broader range of animal (non-linguistic) perception. The notion of animal, non-linguistic cognition (which the medievals call *aestimatio*) is weakly developed even in Aristotle's psychology, and apparently ignored by Plato.

2.5   The unique role of Being

Among the many concepts that the soul must furnish, why is *being* singled out as the one indispensable for truth? For a full answer, we must await the discussion of Being in the next chapter. We prepare for that answer here by examining the role of the verb *einai* in the final argument against Theaetetus' definition of knowledge as sense perception.

Being is said to be the most common of all the *koina*: it is entailed in every case of perceptual judgment or reflection on sensory experience (*malista epi pantōn parepetai*, 186a2). It would seem that Plato has primarily in mind the semantic *is* or truth claim that is basic in predication and implied in every judgment, for this is the notion spelled out in the following examples. In contrast to the tactile sensation of hardness and softness (a qualitative feeling experienced "through the body"), the soul by reflection and comparison tries to judge (*krinein*) "the being (of hardness and softness), and that they are (something), and their opposition to one another, and the being of their opposition" (186b). Here we can recognize three or four examples of conceptual reflection on the sensory event of feeling something hard or soft:

(1) "the being (*ousia*) of hardness and softness." The term *ousia* here can be interpreted in several ways, either as (a) their "existence," and as thus an anticipation of point 2, below; or (b) "what they are" in a strong sense, what is their nature or essence (as an answer to the question "what is X?"); or (c) "what they are" in a weaker sense, as a mere recognition or labeling of them as *hard* or *soft*. Notice that (c), the weakest reading of *ousia* here, is already quasi-linguistic;

(2) *hoti eston*, that they are (something rather than nothing), that there is such a thing as hard and soft;

(3) "their opposition to one another," i.e. that they constitute a pair of opposites; and

(4) the *ousia* or nature of their opposition. If this is to be different from (3), *ousia* must be taken in the strong sense of 1b above.

This elucidation of the concept or *koinon* of Being was preceded by a similar, partially overlapping set of observations referring to the sensations of sound and color (185a8–b5). The earlier argument served to introduce the notion of *koina* as properties common to more than one sense, and hence not the proper objects of any particular sense. Theaetetus agrees that what we perceive through hearing we could not perceive through sight. "Then suppose that you think (*dianoēi*) something about both; you can't possibly be having a perception (*aisthanesthai*) about both, either through one of these [bodily] instruments or through the other?" (185a4–6, trans. Levett). This is precisely what is meant by a *koinon*, a concept that applies to objects of more than one sense. The verb *einai* will appear in all the examples. Thus, concerning sound and color, we can think the following:

(1*) "that they both *are*";
(2*) that each is different from the other, but the same as itself;
(3*) that both are two, but each is one;
(4*) whether they are similar or dissimilar to one another.

These two texts are designed to specify the concept of being that is employed in this final argument. In grammatical terms, the notion of being is illustrated here by six examples of the copula use of *einai* and two existential uses (2 and 1*). But it is clear that for Plato these eight occurrences of the verb represent a single concept, the most universal concept of the language. ("It applies to every case," 186a2.) What all these examples have in common is their propositional form. By propositional form I mean both predicative structure and the force of assertion or truth claim. For Plato we may say that the basic notion of being in this context is "This is how things stand." This was the notion illustrated earlier in the formula cited from Protagoras: man as the measure of "what is, that it is, and of what is not, that it is not." Such a formula is a paradigm of the veridical or "semantic" use of *einai*, which (on my reading) includes both existence for the subject and truth claim or "belonging-to" for the predicate. Propositional form understood in this semantic (rather than merely syntactic) sense is identical with the notion of predication, where the predicate is conceived as a property *belonging to* the (extra-linguistic) subject.[29]

It is propositional form in this sense, including existence for the subject and truth claim for the predicate, that is illustrated in the use of *einai* in all the above examples. And, according to Plato, it is this form that represents both the structure of declarative speech and the structure of judgment and thought. (A judgment is simply a *logos* that the soul speaks to itself.) And in this propositional conception of being, the notion of truth claim is an essential ingredient.

On this reading of *einai* as propositional structure, the final refutation of Theaetetus' definition comes into full clarity. There can be no knowledge without truth content, and no truth content without an element of truth claim. But truth claim requires propositional structure, in other words, being. Hence it is easy to see why "it is not possible for someone who does not even get at being to get at truth" (16c7). *Aisthēsis* alone cannot judge that

---

[29] See further discussion in Chapter Three.

X is anything, or that X is. Therefore *aisthēsis* cannot be true or false, and hence cannot be knowledge.

The refutation is clearly decisive, even though (as I have noted elsewhere) there is an important ambivalence in the notion of being in this argument.[30] On the one hand, *ousia* represents the syntactic-semantic form of statement and judgment just analyzed; and it is this propositional structure that makes it possible to say or judge something true or false. On the other hand, *ousia* can also refer to the state of the world – the way things are – that makes such a truth claim either valid or false. In the full formula for true and false statement in the *Sophist* (263b), as in the thesis of Protagoras, these two notions are expressed by repetitions of the verb: the true statement says (in its claim) the things that are, as they (in fact) are. In the present argument in the *Theaetetus*, these two notions of being are fused rather than distinguished. Both notions operate in the proof that the concept of truth requires access to *ousia*. It is, first of all, the intentional being of propositional structure that is required for a truth claim; and this is the *ousia* that sense cannot provide. But for such a claim to be valid, it must be fulfilled by the objective *ousia* of how things really stand. The concept of knowledge requires *ousia* in both senses.

The final argument elides this distinction, but no fallacy results. To refute *Theaetetus'* definition, it is only the first, intentional notion of being, as the capacity for propositional structure, that is required for a truth claim. And it is precisely this capacity that sensation proper does not provide. But without the notion of a truth claim, the further notion of validity for such a claim does not come into consideration. For the purpose of refutation, then, this ambiguity is harmless.

2.6   Part Two: knowledge as true *doxa* and the problem of false judgment

Since his definition in terms of sensation must be given up, Theaetetus now proposes to define knowledge in terms of the "activity of the soul when it is busy by itself about the things which are (*peri ta onta*)" (187a), that is, in terms of veridical thought (*dianoia*) or judgment (*doxa*).[31]

As we have remarked, one major achievement of Part Two will be the conception of judgment or belief on the model of silent speech (190a). That

---

[30] See Kahn (2007) and Kahn (1981).
[31] I have followed the translators of the *Theaetetus* in rendering δόξα as "judgment," although the more idiomatic equivalent would be "opinion" or "belief."

allows Plato to reduce the problem of false belief to the problem of false statement, which he will resolve in the *Sophist* by his analysis of statements into subject-predicate form. For the history of Western thought, this subject-predicate (noun-verb) analysis of sentence structure will turn out to be of fundamental importance. This solution is not reached in our dialogue; but the mind of the reader is prepared for it by a series of puzzles and paradoxes.

When Theaetetus begins Part Two by proposing a new definition of knowledge as true judgment, his proposal is immediately confronted with three paradoxical arguments claiming to show that it is impossible for anyone to judge falsely. In effect, Part Two of the *Theaetetus* will be devoted to the problem of false *doxa*. Only at the end do we return to the proposed definition of knowledge in terms of true judgment; and this proposal will be quickly rejected. The intervening discussion of false judgment introduces three puzzles and two memorable images: the wax tablet and the aviary or bird-cage.

2.7 Three *Aporias* on false judgment (188a–190e)

I omit here a detailed account of the three arguments that claim to show that it is impossible to judge falsely. These arguments are designed to raise problems to be resolved by a positive theory of truth and error, a theory that will not be presented in this dialogue. On the other hand, two major ingredients of such a theory are introduced here, to be more fully developed in the *Sophist*. The first of these is the interpretation of thought as silent speech (189e–190a), which we have already noticed. The second is the analysis of propositional form into subject and attribute or predicate. The analysis into subject-predicate form is not made explicit in this dialogue, but the need for such analysis seems to be implied, above all in the discussion of the second *aporia* (188d–189b).

The old Parmenidean problem of not-being was mentioned in two earlier dialogues, and it will reappear in the *Sophist*, where it is finally resolved. One of these earlier passages is *Cratylus* 429b, where Socrates reports (and Cratylus immediately accepts) the view, held by many "both now and previously," that speaking falsely is impossible, because it is not saying the things-that-are (*to mē ta onta legein*). This passage in the *Cratylus* looks like an echo of the longer discussion of the problem of falsehood in the *Euthydemus*. There the sophistic claim that falsehood is impossible was described as a view that Socrates has heard "often, and from many people," going back to Protagoras and even earlier.[32] In the *Euthydemus* the denial of falsehood is based on the assumption that if anyone speaks or says something, what they say is one definite thing or being (*on*), distinct from other beings (*onta*). Speaking falsely would be saying what-is-not (*ta mē onta*). But what-is-not is nothing, no object at all. But to say nothing is not to speak. Therefore whenever anyone says anything, they say what-is and speak truly (284a–c).

This denial of false statement in the *Euthydemus* is followed by the equally paradoxical claim that it is impossible to contradict *(antilegein)* what someone else says (*Euthyd.* 285e–286b). This argument is based, like the preceding one, on the assumption of a one-to-one correlation between things and their proper "sayings" (*logoi*): each being (*on*) has its own statement (*logos*) that says that-it-is (or how it is, *hōs estin*).[33] Now if both of us say the same *logos* about the same thing (*pragma*), we are not disagreeing. On the other hand, if neither of us says the *logos* of this thing, we are not even mentioning it.[34] Finally, if one of us states the *logos* and the other does not, or states a different *logos*, we are not contradicting one another.

It has often been recognized that much of the discussion of language in the *Cratylus* is governed by this parallel between naming and describing, a parallel reinforced by the fact that in Greek the term *onoma* means both name and word. Thus, the pursuit of "etymology" in the *Cratylus* is based on the assumption that names should be interpreted as disguised descriptions – as "truthful (*etumoi*) *logoi*." The question arises, both here and in the *Cratylus*, whether Plato is himself misled by these parallels, or whether (as I suppose) he is challenging us as readers to see what goes wrong. Can we successfully distinguish between naming a thing and saying something about it? In the passage just cited from the *Euthydemus*, there is an implicit distinction between mentioning a subject and saying its *logos*. That may be a hint to the reader where the fallacy lies.

As Myles Burnyeat has observed, the material for analyzing these fallacies is presented in the *Euthydemus* in such a way as to call the reader's attention to the structural relation between subject and predicate, and to the importance of this relation for understanding not only false judgment but also more general questions "about the relation of thought and language to the world."[35] Now this relation between subject and predicate corresponds

---

[32] *Euthyd.* 286c. The allusion to Protagoras must refer to his thesis that Man is the Measure, understood as a claim that all judgments are true. Cf. *Crat.* 385e6.
[33] This notion of proper λόγοι, conceived on analogy with proper names, is generally attributed to Antisthenes on the authority of Aristotle, *Met.* 1024b32–34.
[34] *Euthyd.* 286b2: οὐδ' ἂν μεμνημένος εἴη τοῦ πράγματος.   [35] Burnyeat (2002) 50.

precisely to the conception of Being in terms of propositional structure that we have identified in the refutation of Theaetetus' definition. There is more evidence to show that, long before he presents his explicit solution of these problems in the *Sophist*, Plato is fully aware of the importance of subject-predicate structure for both ontology and epistemology. For example, in the refutation of the flux doctrine quoted earlier from the *Cratylus*, Plato's argument repeatedly distinguishes between identifying a subject and attributing properties to it:

> If (something) is always leaving us, would it be possible to address it correctly, <saying> first that it is this (*ekeino*) and then that it is such (*toiouton*)? Or is it necessary, even as we speak, that it become immediately other (*allo*) and leave us and be no longer in the same state (*houtōs echein*)? (439d)

The argument in the *Cratylus* goes on to show that it is not only impossible for there to *be* such a fleeting entity but also impossible for it to be known. For, as the knowing subject approaches, the object "would become another thing (*allo*) and be different in kind (*alloion*)" (440a1). Three times in this text the grammatical distinction between pronoun and adjectival predicate (or, in one case, the adverbial equivalent of a predicate) is used to mark the logical contrast between the thing and its properties, the same distinction that will be articulated in the *Sophist* by the noun-verb construction.

It is important to note, however, that although these passages in the *Cratylus* and *Euthydemus* reflect a clear awareness of subject-attribute structure in propositional thought, no text before the *Sophist* calls attention to the corresponding linguistic distinction between noun and verb. Now it is precisely by means of this latter distinction, focusing on the syntactic connection between subject-expression and predicate-expression within a sentence, that Plato in the *Sophist* will be able to give an unambiguous formulation for the corresponding ontological relation between subject and attribute.[36] If in dialogues before the

---

[36] Our terms "subject" and "predicate" are systematically ambiguous, referring sometimes to extra-linguistic things and attributes, but more often to the corresponding components of a sentence. In the passages cited from *Cratylus* and *Euthydemus* Plato draws this distinction in its extra-linguistic form (as Aristotle does with his term *hupokeimenon* for "subject"). Only in the *Sophist* does Plato introduce the corresponding linguistic distinction between subject and predicate expressions, for which his terms are *onoma* and *rhēma*. It is the latter terminology that is taken over by Aristotle in *De Interpretatione*. Thus, without Aristotle's terminology of *hupokeimenon* and *katēgoreisthai*, the subject-attribute analysis of propositional structure is fully developed in Plato's writings, beginning with the *Euthydemus* and *Cratylus*.

   As Burnyeat (2002) 45 points out, a comparable distinction was also implicit in the contrast between Simmias and his largeness and smallness in *Phaedo* 102b–d.

Sophist Plato has not made this analysis explicit, the reason for his silence may lie not only in a pedagogical preference for readers to work out an understanding on their own (as Burnyeat suggests). He may also have been philosophically disinclined to emphasize the role played by individuals such as persons, as subjects in the realm of change and sense perception. As we shall see, even in the *Sophist* no theoretical account is given of the *subject* of false judgment; we are simply told that both true and false statements are "about Theaetetus."

There may be philosophical reasons for Plato's discretion here. When Aristotle in the *Categories* chooses to take as fundamental principle the subject-predicate analysis, his conception of individuals as primary subjects of predication will serve as the basis for a radically un-Platonic – even anti-Platonic – ontology. Plato's position here is more ambivalent. On the one hand, he needs the subject-predicate analysis of propositional structure to clarify many problems in the theory of meaning and truth. On the other hand, he has no wish to adopt a general, quasi-Aristotelian theory of predication as a fundamental principle for his ontology. For that (as Aristotle will show) tends to identify sensible individuals, including human beings, as primary subjects of predication and hence as primary entities (*ousiai*). But that is not an ontology that Plato could accept. In his most fully developed discussion of subject-attribute structure, in the *Timaeus*, the only individual to be recognized as subject of attributes – the only true "this" – is the cosmic Receptacle taken as a whole (49b–50a). In order to develop his anti-Platonic ontology in the *Categories*, Aristotle had only to embrace Plato's distinction between subject and attribute and apply it systematically to statements about sensible individuals. Plato's metaphysical instinct led him to avoid such an application, and thus to avoid developing a general theory of predication of the Aristotelian type.

2.8   The wax tablet

Among the logical confusions hidden from view in the three puzzles in *Theaetetus* 188a–190e, the complexities of subject-predicate structure will have to await clarification in the sequel dialogue, the *Sophist*. Instead, Socrates now seeks to explicate the notion of "grasping in thought" (*ephaptesthai tēi psuchēi*) by calling attention to a distinction between two kinds of cognition that was overlooked in the first *aporia*. The famous wax tablet of memory is introduced here in order to show why it was a mistake to deny that one could know and not know the same thing. One can be acquainted with Theodorus but fail to recognize him on a particular occasion. (From

191b on, the verb *gignōskein* "to be acquainted with" suggests this weaker notion of cognition, in contrast with the standard verbs "to know": *oida* and *epistasthai*.) The wax tablet of the mind preserves memory imprints (*sēmeia*) deposited there from previous perceptions, which may or may not correspond to the present perception of a person currently in view. The possibility of false judgment is then illustrated by the mismatching of the present perception of one person (e.g. of Theodorus) with the memory imprint deposited from seeing a different person (e.g. Theaetetus). We thus remain as close as possible to the earlier conception of knowledge in terms of sense perception. But by introducing the element of memory, and the possibility that memory may be mistaken, we allow for the dimension of success and failure in perceptual judgment that was missing from the previous definition of knowledge in terms of sensation alone. Of course, we have not dealt with the deeper problems of propositional structure, and so we are not prepared here for any general distinction between true and false judgment. There are other levels of epistemic complexity to be traversed.

The question remains unanswered, how far can the model of the wax tablet be extended. This model locates cases of error "neither in the relations between sense perceptions, nor in thoughts (*dianoiai*), but in the connection of sense perception with thought" (195d1), that is to say, in perceptual judgment. In a later dialogue Plato will show how the interaction between perception and memory can generate true and false judgments over a wider range of cases, not limited to identifying particular persons.[37] At this point in the *Theaetetus*, however, Socrates is impatient to move on to a new level of complexity, where the wax model will no longer suffice.

2.9 The bird-cage

In his description of the wax tablet Socrates had recognized that memory imprints could be derived from thoughts (*ennoiai*) as well as from perceptions (191d5–6). The next stage of our inquiry will be marked by errors of thought alone, without a direct input from sense perception. In effect, we return here to the distinction between the soul's perception through the body and its relation to "common concepts" (*koina*) that it investigates by itself. The new errors belong in this latter category. Plato is here concerned

---

[37] See *Philebus* 38b–e, where true and false δόξαι concerning an obscure visual perception are formulated in silent speech. Sedley (2004) 137 ff. n. 24, points out that the *Philebus* passage uses the *Theaetetus* model but extends it by adding the resource of φαντασία.

with errors deriving not from perceptual judgment but from the domain of concepts corresponding to Hume's relation of ideas and Kantian instances of *a priori* knowledge. The specific examples are number concepts such as seven and five, "not seven and five human beings but five and seven themselves" (196a2). Even if the wax model for perceptual judgment could be generalized, it would not help us to understand errors in arithmetic.

If we bear in mind Plato's general view of mathematics, we see that his treatment here of mathematical error will be confronted with a serious problem of method. Recalling the place of mathematics in the Knowledge Line of *Republic* VI, we recognize that these mathematical examples will carry us up from errors in sensation and perceptual judgment to higher questions concerning rational concepts, and ultimately concerning Forms. Recall how the "square itself" and the "diagonal itself," as object of mathematical thinking (*Rep.* VI, 510d), are located above the division in the Line that separates the visible realm from the intelligible. Now in the *Republic*, as later in the *Timaeus*, the intelligible-sensible contrast in cognition corresponds to the Being-Becoming distinction in ontology. As intelligible entities, mathematical objects will belong in the domain of stable Being. But the ontology of Being is excluded from discussion in the *Theaetetus*. How is false judgment concerning numbers to be analyzed here, if the corresponding objects lie outside the prescribed limits of inquiry?[38]

I suggest that this problem of method, the result of an ontological restriction that defines the project of the *Theaetetus*, explains what is both the most picturesque and most unsatisfying episode in the entire dialogue. The climax of Part Two is the bird-cage model of the mind, in which objects of knowledge are depicted as birds flying around in an enclosed area, like pigeons and doves. The model makes an important philosophical contribution, since it provides a vivid illustration for the distinction between acquiring knowledge as a state (*ktēsis*, "possessing knowledge") on the one hand, and occurrent knowledge (*echein*, "holding knowledge" or having it in mind) on the other hand. It has often been noted that Plato here prepares the way for Aristotle's distinction between potentiality and actuality. That corresponds in the model to the distinction between keeping a number-bird in the cage and catching it in one's hand. The model offers a persuasive picture of how one can both know (as possessing latent knowledge) and not know (not have in mind) the same object, e.g. the number twelve. But,

---

[38] Traveling by a different route, Sedley comes to a similar conclusion: "If Socrates could not get all the way to a solution to the falsity puzzle, his neglect of metaphysics is again to blame" (2004: 149).

somewhat to our surprise, Plato does not allow the birds to represent number concepts, such as the mental "ideas" of seven and five. If he did so, the model could provide a plausible picture (though scarcely an explanation) of mathematical error. Making a mistake in arithmetic would mean simply catching the wrong bird flying around in the cage, i.e. the wrong number.[39] Instead, Socrates introduces the model as an account of "what knowing is like" (*hoion esti to epistasthai*, 197a), so that the birds correspond to items or pieces of knowledge (*epistēmai*). This device is introduced with apologies for the violation of good method, in assuming an account of knowledge before arriving at a definition (196d–197a). The model is ultimately rejected on the grounds that it makes knowledge responsible for error, which is not a rational form of explanation (199d).

Why has Plato avoided what seems to us the natural interpretation of the birds as concepts or ideas corresponding to the number words, and chosen instead to describe the model as composed of bits and pieces of knowledge? There is certainly some philosophical merit in this view. As we have seen, it permits Plato to draw a clear distinction between stored or latent knowledge and occurrent knowledge presently attended to. Besides anticipating Aristotle's distinction between potency and act, the distinction between birds in the cage and birds in the hand offers a vivid contrast between available cognitive resources and current cognitive activity. In this respect the bird-cage model provides a psychological picture that points towards a generalization of the memory and perceptual dimensions of the wax tablet. ("Possessing in the cage" would correspond to memory and "catching in the hand" to perception.) The aviary model shows Plato flirting with the project of a more complete picture of mental activity, a project that he will pursue further in the *Philebus*, where the model of the scribe and the painter are added to account for memory and imagination. But why are the birds conceived here not as number concepts or thoughts but as items of *knowledge* corresponding to the numbers? This looks like a strategic move, designed to prepare for the rejection of the whole search for false judgment as circular, and thus to return us to the quest for a definition of knowledge at 200c–d.

I suspect that there is more at stake here. As a realist in epistemology, Plato has no use for the notion of concepts as psychological entities, like meanings in the mind. It is only by reference to the numbers *themselves* that the number concepts could be distinguished from one another, just as in the

---

[39] There would still be no account of how the birds for seven and five add up to the bird for twelve. But that is true of this model on any interpretation.

Parmenides the thought (*noēma*) of any Form needs to be identified by reference to its object as a definite entity (*hen on, Parm.* 132c). Plato seems unwilling to recognize any identity for particular thoughts or concepts, as subjective or psychological items in the mind, logically independent of their objects. The pieces of knowledge (*epistēmai*) in the bird-cage are designed to play the role that might be played by number-concepts. Their advantage over mental concepts, from Plato's point of view, may lie in the fact that their ontological status is, from the beginning, recognized as problematic. After all, we are engaged in a so-far-unsuccessful search for a definition of knowledge!

That is my best guess as to why Plato's mental birds represent pieces of knowledge rather than number-concepts. It would imply that Plato prefers number-knowledge to number-concepts because (in his view) the notion of knowledge implies successful contact with its object, as the notion of concept does not. But perhaps such speculation is superfluous. Plato might have chosen the notion of number-knowledge simply in order to develop here the distinction between latent and occurrent knowledge.

2.10   Rejecting the definition of knowledge as true judgment

In any event, the rejection of the aviary model brings to an end the long digression on false judgment (187d–200d), and we return to Theaetetus' second definition of knowledge as true judgment (*doxa*).

In the *Meno* true judgment was distinguished from knowledge on the grounds that it is less stable and needs to be tied down by a rational account of the cause (*aitias logismos*, 98a). The *Meno* also implied that only knowledge could make one a successful teacher (99b8). The same distinction (with *nous* instead of *epistēmē* contrasted with judgment) is reasserted on similar grounds at *Timaeus* 51d–e, where it is clear that the relevant *aitia* or causal account will invoke the Forms. The *Timaeus* is thus pursuing the distinction established in *Republic* V, 478–79, where knowledge takes Forms as its object and *doxa* takes sensibles. Now, the Forms were not mentioned in the *Meno*; and of course we do not expect to find them in the *Theaetetus*. Instead, the distinction between knowledge and true belief will be drawn neither on metaphysical grounds nor in terms of a causal explanation but on the basis of the old distinction between teaching and rhetorical persuasion, the distinction that was first drawn in the *Gorgias* (454c–455a): the orator produces persuasion, not instruction. Since this distinction between true opinion and genuine knowledge (exemplified here by the contrast between hearsay and eye-witness report) is such a familiar one, the account of knowledge as true belief can be quickly discarded (201a–c). This leads to Theaetetus' final definition of knowledge.

2.11   Part Three: knowledge as true judgment with a *logos*

Our third attempt to define knowledge, as true *doxa* with a *logos*, returns to the level of analysis reached in the *Meno*. The distinction between knowledge and opinion was of course older, going back as far as Xenophanes (fr. 34) or Parmenides. More recently, this distinction had been treated at length by Antisthenes, in a lost work of which we know only the title.[40] The *Meno* is the first dialogue in which Plato deals explicitly with the distinction, and his statement there of the relation between the two is not entirely clear. The *Meno* has often been thought to include true opinion as a necessary ingredient in knowledge. On this view, knowledge would be understood as true *doxa* plus some additional qualification, as in modern attempts to define knowledge as true belief plus a justification. But this reading of the *Meno* seems profoundly anachronistic; it ignores the traditional contrast between these two cognitive states that goes back to Parmenides. In the *Meno* as in the rest of Plato's work, true *doxa* is properly understood as the stage prior to knowledge rather than a constituent of it.[41]

On either reading, the notion of *logos* in the *Theaetetus*, as the distinctive feature of knowledge, would correspond to the requirement in the *Meno* of *aitias logismos*, "a reasoned account of the cause," as the criterion that distinguishes knowledge from true judgment. The *Meno* tells us nothing further about this criterion. We know from the *Republic* that what distinguishes knowledge from opinion should be some link to the doctrine of Forms. But such a link is excluded on principle from the *Theaetetus*. In this dialogue the relevant *logos* cannot be identified as a *logos tēs ousias*, "an account of being or essence," in the sense of *ousia* that the *Republic* would require (533b3). We look instead for a less metaphysically loaded notion of *logos* – and that turns out to be a fruitless quest.

The first attempt to define knowledge as true opinion with *logos* is the passage known as Socrates' dream.

---

[40] Antisthenes, περὶ δόξης καὶ ἐπιστήμης, in four books! (D.L. VI 17).
[41] Plato's wording is ambiguous. At *Meno* 98a πρῶτον μὲν ἐπιστῆμαι γίγνονται, ἔπειτα μόνιμοι· "[true judgments] first become knowledge, and then become stable" may mean either that knowledge replaces true *doxa* or that it includes and completes it. I think only the first reading can be correct. Since in all other Platonic contexts the two cognitive states are incompatible, it is natural to read the *Meno* passage in a way that is not only consistent with the rest of the Platonic corpus but also respects the tradition going back to Parmenides.

2.12   Socrates' dream: antecedents in the *Cratylus*

As a result of striking parallels to the theory of Logical Atomism developed by Bertrand Russell and others in the twentieth century, the Dream theory has received more attention from philosophers than perhaps any other text in the Platonic corpus. Wittgenstein himself drew the comparison in his *Philosophical Investigations* #46. Quoting our passage from *Theaetetus* 201e–202b, Wittgenstein identifies Plato's primary nameables with Russell's "individuals" and his own "objects" in the *Tractatus*. Similar parallels were discussed by Gilbert Ryle in 1939, before Wittgenstein's own remarks were published. Both similarities and differences between Socrates' dream and these modern semantic theories have been fully discussed by Myles Burnyeat; and I have nothing to add.[42]

Instead of pursuing these modern parallels, I will attempt to clarify this theory by comparison with the related doctrine in the *Cratylus*. Here is another case where the continuity between *Cratylus* and *Theaetetus* proves instructive.

In the *Cratylus* Socrates had been exploring the correctness of names by following the view that the etymology or original form of a word contains a description of the thing named. The principle of correctness is that the name should reveal what the thing actually is (*dēloun hoion hekaston esti tōn ontōn*, 422d). (Plato here illustrates, and perhaps establishes for the first time, the classical notion of *etumologia* as the search for a name's true meaning, its *etumos logos*.) But the components of such descriptions are other, simpler names. The question arises, then, what are the ultimate or primary names? "If someone asks about the terms or expressions (*rēmata*) from which a name is formed, and then about the ones from which the terms are formed, and keeps on asking this again, ... isn't it necessary that the answerer should finally give up?"[43] The right place to stop is when one reaches the primary names, "which are like the elements (*stoicheia*) of other names and sayings (*logoi*)," and which are "no longer composed of some other names" (*Crat.* 422a3, b1).

The word here for element, *stoicheion*, is the usual term for letters of the alphabet, that is, for the letters and phonemes (*grammata*) as alphabetically ordered. But the same term is used for basic components in other ordered

---

[42] Burnyeat (1990) 149–64.

[43] *Crat.* 421d9–e4, translation after Reeve. Compare *Lysis* 219c5, where there is a parallel regress in which the inquirer must finally give up (ἀπειπεῖν) or reach a first principle (ἀρχή). In the *Lysis* passage, the "for the sake of" relation leads to a primary dear (πρῶτον φίλον) which is truly dear, for the sake of which other things are dear.

arrangements, for example, in geometry. The mathematician Hippocrates of Chios, contemporary to Socrates and Plato, is reported to have been the first to present geometry in the form of *stoicheia*, that is, as derived from more basic principles.[44] Hippocrates thus begins the tradition that culminates in the *Elements* (*Stoicheia*) of Euclid.

This mathematical notion of *stoicheia* plays a role in Plato's view, as we shall see. But the most influential of all uses of the term *stoicheion* will turn out to be its application to the first principles of the natural world, that is, to the "elements" of ancient and modern physics. These elements are so to speak the alphabet of nature. We have a report from Eudemus (fr. 31 Wehrli) that Plato was the first to use the term *stoicheion* in this sense, and Eudemus may have had our text from the *Cratylus* in mind.[45] For Socrates goes on to say that, in order to see whether the primary names are correctly assigned, as revelations or imitations (*mimēmata*) of reality, we must not only analyze words into their components but also analyze things into their own elements (*stoicheia*, 424d). He then develops the suggestion of an ideal language in which the systematic arrangement of linguistic components would accurately reflect (by similarity, *homoiōtēs*, 424d6) the systematic structure of the world of things (*onta*). What follows in the *Cratylus* is the first of several texts in which Plato employs the alphabet as a paradigm for the structure of a complex system:

> Shouldn't we thus first divide the vowels, and then, of the others, the consonants and the mutes according to kinds (*kat' eidē*) . . . and also the semi-vowels? And <shouldn't we also see> how many different kinds of vowels there are? And when we have divided all these, <shouldn't we also divide> carefully in turn all the beings (*ta onta*) to which names must be assigned, <to see> if there are as it were elements (*stoicheia*) to which all of them are referred and out of which they can be seen to be composed, and if there are kinds (*eidē*) among them [sc. among the beings] in the same way as among the letters? (*Crat.*424c5–d4)[46]

The notion of dividing the letters into phonetic kinds (*eidē*) will serve again in the *Philebus* to illustrate the dialectic of Division and Collection,

---

[44] Proclus, *in Euclidem*, p. 65, cited Heath (1921) I, 170. For the importance of this mathematical notion for Plato's conception of στοιχεῖα, see Morrow (1970). In Plato's *Timaeus*, the elementary triangles are called στοιχεῖον (54d6 and *passim*).

[45] Alternatively, Eudemus may have been referring to the use of στοιχεῖον for elementary triangles in the *Timaeus*, since that context reflects the transfer from the mathematical to the physical sense of element.

[46] The text here is compressed and some words may have dropped out, but the thought is clear. In 424d1, I put a comma after διελώμεθα, retain τὰ ὄντα (despite Burnet's brackets), and understand διελέσθαι again after εὖ πάντα.

presented there as a general method of rational analysis (*Phil.* 16b–18d). The terminology of that later method is also suggested here by repeated use of the language of division and combination.[47] In the present context, however, there is no mention of dialectic. Our attention is directed to kinds of names corresponding to kinds of things named, with primitive names (i.e. letters) corresponding to elements, more complex linguistic forms corresponding to elemental compounds.

Plato is here appropriating the notion of physical elements, as the enduring constituents of perishable compounds, that was developed by the fifth-century cosmologists in response to Parmenides' attack on coming-to-be. Empedocles had used the image of the painter blending colors to explain how a small number of elements could produce such immense phenomenal diversity; the atomists seem to have invoked the letters of the alphabet for the same purpose.[48] Plato echoes here Empedocles' comparison to the painter (424d7), while at the same time making use of the atomist analogy to the letters (*hōsper ta stoicheia*, 424d2). In thus taking over the Presocratic concept of element, Plato baptizes it with the classical term *stoicheion*, destined to become *elementum* in Latin. The concept comes from fifth-century cosmology, but the terminology is new with Plato and reinforced by its association with geometry.

In the *Cratylus* Plato's innovation is to combine this notion of physical element with a linguistic theory according to which the function of names, and of words generally, is to reveal the true nature or *ousia* of things, which they do by imitating or resembling the things named. Relying on this principle of correctness, Plato briefly sketches the notion of an ideal language in which the analysis of names would mirror and reveal the ramified structure of reality. (He thus anticipates in the *Cratylus* the view to be presented in the *Theaetetus* as Socrates' dream.) A more fruitful version of this conception can be recognized in Plato's own conception of dialectic as Division and Collection, to be most fully described in the *Philebus*. As presented in the *Cratylus*, however, the theory gives no positive results. It leads to a ridiculous view of primitive names according to which the letters "r" and "s" are interpreted as natural signs for the doctrine of flux. That

---

[47] See διαιρέσεως at *Crat.* 424b7, διελέσθα c6, διείλοντο c2, διελέσθαι c6, διελώμεθα d1, διαθεασαμένους d5, διελομένους 425b1. These divisions are balanced by a certain number of collections: συγκεράσαντες 424e1, συντιθέναι 424e6, 425a1, a6, σύγκειται a6.

[48] Emped. DK 23; Leucippus DK 9 (= Arist. *De Gen. Corr.* 315b14): tragedy and comedy are composed of the same letters. Aristotle speaks here of γράμματα rather than στοιχεῖα. Since for the atomists there were an unlimited number of different atomic shapes, it would be the letters or markings (γράμματα) generally rather than the alphabet proper that provided them with an appropriate model for the elements.

would be bad enough. But there is also phonetic evidence pointing in the opposite direction: basic sounds that indicate stability rather than motion. Socrates apologizes repeatedly for the application of this likeness principle to these primitive phonemes. I take Socrates' embarrassment here to be Plato's hint to the reader that the whole theory of names as natural signs should be regarded as a ridiculous mistake.[49] But if the account of primitive names is implausible and inconsistent, the whole enterprise is suspect. In the end, the *Cratylus* concludes that the study of language cannot offer a sound basis for the analysis of reality (439b–c).

2.13   Socrates' dream: positive contributions

The discussion of Socrates' dream in the *Theaetetus* begins and ends with an echo of the *Cratylus* passage just discussed. The common point is the notion of physical element understood by analogy with the letters of the alphabet. Thus, the Dream theory begins with "primary things (*ta prōta*), as it were the *stoicheia*, from which we and other things are composed" (*Theaet.* 201e1). The term *stoicheia* here designates both letter and element; as in the *Cratylus*, the alphabet is taken as the model for an analysis of complexes into their basic constituents. The Dream theory suggests a more complex structure, invoking the notion of whole and part, but the most important connection between these two texts lies in the parallelism of their conclusions.

Since, according to the *Cratylus*, other names depend on the primary names for their descriptive role, there is no way to know the rightness of other names unless one knows the rightness of those that are prior. "Anyone who claims to be an expert (*technikos*) on these matters must be able to give the purest and best account of primary names, or we may be sure that he is talking nonsense about the rest" (426a–b2). (Hence Socrates' elaborate apology for his account of primary names is designed to cast doubt on his account of names in general.) This skeptical conclusion is echoed in the final rejection of the Dream theory: "if anyone says that a syllable is knowable, but a letter (*stoicheion*) is by nature unknowable, we will think that, intentionally or unintentionally, he is joking" (*Theaet.* 206b9). Taken literally, the Dream theory that complexes are known by analysis into

---

[49] *Crat.* 425d1: the imitation of reality by letters and syllables will appear laughable (γελοῖα). This echoes the warning at 422c3 that the account of rightness for primary names may be talking nonsense (παραληρεῖν). The apology is repeated at 426b6: Socrates' account of primary names seems to him ὑβριστικὰ καὶ γελοῖα.

unknown simples is found to be ridiculous, just like the *Cratylus* theory of linguistic meaning based on natural signs. But the rejection in each case leads to a positive conclusion about the systematic structure of knowledge. As Aristotle will put it in the *Posterior Analytics*, the elements and first principles of any science must be "more knowable" (*gnorimōtera*) than what is derived from them.⁵⁰

In the *Cratylus* this conclusion is implicitly confirmed by the failure of the whole etymological enterprise. In the *Theaetetus* the corresponding conclusion – the impossibility of knowing syllables when letters are unknown – is formally established by a series of three arguments. The first and briefest refutation of the Dream theory simply identifies the first syllable of Socrates' name with the letters S and O and concludes that, in order to know the syllable consisting of the two, both letters must be known first (*Theaet.* 203c4–d10). The third argument is drawn from the experience of learning to read. The beginning reader must first learn to identify the individual letters, regardless of their position in different syllables; and a similar skill is required for identifying notes in music (206a). In between these two brief arguments comes the second, most fully worked-out refutation, in which Socrates develops a problematic dilemma designed to show that letters and syllables must be either equally knowable or equally unknown (204–5). Taking the syllable as a model, this argument rejects the epistemic asymmetry of the Dream theory for any complex structure (*sullabē*) conceived as a whole of parts. If the whole syllable is a single form (*eidos*), with a structure (*idea*) of its own distinct from the parts, then it is just as unknowable as its parts. On the other hand, if the whole is the same as its parts, whole and parts must be equally knowable.⁵¹

As a result of these arguments the Dream theory is rejected, and with it the notion of elemental principles that could be perceived but not known. By a kind of ring composition, this negative result echoes the anti-empiricist conclusion of Part One: one cannot get to knowledge by starting from perception. Nevertheless, important positive insights have been developed in the statement and refutation of this theory.

1. The concept of knowledge is presented as a ramified structure, with primary principles or elements serving as foundation for the whole system. Both here and in the *Cratylus*, the letters of the alphabet provide the model for elements (*stoicheia*) in any area of cognition (204a3, 206b6–9). However,

---

⁵⁰ *Post. Anal.* I.2, 71b21, cited in this connection by Morrow (1970) 332. Compare Aristotle's elaboration of this point in the first chapter of the *Physics*.
⁵¹ For analysis of this argument see Harte (2002) 32–47, following Burnyeat (1990) 191–208.

the structure of knowledge is conceived in two different ways, corresponding to two different notions of dialectic.

On the one hand, the term *stoicheia* suggests mathematics as a model for systematic knowledge. This is the deductive model developed as the method of hypothesis in the *Phaedo*, and more fully in the epistemology of *Republic* VI. The *Republic* passage makes clear that first principles must be grasped not by perception but by intellection (*noēsis*). Since the first principle will serve as basis for everything else, it must itself be known non-hypothetically (*Rep.* 511b–e), that is to say, more firmly known than the truths derived from it. In the *Timaeus* this view of principles will be applied to physics. Perceptible elements such as fire are there denied the right to be called *stoicheia* (i.e. letters): a reasonable person would not even count them as syllables! (48c). These visible elements are to be explained in terms of their underlying geometric structure, and ultimately in terms of two elementary triangles. According to the *Timaeus*, it is these latter that are the true *stoicheia* (54d6–55b4).

This is the Platonic view of knowledge that takes mathematical *stoicheia* as the model for systematic order. On the other hand, a rather different conception of the structure of knowledge, again taking the alphabet as an example, is developed in the theory of dialectic in terms of Division and Collection. In this case the paradigm for rational method is provided not by mathematical deduction but by whole-part analysis, that is, by the division of complex unities into successive levels of plurality, by way of types and subtypes. This pattern was prefigured in the *Cratylus*, as we have seen, by repeated reference to the division of letters and things into kinds (*eidē*). There is no similar emphasis on division into kinds in the *Theaetetus*, but a comparable concern with one-many relations is represented here in the analysis of unities into wholes and parts.

2. The theory of meaning in the *Theaetetus* marks a fundamental advance over the *Cratylus*. In the *Cratylus* there is no separation in principle between names and descriptions, whereas the sharpness of that distinction is the central semantic achievement of the *Theaetetus*. The recognition that a *logos* is more than a name, that it is in fact a weaving-together of names (*sumplokē onomatōn*), points the way to the theory of propositional structure to be completed in the *Sophist*. The concern there with the Late-learners' confusion, which makes predication impossible, is anticipated in the *Theaetetus* in the list of forbidden predicates ("is," "it," "that," "this," "each," "only") and in the reference to Antisthenes' theory of "proper *logos*" (202a). Plato's theory of predication (*prosagoreuein*) becomes explicit only with the discussion of the Late-learners in the *Sophist*, but there are clear anticipations in the *Cratylus* and *Theaetetus*.

3. The notion of weaving-together prefigures another development of the *Sophist*: the conception of Forms as a network of interrelations. That new point of view is represented here by its negative counterpart. It is because the first principles of the Dream theory are simple and incomposite (*asuntheta, monoeideis, amerista* at 205c7–d2) that they cannot be known or described. By way of negation, then, this points towards the doctrine of *Sophist* 259e: that *logos* is given to us by a weaving-together of Forms with one another (*hē allēlōn tōn eidōn sumplokē*). For another flagging of this unsatisfactory conception of the Forms as incomposite and indivisible, see *Parmenides* 129a–e (discussed above, p. 4).

2.14 Fruitless attempts to interpret *logos*

The dialogue ends with a survey of three meanings of the term *logos*, none of which succeeds in identifying the gap that separates knowledge from true judgment. In contrast with the rich history of the term *logos* and its importance in earlier Platonic dialogues, these three attempts to interpret the word are strikingly feeble. They serve to remind the alert reader that the relevant notion of *logos* (namely, *logos tēs ousias*, in answer to the question "What is it?") cannot be introduced here, since that would imply a reference to the stable concept of being connected with the theory of Forms.[52] Hence no adequate account of *logos* can be given without violating the hypothesis of the *Theaetetus*, namely, that knowledge is to be defined in isolation from any notion of unchanging, intelligible reality. Under these conditions, any attempt to introduce the notion of *logos* can make no real contribution to the definition of knowledge.

Of the three proposed interpretations the first, taking *logos* as language, offers nothing new; it simply recalls the notion of speech as the public image of thought (*dianoias eidōlon*, 208c5): putting one's thought into words.[53] Since everyone who is not deaf and dumb can put their opinion into words and phrases, this sense of *logos* will not mark a gap separating knowledge from true opinion.

---

[52] There may be a hint of this more Platonic sense of λόγος in the repeated reference to the οὐσία of wagon at 207c1 and 3.

[53] "To declare one's thought through voice, by means of words and phrases" (μετὰ ῥημάτων τε καὶ ὀνομάτων, 206d). As in *Apology* 17c1, ῥήματα τε καὶ ὀνόματα is a standard formula for verbal elaboration. Given its formulaic character, there is no reason to translate the expression here as "by means of nouns and verbs," and thus obscure Plato's radical innovation in the *Sophist*, where for the first time he introduces the noun-verb analysis of sentence structure as a preparation for his theory of truth. (See below, p. 125.) A similar mistake is made by reading Plato's later notion of *onoma* and *rhēma* into *Cratylus* 425a1; cf. ῥήματα at 431b5.

The second interpretation of *logos* might seem to suggest the notion of a Socratic definition. It interprets *logos* as an account or enumeration of elemental constituents, "a path through the *stoicheia*." But elements are understood here only as physical parts. Socrates' example is from Hesiod, whose expert wagoner will know that "a wagon has one hundred timbers": wheel, axle, yoke, etc. (207a–c; cf. *Works and Days* 456). Such a definition, limited to sensible parts, will lack the required generality. This point is illustrated by an example from spelling, where the *stoicheia* are the letters. Thus, even if a person can list the parts of Theaetetus' name, that is, the correct set of letters, he does not have knowledge of the syllable *theta+epsilon* if, when he encounters it in Theodorus' name, he mistakes it for the syllable *tau+epsilon*. Knowledge implies generality, the capacity to identify sameness and difference for constituent elements in different combinations. But the notion of "same letter" implies more than a physical resemblance between two marks. It denotes a plurality defined by some principle of unity, a single position in an ordered system of signs. There may be different visible representations of the letter *alpha*. What unifies these visible symbols is their position in the alphabet – in a rational structure that is no longer an object of sense perception.

The third and final attempt to specify *logos* might seem to come closer to a satisfactory account, since it introduces the notion of a differentia or distinguishing mark (*sēmeion, diaphora*), a property by which the object in question differs from everything else (208c7). Thus, the *logos* of the sun would be "the brightest thing in heaven circulating the earth." To identify Theaetetus one might specifying his appearance, including his snub nose (209a–c). Such a feature will remind us of Theaetetus when we meet him again. But if this reminder is to provide more than right opinion, it must include the recognition that this snub nose belongs to Theaetetus. But such recognition (*gnōnai*) implies acquaintance and is thus a form of knowledge. So this definition of *logos* in terms of a distinguishing mark turns out to be circular. That the mark in question belongs to Theaetetus must itself be known, not simply opined, in order to elevate this case of true opinion to the level of knowledge.[54]

The failure of this attempt to define knowledge leaves open the possibility of a better approach in the future (210c1). The implied conclusion,

---

[54] As a rhetorical device, Plato relies here on the contrast between personal acquaintance and mere belief about Theaetetus in order to illustrate the distinction between knowledge and true opinion. There is a similar contrast in the *Meno* between eyewitness and hearsay evidence. In both cases the epistemic contrast is clear enough; but in neither case is the representative of ἐπιστήμη an example of knowledge in the strict sense, as a function of reason rather than sense perception.

then, is not that a definition of knowledge is impossible but that it is impossible under the conditions imposed on the present project. We cannot specify the nature of knowledge without identifying its object as a reality exempt from change, a reality accessible to reason but lying beyond the scope of sensory experience. In the examples considered and rejected, the subjects to be defined are always sensible individuals: a wagon, the sun, or Theaetetus and his snub nose. For Plato, these cannot be objects of knowledge in any strict sense.

The *Theaetetus* thus remains faithful to its anti-rationalist beginnings with the conception of knowledge as sense perception. This empiricist bias has been systematically preserved in the three readings of *logos* that conclude the dialogue. In view of the emphasis on mathematics in the introductory conversation with Theaetetus and Theodorus, we might be inclined to ask: Why is there no attempt here to take account of the richer notions of *logos* ("ratio") and *stoicheia* ("elements") as principles of rational order in mathematics? The answer, I suggest, is that any adequate account of such notions would require some reference to intelligible structure with a basis in stable Being. But for such a basis we must look beyond the *Theaetetus*. We turn, then, to the *Sophist*, which announces itself as the promised continuation (210d4, 216a1).

Appendix 1   On the narrow conception of *aisthēsis* in the central argument

In the *Theaetetus* as elsewhere, the term *aisthēsis* is often taken to apply to perception generally, including not only perceptual judgment but also affective states such as pleasure and pain, desires and fears (*Theaet.* 156b4–5). It is important to distinguish this broader notion of perception, which we meet throughout the corpus, from the very restricted sense of *aisthēsis* presupposed here in the central argument of the dialogue (184b–186e).

In his final refutation of the claims of perception to constitute knowledge, Socrates is careful to limit the conception of *aisthēsis* to sensation proper, as a strictly passive form of cognition received through the special organs of sense. Thus, *aisthēsis* is taken here in its elementary form, as perception of the proper sensibles. The content of *aisthēsis* so understood is identified as the direct object of the bodily sense modalities: color, sound, smells, tastes, and the properties of touch (hot/cold, dry/wet, hard/soft, rough/smooth, etc.).

It is sensation in this precise sense, as distinguished from perceptual experience in general and from judgments about the content of perception, that is isolated in this passage in defining the thesis to be refuted. (Perceptual judgments generally will then be included under *doxa*, which becomes the topic for the remainder of the *Theaetetus*.) Such a careful distinction was not drawn in the original statement of the theory at 156–57, which was formulated generally to cover all forms of perception. (For example, it was implied at 157d8 that *aisthēsis* included judgments of goodness and beauty.) The discussion at 186c is probably the first time that Plato – or any philosopher – drew a careful distinction between sensation narrowly understood, as passive reception of qualitative differences in the bodily sense modalities, and perceptual judgment in general. (For a partial anticipation, see Democritus fr. 11.)

The objects of *aisthēsis* strictly understood are now identified as those which the soul considers "through the powers of the body" (*Theaet.* 185e7), in contrast with the objects of conceptual judgment, which the soul considers on its own ("itself by itself"). The former are described as experiences (*pathēmata*) naturally available to humans and animals as soon as they are born, and which "reach through the body to the soul" (186c1).[55]

Plato does not attempt to specify at what point exactly this passive faculty of sensation is enriched by the conceptual complexities of perceptual judgment, which accordingly introduce the activity of *logos* and *doxa*. But for his refutation of the empiricist claim to define knowledge in terms of sense perception, it is necessary for Plato to take *aisthēsis* in its most elementary, entirely passive form, by reference to the bodily organs of sense. On the other hand, it is the broader notion of *aisthēsis*, including both feelings in general and perceptual judgment, that is usually under discussion in the *Theaetetus* and elsewhere. It is this broader notion that is invoked in the standard contrast between sense and intellect. Only in the argument of 185–86 does Plato carefully reduce *aisthēsis* to this strictest notion, as passive reception of information from the sense modalities. It is essential for him to show that from *aisthēsis* alone, in this sense, there is no account of knowledge to be derived, nor any picture of the natural world.

For a partial parallel, see the contrast at *Philebus* 21b–c between the experience of pleasure as such and its interpretation in judgment (*doxa*) and awareness (*phronēsis*). As in *Theaetetus* 185–86, Plato is here concerned

---

[55] Notice that in other contexts this last expression can apply not only to the special objects of the sense modalities but also to feelings generally, including the sensations of pleasure and pain. Thus, in the *Timaeus* the confused experience of the newly incarnate soul is ascribed to "motions (κινήσεις) that are carried through the body and hit against the soul" (43c4). It may be that also in the argument of *Theaetetus* 185–86 the sensation of bodily pleasure/pain is similarly included in the notion of αἴσθησις narrowly understood.

to distinguish the sensory experience itself from its cognitive interpretation. The former without the latter, he says, is the life of a clam or a medusa, not that of a human being.

Appendix 2   The digression

The long digression (from 172c to 177b) is concerned with the contrast between two lives, that of the philosopher and that of the successful politician, with their respective rewards and punishments. The passage is a sustained exercise in rhetorical prose, and (as Theodorus observes) it provides a welcome relief from the rigorous critique of Protagoras' thesis. Since this digression contains many echoes of earlier dialogues, its interpretation has a direct bearing on the question how the argument of the *Theaetetus* is related to the conception of knowledge in those other works.

The digression follows Protagoras' brief and partial reappearance at 171d1 ("from the neck up") and constitutes an intermission between the two careful arguments: the general refutation of Protagorean relativism (known as the *peritropē*) and the specific refutation of the claim that all judgments concerning the future could be true (178a–179a). This digression was directly provoked by the modified restatement of Protagoras' view in his final, partial reappearance. There he concedes that judgments of what will be healthy or advantageous (*ta sumpheronta*) may be in error, but insists there can be no natural criterion for what is hot or cold, or right and wrong. The issue concerning the status of sense feelings such as hot and cold will be discussed later, in the theory of twin motions. On the other hand, this digression constitutes Plato's only response in this dialogue to the relativist denial of the distinction between what is just and unjust, right and wrong. Thus it is the only answer here to the moral challenge faced by Socrates in the *Gorgias* and in the first book of the *Republic*.

The digression opens with a reference to the philosopher who, when he appears in court, must make a ridiculous appearance as an orator. This sounds like an allusion to Socrates in the *Apology*, but the reference is not exact. For the model philosopher is described here as one who does not know his way to the agora (173d1), which is scarcely characteristic of Socrates. This indirect and partial form of allusion is typical of many echoes here of topics from earlier dialogues, including reminiscences of Callicles, Polus, and Thrasymachus. But these allusions are never precise enough to constitute an immediate reference. Thus, the digression introduces a contrast between two stereotypes. On the one hand, we have the unworldly philosopher, concerned with questions of "justice itself and injustice, what each of them is and how they differ from one another," and how kingship is related to human happiness. On the other hand, our philosopher is confronted with the ruthless practical politician, who becomes dizzy when he is obliged to answer such questions and forced to rise to these intellectual heights (175c–d). The contrast includes many vague reminders of Socrates' confrontations with Callicles and the sophists.

This mode of indirect allusion to themes from earlier dialogues continues in the positive doctrine that concludes the digression. We have first a passionate echo of the otherworldly atmosphere of the *Phaedo*, with an offer of escape from the evils of this world by *homoiōsis theōi*, the imitation of the divine in a life of justice and wisdom (176b). This new theme of *imitatio dei* is reinforced by an allusion to the myths of punishment in *Phaedo* and *Republic*. Thus, for moral ignorance and wrongdoing there is said to be a punishment in store "that it is impossible to escape" (176e1). The notion of divine justice is represented here by a cosmic image vaguely reminiscent of the theory of Forms: "There are two models established in reality (*paradeigmatōn en tōi onti hestōtōn*), one divine and most happy, the other godless and most miserable." What constitutes the inevitable punishment for an unjust life is to become assimilated to the second model. Hence, when the unjust die, "the place that is pure of evils will not receive them" (177a). This echo of the punishment myths is linked here to the contrast between philosopher and politician by a final reference to the fate of Socrates' opponents, who are unable to maintain their position under scrutiny from the Socratic test of "giving and receiving an account (*logos*)" (177b).

Thus, the digression provides us with a vivid reminder of the moral doctrine of the *Gorgias*, *Phaedo*, and *Republic*, including an allusion to the myths of judgment. But the metaphysical restrictions of the *Theaetetus* are faithfully respected, even in the hint here of "two models established in reality." This mention of *paradeigmata* is carefully formulated to avoid any reference to the distinction between Being and Becoming, or to anything else that would imply a distinctly Platonic account of knowledge. This is Plato's solution to a difficult problem of method. On the one hand, he cannot leave the moral implications of Protagorean relativism unanswered. On the other hand, he cannot give a full defense of Socratic morality without violating the philosophical limitations of the *Theaetetus*. The digression is a cunning device for resolving this dilemma. It does so by recalling the moral argument of the *Gorgias*, *Phaedo*, and *Republic* without explicit reference to either the mythical or metaphysical doctrine of these dialogues, but with unmistakable allusions to both.

Appendix 3   Sense perception as a system of motions

In the *Timaeus* we will find a detailed account of the perceptual modalities but no general theory of sense perception. Plato's fullest account is given in a curious passage of the *Theaetetus* where perception is described in terms of a system of active and passive motions.

In other contexts, perception is generally characterized as "motions (from external sources) that are carried through the body and hit against the soul."[56] Thus, in the *Philebus aisthēsis* is defined as a motion in which "body and soul come together in a single *pathos* and are moved in common (*koinēi*)" (34a). Here Plato distinguishes the affects (*pathēmata*) that are extinguished in the body before they reach the soul (and hence leave the latter unaffected, *apathēs*) from those that go through both body and soul "and induce as it were a quaking (*seismos*) that is common to both and proper to each" (*Phil.* 33d).

Implicit in such texts is a recognition of three or four distinct components in sense perception. There is first of all (1) the active property or power (*dunamis*) of the object (which, in the *Timaeus*, will be explained in terms of elemental triangles); and (2) the passive affect (*pathēma*) on the sentient subject. This affect consists of two elements: (2a) the mechanical impact on the body, and (2b) the corresponding impact on the psychic capacity of sense: the qualitative reception of color, sound, or the like. But it is an essential feature of 2b, and the distinctive mark of perception in general, that (3) the quality in question is perceived as belonging to the initial object or source (1 above). This objective reference of perception (3) is the distinctive work of the sensory soul – a work that the body alone cannot carry out. It is in virtue of this feature that, as Timaeus will point out, it is plausible (*eikotōs*) that both items 1 and 2 are called by the same name, e.g. "hot."[57]

Notice that although items 1 and 2a involve only the bodily object and the bodily organ, items 2b and 3 involve the psychic faculty of sense. It is this complexity that is reflected in Plato's description of sense perception as moving "through the body to the psyche."

Now the only passage in the dialogues where these four components are clearly distinguished is a picturesque text in the *Theaetetus*, in Plato's discussion of the proposed definition of knowledge as sense perception. That definition is supported here by an elaborate theory in which the whole

---

[56] *Timaeus* 43c. Cf. *Theaet.* 186c: sense perceptions are "affects" (παθήματα) that stretch through the body to the soul.
[57] *Timaeus* 62a4.

of nature is interpreted as a system of motions. In this context no distinction is drawn between bodily and psychic components; the entire analysis is carried out in terms of neutral motions. (Since the context is a discussion of perception, no account is given of bodily impact in which sensation does not occur.)

The physical conditions of perception are described in terms of two motions, one passive (the perceiver) and one active (the external cause of perception). The corresponding psychic factors will be represented by the twin products of contact between these two bodily motions:

> There are two kinds of motion, each one unlimited in multitude but distinguished in power (*dunamis*), the one active the other passive. And through the intercourse and mutual friction of these two there comes to be an offspring infinite in multitude but always twin births, on the one hand what is perceived, on the other, the perception of it, the perception in every case being generated together with what is perceived and emerging along with it.

The perceptions include sight, hearing, feeling hot and cold, but also pleasures and pains, desires and fears:

> For each of these perceptions <there are> perceived things born of the same parents: for diverse visions diverse colors, for diverse hearings diverse sounds, and so on, for different perceptions different things perceived the same in kind (*suggenê*). (156a5–c3, trans. after Levett-Burnyeat)

Thus, Socrates presents sensation as the joint product or offspring of two factors, two slow motions, constituting an internal subject (such as the eye or the ear) and an external object (the thing seen or heard, such as a piece of wood or stone). The interaction between these two factors produces two swift movements, one projected back onto the internal subject and the other thrown forward onto the external object or cause of sensation. The result of these movements is a pair of twin qualities: the eye is filled with a vision of whiteness, and the stick or stone is seen as white:

> Thus the eye and some other thing – one of the things commensurate with it – which has come into its neighborhood, generate both whiteness and the sensation that is linked to it by nature (*sumphuton*) . . . In this event, motions arise in between, sight on the side of the eye and whiteness on the side of that which cooperates in producing the color. The eye is filled with sight; at that moment it sees, and there comes into being, not indeed sight, but a seeing eye; while its partner in producing color is filled with whiteness, and there comes into being not whiteness but white, a white stick or stone or whatever

it is that happens to be colored this sort of color. (*Theaet.* 156d–e, Levett-Burnyeat translation slightly revised).

We have already discussed the function of this text in the argument of the *Theaetetus*. (See above, p. 53.) What concerns us here is this passage as an account of the phenomenology of perception represented in the fast motions, as distinguished from the physicalist account of organ and object reflected in the slow motions. The role of the psyche is not mentioned in this context, but silently implied in Socrates' account of the two fast motions. It is the physical eye and the physical object that are identified here as slow motions – slow, because nothing in this theory is allowed to stand still.[58] But the twin qualities produced by this physical marriage between subject and object correspond, on the one hand, to a private ("subjective") sensory experience of whiteness that results from the projection inwards onto the percipient subject; while, on the other hand, in the corresponding twin motion, the *same* qualitative content is projected outwards onto the object, thus providing "objective" information about the world as seen. Such qualitative information is in principle reliable, since both internal and external twins represent the object-as-perceived.[59]

The exceptional power of Plato's model here is that it both admits and overcomes the interpretation of qualitative experience as subjective, located only in the percipient. It overcomes this interpretation by reproducing the very same quality in the twin structure of the external offspring. The sensory quality of color or sound is thus not only experienced by the subject of perception; by the same act it is projected onto the external object. The *Theaetetus* model thus does justice to the fundamental nature of perceptual experience: that sensory qualities, despite their subjectivity, are actually perceived as belonging to the external world. This twin feature reflects the basic function of perception, namely, that sensory information turns out to be useful in dealing with the world. Thus, Plato's model for the twin structure of perception takes full account of a fact that may well seem inexplicable from a post-Cartesian point of view: namely, that the world is systematically and beneficially perceived as qualified – that the rain is perceived as wet, the fire as hot, the honey as sweet, and that such

---

[58] These slow motions would correspond in the *Timaeus* to an account of organ and object in terms of elemental solids. There may be a hint here of such atomic structures in the unexplained reference to many "aggregates" (ἀθροίσματα) at *Theaet.* 157b9, composing what "people call 'man' or 'stone,' or to which they give the names of the different animals and sorts of things" (trans. Levett-Burnyeat).

[59] This qualitative identity between perceptual twins corresponds to the double use of the term "hot" for feelings and fire recognized in the *Timaeus*. To this extent there is an exact correlation between the accounts of perception in the *Timaeus* and the *Theaetetus*.

perceptions regularly provide the basis for successful encounters with the external world. These qualities that our modern critique tends to regard as purely subjective are in fact usefully perceived as properties belonging to the external object. That is why, as Timaeus will point out, it is natural to assign the same name both to our feeling of heat and to its external cause.

It is this phenomenal correlation between the inward experience and the outward reference of sense qualities that is so vividly represented in Plato's twin structure for the fast motions. It is the fast motions that represent the manifest image, whereas the slow motions correspond to the scientific (e.g. atomist) account.

Neither Plato's model nor modern dualism resolves the mystery of how we succeed in recognizing the qualitative diversity of the perceived world with, in general, a good deal of reliability, despite the highly specific limitations on our perceptual apparatus as scientifically described. But at least Plato's model takes account of this success, whereas modern dualism (by insisting on the merely mental-subjective status of the fast motions) tends to make such success inexplicable.

CHAPTER 3

Being and Not-Being in the Sophist

In the *Theaetetus* Socrates insisted on avoiding the discussion (which Theaetetus had requested) of Parmenides' doctrine of Being. As the promised sequel to the *Theaetetus*, the *Sophist* is designed to fill that gap. A significant change in style suggests that a considerable lapse of time may have occurred between the composition of these two dialogues. Nevertheless, the reappearance of Theaetetus as interlocutor in the *Sophist* is a clear reminder of continuity in this project.

It was presumably with these Parmenidean issues in view that Plato chose to replace Socrates as chief speaker with a visitor from Elea. One of Plato's principal tasks in this dialogue will be to correct Parmenides' account of Not-Being. The choice of a spokesman from Parmenides' own school will serve to guarantee an atmosphere of intellectual sympathy for the doctrine to be criticized.

3.1 Limits of this Dialogue

In the *Sophist* Plato will discuss Being, as well as Not-Being, within the limits of a specific range of problems. The constructive section of the dialogue will explore a network of positive and negative relations between forms as constituents of *logos*, that is to say, between linguistic structures considered as an account of reality. This network presents the object for a new conception of dialectic in terms of Collection and Division, a conception proposed in the *Phaedrus* and illustrated now in the *Sophist* and *Statesman*. The forms are presented here precisely as objects of dialectic, of rational combination and separation. Despite the focus on Being, the Eleatic Stranger will discuss neither the metaphysical status of these forms nor their instantiation in the sensible world. (Accordingly, in this chapter I will generally refer to "forms" without a capital "F".) Thus, the *Sophist* stops short of full ontology, just as it avoids a discussion of cosmology and physics, except in the report of earlier theories. With its specific goal of

94

defining the Sophist and distinguishing him from the philosopher, this dialogue tends to treat forms almost exclusively as items of rational discourse and thought. The hints of a more robust, more Platonic metaphysics are limited here to the critical review of the doctrines of the Friends of Forms, and also to a brief glimpse of the philosopher "always clinging through his reasonings to the form of Being forever."[1] This last formula strongly suggests the metaphysical status of the forms, familiar from earlier dialogues. But Plato's classical doctrine of Forms is seen here from a critical distance, as it were from Elea.

The dialogue, then, has a limited goal: to give an account of Being, via the analysis of five forms, that can clarify the notions of Not-Being and negative predication, in order to validate the concepts of false appearance, false statement, and false judgment. There is a special concern for a solution to the problem of false judgment, which has been so elaborately canvassed in the *Theaetetus*. There is no attempt to give an account of – neither to affirm nor deny – the levels of reality and cognition distinguished in *Republic* V–VII and recognized again in *Philebus* and *Timaeus*. Similarly, no attempt is made to clarify the relations between Motion and Rest, except for their mutual exclusion. The necessity of both forms for knowledge is recognized, but treated summarily. Theories of Motion and Rest are discussed only in the report of earlier doctrines. If that report leads us to expect a solution to the physical and metaphysical problems surveyed, our expectations will be disappointed. Instead of physics and metaphysics, what we have in the constructive doctrine of the *Sophist* is an account of Being and Not-Being as predicate concepts or kinds (*genē*), in the context of a general theory of predication and truth. I have the impression that, in order to resolve these conceptual problems with a sufficient level of clarity, Plato has simply put aside all metaphysical issues concerning the relations between Being and Becoming. Thus, the problem of cognition for objects involved in change and Becoming, discussed at such length in the *Theaetetus*, is noticed here but left unresolved.

3.2 Analysis of *einai*

It is the corollary about Not-Being that Plato chooses as his route of entry into the new survey of theories of Being. This problem has been on his mind for some time, as we can see from the paradoxes surveyed in earlier dialogues

---

[1] *Soph.* 254a 8–9 τῇ τοῦ ὄντος ἀεὶ διὰ λογισμῶν προσκείμενος ἰδέα, with deliberate ambiguity in the syntax of ἀεί, modifying both ὄντος and προσκείμενος.

(above, pp. 69–70). To understand why this subject of Not-Being is so critical for Plato we must return to the Parmenidean conception of Being that he had adopted for his own metaphysics. Modern scholars have sometimes interpreted Parmenides' notion of being as a fusion, or confusion, between existential and copula uses of the verb *to be*. I have argued elsewhere that this distinction provides an inadequate framework for interpreting the role of *einai* in Greek. In the preceding chapter I suggested that the basic sense of being for Plato was something like propositional structure, involving both predication and truth claim, together with existence for the subject of predication. In support of this analysis, I will here summarize my account of the verb from a linguistic point of view.[2]

We can distinguish one syntactic and three semantic functions of the verb *to be* (*einai*) in Greek. The syntactic function of *einai* is its basic role as grammatical copula in sentences of the form *S is P*. In recent discussion, this copula construction has often been called the "incomplete" use of *einai*, since it needs to be completed by the addition of a predicate term. The semantic uses, on the other hand, are typically "complete" in this respect, in that they do not need an additional predicate. I find the terminology of "complete" and "incomplete" misleading; it refers in any case only to surface structure. For Plato as for Aristotle, *to be* is always to be something or other. Hence, every use of *einai* is logically incomplete. (This is made explicit in transformational analysis, which shows that the apparently "complete" semantic uses, e.g. for existence, presuppose an underlying copula construction in which the verb is formally incomplete.) Hence, it is the "incomplete" or copula construction *S is P* that is fundamental for all uses of *einai*. And this copula construction is by far the most common use of the verb *be* in every period of Greek, as in English.

The three semantic functions of *einai* are (1) existential, for assertions of the subject, claiming *that S is*; (2) instantiation, for assertions of the predicate, claiming *that P is, or occurs*; and (3) veridical, for asserting the whole sentence, i.e. claiming that it is the case *that S is P* (or that it is true *that S is P*). These three semantic functions are all second-order uses of the verb, focusing attention on a particular aspect or implication of an *S is P* sentence, when the latter is asserted. Thus, the second-order uses all take as their target a first-order sentence of the form *S is P*. In this regard, the predicative ("incomplete") function of the verb is fundamental for the whole system of uses of *einai*.

---

[2] In what follows I report the results of my linguistic analysis, presented in Kahn (2004) 381–405. Fuller references in Kahn (2003).

In the light of this analysis, we must understand Parmenides' concept of Being as taking predication as its basis but also including all three semantic values of *einai*. Thus, regardless whether the surface grammar of the verb is complete or incomplete, an occurrence of *is* (*esti*) or *being* (*eon*) in Parmenides' poem presupposes a predication of the form *S is P*, and asserts (1) the existence of a subject; (2) the instantiation of a predicate; and (3) the combination of the two in a state-of-affairs. That is the logical structure of the concept of Being in Parmenides, and in Plato as well, as formulated in the terms of modern linguistic analysis. It corresponds closely to the philosophical interpretation of Being in terms of propositional structure that I have proposed in the preceding chapter.

In Plato's own discussion, the *S is P* basis for predication is taken for granted, although of course not expressed in this modern form. What we find in the *Sophist* is an analysis of being as predication from two points of view: first at the level of high theory, in terms of the mixing or connection between forms; and later at the level of concrete examples, in terms of the noun-verb and subject-predicate composition of simple sentences, such as *Theaetetus sits*, in which the verb "to be" does not actually appear.

Before turning to Plato's text there is more to be said about the pre-philosophic connotations of the verb *einai*. In addition to the formal functions discussed above, there are other aspects of the verb that need to be taken into account. It is significant that the verb "be" is represented in Greek only by the present-imperfect stem **es-* with its durative-stative value, in contrast to verbs with the mutative-kinetic value of "becomes." (In Greek the mutative copula is normally *gignesthai*, but sometimes *phunai*.) This durative sense for being, as expressed by *einai* and other forms derived from **es-*, is particularly strong in Greek, which, almost alone among Indo-European languages, has not incorporated a mutative stem into the conjugation of *einai*. (Thus, there is no Greek suppletive form corresponding to *fuisse* in Latin, *be* and *was* in English). This durative-stative aspect of the verb provides intuitive support for the philosophical notion that Being, to be knowable, must be stable and unchanging. Plato can thus rely on Greek linguistic intuition to support his claim that being as the object of knowledge must be in some respect unchanging. But of course this is a thesis that Plato has also defended by systematic argument, in his refutations of unlimited flux in the *Cratylus* and *Theaetetus*. (The issue of stability for Being comes up again in the *Sophist* discussion of the two Forms Rest and Motion, where the Eleatic Stranger will insist that Being must include both.)

Furthermore, for Parmenides and all pre-Platonic thinkers, we must add the locative value of *einai* as being-somewhere. Parmenides' Being is unabashedly spatial ("equally balanced from the center in every direction, like the bulk of a well-rounded sphere," fr. 8, 43). And a similar spatial attribute is ascribed by Anaxagoras to his principle of Mind (*nous*), which is said to be "in the same place as everything else" (fr. 14). Plato is the first philosopher to deny this locative value that is intuitively associated with the Greek notion of reality as expressed by *einai*.[3] Even Plato, however, preserves this value metaphorically by locating his Forms in the space of concepts: in the *noētos topos* (*Rep.* 508c1).

(In his critical response to my book, the linguist C.J. Ruijgh argued at length that the fundamental value of *einai* was locative ("*être présent, être là*"). See Ruijgh (1984) 264–70. See also Ruijgh (1979) 43–83. I agree that the locative value is basic, but not universal. There is nothing locative in a noun-adjective or noun-noun use of the verb, such as *Socrates is wise* or *Socrates is a philosopher*. We have no knowledge of a stage of Greek in which the verb was not so used.)

There is one more complexity in the notion of Being that Plato has inherited from Parmenides. As we saw in discussing the final argument against sense perception in Chapter 2, there is a certain ambiguity in the veridical notion of being as being-the-case – the notion of being that knowledge requires and that sense perception cannot provide. On the one hand, being is needed for the propositional structure that can express a truth claim, whether in statement or in judgment; on the other hand, being as an objective state-of-affairs is what can make such a claim true. It is being in the former sense, as propositional structure, that we have analyzed here in the semantic values 1–3. Being as state-of-affairs is not a linguistic structure at all, but whatever in the world serves to justify or refute such a truth claim. Like Parmenides, Plato needs to include both propositional form and objective being-so in his conception of Being. Plato nowhere makes this distinction explicit. But, as we shall see below in section 14, in the double clauses of his definition of truth Plato recognizes an implicit distinction between the two.

3.3   The topic of Being in the *Sophist*

The ontological discussion of the *Sophist* divides into two parts. The first, aporetic part (my sections 3–8) surveys a range of problems, beginning with

[3] See *Symp.* 211c8: the Beautiful itself is "not anywhere in something else, for instance in a living thing or in earth or in heaven or in anything else." For the locative sense of being in Greek see Kahn (2003) 156–67.

a series of paradoxical arguments concerning Not-Being (sections 3–4) that develop issues about negative predication raised earlier in the *Theaetetus* and other dialogues. On the pretext of recognizing problems about Being as well as about Not-Being, the Stranger then passes in review ontological disputes between monists and cosmologists (section 5) and between materialists and Friends of Forms (section 6). He concludes this survey of problems in ontology with two issues concerning predication: a problem of negative predication between forms (section 7) and the radical challenge to predication posed by the doctrine of the Late-learners (section 8).

Only in section 9 does the Eleatic Stranger begin to deal constructively with the issue of Not-Being in his refutation of the Late-learners, where he shows that some forms must combine, while others do not. This second, more positive part of the discussion then presents an account of true and false predication, formulated against the background theory of a network of forms that connect with one another in various ways. Sections 10–12 resolve the problem of Not-Being by providing an account of predication, both positive and negative, within the framework of this network of forms. We can then return to the topic of falsehood for statement and judgment, raised earlier as a problem in the *Theaetetus* and required now for the definition of the *Sophist*. The discussion concludes in sections 13–14 with the definition of true and false statement (*logos*), a definition that can easily be applied to judgment (*doxa*) as well.

Notice that this constructive work of the dialogue resolves the problem of Not-Being only as an issue for language and thought, not for ontology proper as concerned with the nature of things. Fundamental issues in cosmology and metaphysics are canvassed in the aporetic preliminaries (sections 3–8) but scarcely mentioned in the constructive exposition that follows (sections 9–14). The network of forms is presented as a clear reality, but left without any definite relation to the realm of change and sense perception. Thus, the nature of the world is raised as a problem, but not addressed by any constructive solution. It is elsewhere that Plato will deal with these cosmic questions, namely, in the *Philebus* and *Timaeus*, and to some extent in *Laws* X.

3.4 The *aporias* concerning Not-Being (237b–239b)

We turn now to the conception of Being presented in Plato's text, beginning with the negative concept of Not-Being. In order to see what kind of problems Plato will confront in dealing with Not-Being, we need to take account of the logical asymmetry between positive and negative applications of the semantic distinctions that I have recognized in my own analysis of *einai* (above, section 2). On the one hand, it is possible to combine the three logical components of propositional structure (existence for the subject, instantiation for the predicate, validity for the truth claim) in a single positive concept, roughly the notion of a fact. In this notion of propositional being we can also include the durative aspect and even the proposition/fact ambiguity. What results from this combination is a coherent conception of enduring reality with quasi-linguistic structure. This is the positive concept of Being that Plato has inherited from Parmenides: a stable entity, or type of entity, with something like propositional structure. On the other hand, the prospects are quite different for any combination of these same linguistic components in their negative form. Taken as negations, the three semantic uses (non-existence for the subject, non-instantiation for the predicate, falsehood for the truth claim) fall apart, and yield only blank nonentity. They do not combine to define a unified notion; and an additional denial of the durative aspect would not improve the blend. As a consequence the notion of Not-Being, if left unrestricted, will be fundamentally incoherent. That is, I suggest, what Parmenides saw in his rejection of Not-Being. And it is precisely this incoherence that Plato's *aporias* are designed to display.

The problematic status of Not-Being is established here by a triple set of arguments. The first *aporia* begins with an unqualified expression of Not-Being. There is nothing to prevent us from uttering the words "what is in no way at all" (*to mēdamōs on*). The problem is to attach a meaning to this phrase, to take it as signifying something definite:

> Now suppose someone putting his mind to this question seriously, and not with a view to controversy or amusement, were to ask: to what should one apply (*epipherein*) this name "what is not"? Of what and what sort of thing might we expect him to use it, and what would he indicate (*deiknunai*) to his interlocutor? (237b10–c4, trans. after L. Brown)

We are to imagine a situation in which one speaker tries to identify an item for his interlocutor by means of a speech act conceived on the model of naming. The word-thing relation is taken here in its most general form; there is no distinction implied between sense and reference, no distinction between abstract entities and concrete objects. The argument aims to show that a speaker will not succeed in naming or describing anything by uttering the expression "what is not at all" (or simply "what is not" without qualification). There is nothing of which this expression could be the name or the description. The negation is so general that it excludes anything that one might wish to apply it to.

This notion of "applying" (*epipherein*) not-being to being – the act rejected here as impossible (237c7–9) – is not unambiguous. But it is more natural to take it as a word-thing rather than a thing-thing relationship. Starting with this linguistic expression "what is in no way at all," we ask if there is anything to which this can be successfully applied. ("Successfully" need not mean "truthfully." To succeed in referring to an object would be enough.) The point of this first *aporia* is that, by excluding being in every respect, the expression in question cannot name or describe an object with any property whatsoever. There is no being (*on*), no something (*ti*), that could be picked out by this expression:

> This much at least is clear: what-is-not (*to mē on*) is not to be applied to any of the things-that-are (*ta onta*) . . . Neither would it be correct to apply it to something (*ti*) . . . (since) whenever we say this "something" (*ti*) we say it of a thing-that-is (*on*). For to say it [namely, *ti*] alone, as it were naked and isolated from everything-that-is, is impossible. (237d, trans. after Brown)

Here we have a clear distinction between uttering the words and using them to refer or designate; it is the latter that is impossible. This point is reinforced by bringing in the singular form of *ti* ("something"), to show that a denial of *ti* would be a reference to nothing, with a word-play on the etymology of *mēden* ("nothing"). Since the expression *ti* is the sign of something singular, i.e. one, to say "not *ti*" is to say "not even one" (*mē d' hen*), i.e. to say absolutely nothing (*mēden*). So when the speaker tries to utter "what is not" he is not saying anything – he is not even speaking! (237e).

The first *aporia* thus ends with the echo of a paradox from the *Theaetetus*: to judge (*doxazein*) what-is-not is impossible, because it is to judge nothing, and hence not to judge at all (*Theaet.* 189a). In terms of our analysis of *einai*, since such arguments negate every mode of being, they have the effect of denying existence both for any subject and also for any attribute, and thus make propositional assertion impossible. (Even a false statement requires a subject and a predicate.) The *aporia* implied in the *Sophist* text takes a slightly different line. It points rather to the notion of an underlying link or connection between forms, and in particular to the claim that any form must be linked both to Being and to One. In effect, by excluding any connection with Being, unqualified Not-Being denies any possibility of existence for either subject or predicate. Hence, there is nothing to assert, and accordingly (as the *Theaetetus* pointed out) nothing to judge. In the

Parmenides Plato has shown that forms do not exist in isolation (*chōrismos*) from one another. Every form must be connected with the form of Being, and also with the form One. These two kinds are connected both to one another and, by implication, to everything else. The present argument aims to show that a form named by "what is not at all," or described as "not something (*ti*)," could not be connected to anything. But a form so unconnected will not be a being, and hence not a form. (We are about to meet the claim that language depends on *sumplokē eidōn*, the interconnection of forms.)

Thus the first *aporia*, which began with the analysis of "applying" as a word-thing relation, ends with the notion of a thing-thing connection between forms or concepts as underlying any successful reference or description. This alternative construal in terms of a thing-thing relation is confirmed now by the term *prosgenesthai*, "be attached to," that will replace *epipherein* in the second *aporia*.

The second *aporia* begins with a premise in other respects like that of the first. Since being and not-being are contradictory, the former cannot be attached (*prosgenesthai*) to the latter (238a7). Furthermore, since every number is a being, neither one nor many can be attached to not-being. But it is impossible to say what-is-not without making this term either singular or plural in form. And that would be to attach some being – either one or many – to not-being. Since (as the *Theaetetus* has pointed out, and this dialogue will confirm) the form of thought is directly dependent on the form of speech, not-being is not only unspeakable but also unthinkable (238c).

This argument relies upon the fact that we cannot take not-being as the subject either of speech or of thought without making it numerically definite. That is a truth about the linguistic forms for Being in Greek (*on* and *onta*, singular and plural, respectively), and hence also for Not-Being. Beyond the facts of grammar, however, the philosophical claim is that the choice of a singular or plural ending for the subject expression reflects a numerical choice between the one and the many as attributes of the alleged non-linguistic subject. But either choice would be illegitimate, because it would attach a being (being one or many) to unqualified not-being.

A modern reader might be tempted to reject this inference as reflecting a use-mention confusion, since it argues from the grammatical form of the subject expression in Greek to the nature of the corresponding object. But such an inference need not be fallacious. The point is that unqualified Not-Being cannot be grasped as a subject for either thought or speech *because* it is (as it were "by definition") wholly indeterminate. You cannot succeed in specifying a subject for speaking or thinking without giving it a degree of definiteness (as one or as many) that is strictly incompatible with the unqualified notion of not-being.

The third *aporia* relies on the same reasoning but deploys it now to deny the coherence of any attempt to *reject* not-being. There is no way even to refute this notion without contradiction, since to refer to it as "it" or "this" (*touto*) or describe it as "unspeakable" (*arrēton*) is to take it as singular, and hence as a determinate form of being. Even worse, to claim that not-being is irrational (*alogon einai*) is to say *that it is* (*einai*), and thus to contradict the very notion of not-being, namely, *that it is not in any way.* Despite appearances, what is at stake here cannot be dismissed as an equivocation between copula and existential verb. Since the unqualified negative thesis will also deny the *is* of predication understood as sentential truth claim, it makes all assertion impossible. Even a negative predication will require the semantic *is so* of a truth claim.[4]

What the triple *aporia* has established, then, is that unqualified not-being is a hopelessly incoherent notion, which cannot even be denied without contradiction. In this respect the concept of not-being offers a significant parallel to the doctrine of unqualified flux, which, as we saw in Chapter 2, is also impossible to formulate without contradiction. We have here in Platonic metaphysics two significant examples of what we might count as Transcendental Arguments, arguments that proceed by a form of *reductio* to show that a given thesis is incompatible with the facts of human language and cognition. Just as the refutation of flux shows that both knowledge and being require an element of stability, so the current argument concludes that both language and thought are impossible without some limits on the negation of being. The concept of unrestricted flux thus provides a kind of image or metaphor for unqualified Not-Being.

3.5 The *aporias* concerning Being: cosmologists and monists (242c–245e)

Having abandoned the notion of unqualified Not-Being, the rest of our dialogue is devoted to salvaging some more limited uses of *is not.* But the elucidation of *is not* will require some preliminary clarification of *is.* The Eleatic Stranger begins by showing that the notion of Being is just as problematic as Not-Being, so that the two notions must be clarified together. (The required clarification begins only below, section 9.) This

---

[4] That is a point made by Plato in the *Parmenides* in connection with Deduction 5. See above, p. 36.

new set of *aporias* concerning Being will take the form of a survey of previous philosophical theories, beginning with the cosmologists (242c–243b) and monists (244–245), and continuing with the corporealists (246a–247e) and the Friends of Forms (248a–249d).

The question addressed to the cosmologists (including Heraclitus and Empedocles) is: What do they mean by saying of two elemental principles, such as the hot and the cold, that they both *are*? Do they mean that they are really one thing, namely Being? (244a1). The point of this objection is not immediately clear. But in the light of what follows we can see that Plato is introducing here the distinction between two ways of *being F*, namely, either being the nature of F or having F as an attribute. The hot and the cold are not identical with the form or nature of Being, but they both have being as a property. In terminology familiar from the *Parmenides* (and which will reappear later in this dialogue), hot and cold both share in Being (*metechein tou ontos*) without being Being itself. Thus, we have a first hint here of the distinction between *being F per se* and *being F per aliud* that will be introduced later.

Turning now to the monists, the Stranger asks them whether Being will have the one as an attribute (*pathos*), and, if so, whether Being and the One will each have its own nature (*phusis*) and thus be two rather than one (245a). The discussion is further complicated by a quotation from Parmenides which suggests that being is a whole of parts, so that its unity would be that of a whole. The monists are then challenged by an intricate argument designed to show that the three concepts of Being, One, and Whole are so interrelated as to be incompatible with the claim that Being is strictly one (244e–245d).[5]

At this point the Eleatic Stranger is less concerned to clarify the relation between these three forms than to show that they are distinct from one another, and hence that "each one has its own separate nature" (245c9). Here, for the first time, the Stranger explicitly draws the distinction between a form itself – that is, its essence or nature (*phusis*) – and the corresponding attribute (*pathos*). The immediate aim is to show that unity is an attribute of Being, and hence that One and Being are two distinct forms. (Similarly for the distinctness of Being and Whole.) "Since Being has the attribute of

---

[5] For a full discussion of this difficult argument, see Harte (2002) 100–18. The reasoning is aporetic, and probably not all claims are designed to stand unchallenged. In particular, the statement that "the one itself" or "the truly one" would have no parts (245a) seems problematic. Plato's considered view, formulated in the *Philebus*, is that every form is a combination of one and many. But perhaps "the truly one" here is a hint of the absolute One of the so-called unwritten doctrines, a One that would be more fundamental than the Forms.

somehow being one (*peponthos to on hen einai pōs*), it will turn out to be not the same as the One" (245b7). Since we are criticizing the monists here, the focus of the argument is on the plurality of entities rather than on the distinction between the form itself and its role as attribute. But we could not ask for a sharper statement of the contrast between two ways of being one: being the One itself, or being something else that has unity as an attribute. This contrast prepares the way for the fundamental distinction between being *per se* and being *per aliud*, which will be presented later (beginning at 250c6).

3.6 The battle between gods and giants: corporealists and Friends of Forms (246a–249d)

The constructive account of Not-Being still lies ahead, in the systematic treatment of the five "greatest kinds." First we have the discussion and critique of two theories of Being from rival schools, the materialists and the Platonists. Their conflict is staged as a battle between the gods and the giants, the gods being the Friends of (Platonic) Forms, whereas the giants are thinkers who claim that all being is bodily and that nothing is real except what they can grasp with their hands. Instead of confronting the latter directly, the Stranger offers to reconstruct them as enlightened materialists who will acknowledge a reality not strictly conceived in bodily terms. In order to engage these reformed materialists, the Stranger proposes as a distinguishing mark (*horos*) of beings (*ta onta*): whatever has the power or capacity (*dunamis*) to act or be acted upon (247e1). However, this definition of Being in terms of *dunamis* will be rejected by the classical Platonists, who allow it only as an account of Becoming (248c).

It is at this point that we get our first hint of a significant innovation in Plato's late ontology, allowing for a mixed level of reality in between the changeless Being of the Forms and the flux of sensible Becoming.[6] What is suggested by this formula for the capacity to act or be acted on is in fact a wider conception of Being that will cover the realm of change. This more generous notion of Being is probably designed to prepare the way for a mixed type, destined to appear in the *Philebus* as a blend of Being and Becoming, to be distinguished there from the eternal Being of the Forms.

Because of his familiarity with the Platonists, the Stranger knows in advance that they will reject this notion of power as an account of Being

---

[6] There is an anticipation of this formula for "the capacity to act and be acted on" in the sketch of a scientific study of nature in *Phaedrus* at 270d. See below, p. 138.

(248b8). Acordingly, the Stranger now turns to these Platonists and poses two problems for the classical doctrine of Forms. The first *aporia* continues with the notion of power developed in the exchange with the materialists. The doctrine of the Friends of Forms is that "by sense perception we communicate (*koinōnein*) with Becoming, by reasoning we communicate with real Being" (*ontōs ousia*, 248a11). But what is this cognitive power that is common to both? Is it a power to act or be acted upon, as specified in the previous account?

The Platonists' answer is complex. In regard to Becoming they accept a definition in terms of causal action and passivity. However, for the unchanging reality of true *ousia* this account is unacceptable, for it would imply change in both subject and object. But the Forms are by nature unchanging. Hence, knowing and being known are not genuine cases of acting and being acted upon. Unlike sensation, intellectual cognition is not a transitive act that causes change in either subject or object, or both. Hence, instead of being an objection for the Platonists, the definition of reality in terms of *dunamis* turns out to be the beginning of an acceptable account for the mixed being of the phenomenal world.

The second challenge to the Platonists begins from their answer to the first *aporia*. Granted that in an act of intellectual cognition no change occurs in the object, is this true also for the knowing subject? And what would this imply for the presence of knowledge among the unchanging Forms?

"Are we going to be easily persuaded that change (*kinēsis*) and life and soul and understanding (*nous*) are not present in what is completely real (*to pantelōs on*), but that it neither lives nor thinks (*phronein*) but stands there motionless, as solemn as a sacred statue, without understanding?" (248e6–249a2) The Stranger insists that knowledge and understanding (*nous*) can only exist in the soul of something alive (*empsuchon*), and that this is impossible without change. The conclusion is that, for there to be understanding in the world, change and motion (*kinēsis*) must be admitted among *ta onta*, the things-that-there-are (249b).

The full import of this conclusion is not entirely clear, and the text that follows offers no clarification. The weaker conclusion seems unproblematic. Reality must include a knower, that is to say, a subject possessing *nous*. And since knowledge and understanding can be found only in a psyche, that subject must be alive (*empsychon*). The knowing subject may be a human being, or perhaps a god, or even the World Soul of the *Timaeus*. (Could it be the Demiurge himself?) But the text seems to imply something stronger. Plato's wording here suggests that, if the living, knowing subject must be present to what is "completely real," then it must have its place *among the*

Forms. But the Forms are by definition unchanging. How are these claims to be reconciled?

We can understand the temptation here of a solution like that of Plotinus: to recognize a divine *nous* that will take the Forms as its object of cognition, and thus to define a unified level of reality for the Forms and their supreme knower – but a noetic level of *unchanging* reality, above the changing level of psyche and vital motion. If we prefer to stop short of this Neoplatonic interpretation, involving a radical division between psyche and *nous*, we might at least admit that Plato seems to have left open here the possibility of a cosmic Mind, perhaps the equivalent of the Demiurge in the *Timaeus*, to guarantee an eternal Knower corresponding to the eternal knowability of the Forms. But there are also problems with this interpretation. Such a divine *nous* would seem to require the immobility and freedom from change that is definitive of the Forms. But then we would again lose the essential link between *nous* and psyche (as principle of motion and life) that is repeatedly affirmed in the dialogues.

We are left with this dilemma unresolved. The Stranger's critique of the Friends of Forms concludes with a dramatic appeal not to leave the Forms standing there like statues, bereft of knowledge and understanding. That appeal is presented to us as a challenge, with no clear response in the dialogue.

The passage ends, however, with a positive conclusion: we cannot allow that everything is in motion, nor that everything is standing still, but like children asking for "both," we must say that "being and the all are both, what is unmoved and what is in motion" (249d). The final conclusion, then, is that the notion of Being (*to on*) is now officially extended to include the realm of change.[7]

3.7   Final *aporias* about Being: (i) two modes of predication (249e–250e)

The constructive analysis of the five greatest kinds is preceded by two final *aporias*. The first concerns the connections between Being, Motion, and Rest. The second presents the denial of predication by the Late-learners. Both *aporias* serve directly to prepare for the new account of dialectic in terms of the weaving-together of forms. Looking ahead, we can see that this

---

[7] There are occasional anticipations of a wider use of "being" in earlier dialogues, for example in *Phaedo* 79a6: "Let us assume two kinds of beings (*onta*), one visible, another invisible." In general, however, Plato had previously refrained from using the term "being" to describe things that change.

new conception of a network of forms will provide the framework for an analysis of the five "greatest kinds," an analysis that will culminate in the definition of Not-Being as a member of this network and a form in its own right.

In the first *aporia* the Eleatic Stranger, having identified Being as a third form distinct from Motion and Rest (since it is predicated of both), declares that Being is neither in motion nor at rest "in virtue of its own nature" (*kata tēn hautou phusin*, 250c6). With this denial the Stranger introduces the notion of *per se* predication: what is true of a kind (*genos*) in virtue of its own nature or solely because of what it is, in contrast to what it is by connection with another kind.[8] The denial of motion and rest for Being introduces a basic mode of negative predication, equivalent in this case to a denial of identity, that the Stranger needs to salvage as a valid function of *is not*. "Being is not Motion and Rest together, but something different from them … In virtue of its own nature, Being is neither in motion nor at rest" (250c3–6).

Although it happens that the verb *einai* does not actually appear in the Greek of this last sentence, the claim that Being is neither in motion nor at rest "in virtue of its own nature" presents the general form of a negative *per se* predication. It is this form that Plato will employ later in the decisive set of examples for Not-Being, that is to say, for negative assertions of *einai*. In the present context there is no immediate hint of what is at stake. But Plato calls attention here to this special form of negative predication (for a feature that does not belong to a subject "in virtue of its own nature") by making it seem paradoxical. The Stranger asks: If something is not in motion, won't it be at rest? And if it is not at rest, won't it be in motion? After all, we know that Being is connected to both forms. The Stranger has just insisted that Motion and Rest both *are*, that is, are beings. (In terms of our analysis, they are both instantiated as predicates.) Correspondingly, he argued earlier that Being includes them both. So the denial of motion and rest to Being is designed to seem puzzling here, and hence, to alert us to the distinct category of predicates that are (or are not) directly true of their subject by virtue of its nature. We will later recognize these as "beings said in virtue of themselves alone" (*onta auta kath' hauta legomena*) in contrast to "beings always said in reference to something else" (*onta pros alla aei legomena*, 255c12).

---

[8] See the discussion of *per se* predication above, pp. 24–27.

3.8 (ii) The last *aporia*: the paradox of the Late-learners (251a–c)

The final *aporia* is concerned not with particular forms or kinds but with the general problem of predication. This is the famous paradox of the "Late-learners." (The term presumably refers to Antisthenes, an older follower of Socrates, and to his followers if any.) Plato introduces the problem by way of the semi-technical term *prosagoreuein* "to address or describe," with which he anticipates Aristotle's concept of predication (*katēgorein*): "How do we address one thing with many names?" As Plato formulates it, the thesis of the Late-learners combines (and confuses) the problem of word-thing predication with the problem of a connection between two distinct predicate terms or forms. The initial examples belong to the former class, attributing names or descriptions to objects:

> We speak of a human being, for example, and we name him many things (*poll' atta eponomazontes*), applying (*epipherontes*) colors to him and figures and magnitudes and vices and virtues . . . We say not only that he is a human being but also that he is good, and an unlimited number of other things . . . We thus take each subject (*hupothemenoi*) as one, and also call it many things and by many names (251a–b).

Plato is taking for granted here the archaic concept of naming but reshaping it with an eye to his new subject-attribute analysis of predication. The subject is taken as a thing – here a human being – and the attributes are conceived as so many properties, expressed by so many "names," i.e. so many linguistic expressions.[9]

Predication is thus understood as a thing-thing relation, between a person and his or her properties; but it is analyzed in terms of what the person is called, and hence in terms of a thing-word (or thing-name) relation. The term *epipherein* here, for attributing properties to the person, is the same verb that was used earlier for the (invalid) application of the expression "not being" to a being, to something-that-is (237c). In both cases it is an ontological, thing-thing relation that is intended. But of course the attribute in question can be specified only by means of the corresponding word or name (*onoma*).

The paradox of the Late-learners is described as a refusal to admit that one thing can be many, or many things one. Hence, they do not want to say that a human being is good, but only that something good is good, and that the human being is human (251b7–c2). The point here is not some fixation

---

[9] Note the anticipation in ὑποθέμενοι at 251b3 of Aristotle's concept of the ὑποκείμενον, an extralinguistic subject of predication.

on the *is* of identity, as if this were a thesis about the meaning of the word "is." Instead, what is at issue is the conception of predication as a form of correct naming. Hence, the Late-learners insist that for any one thing there can be only one true name, and that will be the name which expresses the thing's nature or essential property.[10]

On the view in question, if many different names are assigned to the same thing, all but one of them will be false. There are, so to speak, no accidental properties. The thesis is logical and ontological, not primarily linguistic; but it has the effect of making language impossible. And Plato's fundamental response – the weaving-together of forms – implies a corresponding link between grammar and metaphysics. Plato's aim is to show that the combination of words in a statement (or of thoughts in a judgment) implies a corresponding connection between forms, that is, between beings. That is why the Late-learners are included among this survey of "those who have ever said anything whatsoever about being" (*peri ousias*, 251d1). Since these thinkers (as Plato construes them) deny that one thing can be many, they offer the most radical possible challenge to his new view of forms as a network of connections.

3.9   Refutation of the Late-learners: some Forms combine (251d–252c)

The transition to Plato's positive account of Being and Not-Being begins with the rejection of the Late-learners' view that no forms combine. This view is refuted by two distinct arguments. The first argument shows that a connection between forms, and in particular a connection with Being, is required for any positive claim. The second argument shows that the Late-learners' thesis is self-contradictory.

The first refutation refers back to the cosmological views discussed earlier, all of which make assertions about things moving or being at rest. The argument begins by claiming that if Motion and Rest had no share in Being, they would not *be* at all (252a2), that is, they could not be subject or attribute of anything. This connection to Being can be understood in three ways, and I suggest that all three interpretations are intended. First of all, unless Motion and Rest exist as subjects, nothing can be true of them.

---

[10] This again is a view associated with Antisthenes: everything has its own proper *logos*. Like the discussion of meaning in the *Cratylus*, Antisthenes' thesis makes no distinction in principle between a name and a description: names are understood as condensed descriptions, and so they will be either true or false.

Secondly, unless they can be instantiated as attributes, nothing can move or be at rest. Finally, there is the general connection to reality implied in any truth claim. That claim is represented here by two "veridical" uses of *einai*, reinforcing the basic assertion about motion or rest. All of these theorists make use of a connection with Being, "some saying that things really move (*ontōs kineisthai*), others saying that they are really standing still (*ontōs estēkot' einai*)" (252a9–10). Thus, all three semantic values of *einai* – existence for the subject, instantiation for the predicate, and truth claim for the connection between them – are implied in the claim that Motion and Rest must both *be*. These consequences are then applied to the theories surveyed in the preceding sections. Neither the doctrines of the cosmologists nor those of the materialists and Platonists can be maintained without assuming the reality of Motion or Rest or both, and hence without a connection of at least one of these forms with Being.

The second refutation makes explicit reference to the language in which the doctrine of the Late-learners can be expressed. Their thesis is reported in Plato's semi-technical term for predication: "they do not allow us to address or describe (*prosagoreuein*) anything by means of a share (*koinōnia*) in a different attribute (*pathēma*)" (252b9). The refutation points out that this restriction on descriptive language makes it impossible for them to formulate their own view without self-contradiction. They will not be able to state their thesis without making use of terms like "being," "separate," and "from the others," all of which apply to more than one subject. It is not simply that their vocabulary will be hopelessly impoverished by their restrictive thesis. Their refusal to allow connection or blending (*summeixis*) will make it impossible for them to formulate any assertions that go beyond a stuttering reiteration of the subject term. Hence, they cannot assert their own thesis. This final argument shows that the Late-learners' view has this feature in common both with the unqualified notion of Not-Being and also with the doctrine of universal flux; like them, this theory too cannot be stated without self-contradiction.

3.10   Not all Forms combine: Motion and Rest do not (252d)

Therefore, we conclude, some forms can be combined. Will this be true of all forms? Here Theaetetus knows the answer. Motion and Rest will not fit together because, if they did, "motion itself would absolutely stand still and rest would be in motion." But that is impossible "by the greatest of necessities" (252d9), in other words, by the law of non-contradiction, construed here as non-contrariety. Plato elsewhere expresses this principle in terms of the impossibility of opposites to be true together. (See *Rep.* IV,

436, where it is precisely motion and rest that are named as the opposites in question.) So the impossibility here of a connection between Motion and Rest represents the principle that as contrary attributes they exclude one another: they cannot apply to the same subject in the same respect. The immediacy of Theaetetus' response makes clear that the kinds are understood here as predicate concepts or attributes, not as abstract objects. For if they were conceived as isolated objects of knowledge (like the monads of the *Philebus*), it would not be absurd to claim that the Form of Motion was standing still. Stability was in fact required for the objects of knowledge in an earlier passage of this very dialogue (249b–d).[11] So it is not as isolated concepts or objects of knowledge that Motion and Rest exclude one another, but as positions in a logical network, potential predicates for the same subject.

3.11   Network of Forms (252e–254b)

The constructive section of the dialogue opens now with a sketch of the revised theory of forms or essences as a network of concepts, introduced as object for the new conception of dialectic. This is dialectic conceived in terms of Division and Collection, the conception first presented in the *Phaedrus* and illustrated at length in earlier sections of the *Sophist* (to be discussed in the next chapter). Whereas the classical theory spoke only of the relation between forms and their sensible homonyms, the new dialectic takes as its object a conceptual system within which the forms are defined by their relations to one another.

Plato's new account of dialectic begins with the proof, against the Late-learners, that some forms combine and others do not. But what is meant by a connection between forms or kinds? The conception of *genos* and *eidos* employed here is be understood in terms of both syntax and ontology, just as in the earlier account of predication. Since the agreement and disagreement between kinds is mirrored in the positive and negative combination of the corresponding terms, the words for "connection" or "fitting-together" will apply both to the sentential connection between words and also to the corresponding objective connection between kinds.[12] Sentential

---

[11] I follow Michael Frede in recognizing an oblique reference here to the conception of Motion as a form standing still at 256b7: "If in any way Motion itself were to share in Rest, it would not be strange to describe it as stable (στάσιμον)." See Frede in Kraut (1992) 397–424.

[12] In using the terminology for fitting-together, Plato may sometimes have in mind a third relation: the semantic notion linking words to the corresponding kinds. I have found no unmistakable example of this third notion. But see the discussion of ἐπιφέρειν in the first *aporia* at 237c, above, p. 101.

connections between linguistic signs will be systematically interpreted in terms of the objective connections that would make them true. Thus, the agreement and disagreement between forms will be expressed in the positive and negative combination of the corresponding terms.[13]

The refutation of the Late-learners leaves us with the conclusion that some forms combine, some do not, and that it will be the task of the dialectician to know which is which. In a familiar Platonic simile the forms are compared to the letters, some of which fit together while others do not.[14] The new thought here is that some forms will be like the vowels, which are required for every combination of letters into syllables, as a link (*desmos*) running through all alphabetical connections. In the same way, some vowel forms will function throughout "to hold things together, so that they can be mingled, while others, in divisions, are responsible for dividing forms into whole groups (*di' holōn*)" (253c).

We are not told as much as we would like about the nature of these forms, not even their identity. We are given only a tantalizing sketch of the conceptual landscape, within which the dialectician will be able to discern "one feature (*idea*) extended everywhere through many forms (*eidē*), each one of them lying apart (*chōris*), and many features different from each other, embraced from without by a single one [e.g. by the form of Being?], and again one feature running through many wholes, joined into a unity [by the form of One], and many features wholly divided apart [by the Different?]. And <skill in dialectic> is to know how to distinguish according to kinds (*diakrinein kata genē*), in what way each group can combine and in what way not" (253d, trans. after Brown).

The vowel forms described here as connecting all others must include Being and One. The form One is not mentioned in this context, but it has appeared earlier (with Being and Whole at 244c–245b). Its universal role, parallel to Being in its application to all other forms, was demonstrated at length in Part Two of the *Parmenides*. Same and Different must also count as vowel forms, necessarily connected to every form. It is by way of the Different, as we shall see, that the form of Not-Being serves to separate every form, and every group of forms, from all the others. What we have, then, as object of dialectic, is the sketch of a system of *a priori* conceptual relations,

---

[13] Plato does not always distinguish between the linguistic and ontological levels, but I doubt that any of his constructive arguments depends upon a confusion between the two. A few pages later, the Eleatic Stranger will signal a very sharp recognition (and avoidance) of the possibility of use-mention confusion. See 257c1–3.

[14] The comparison here to the letters echoes the use of the alphabet in *Cratylus* 422a–24d and *Theaetetus* 202e–205b; it is carried further in *Philebus* 18b–d.

presupposed both in the structure of the universe and also in our human understanding of this structure. In short, this is the conceptual system that represents the content of *nous* and *logos*, where this content is taken both subjectively (as the structure of human rationality) and objectively (as the order of the world).

Plato's account of dialectic here is left deliberately incomplete; we are given only the intriguing outline of a fundamentally new system. In the older, more Socratic conception of dialectic, the search for a definition sought to locate an *eidos* within a wider *genos*, from which it will be distinguished by a specific differentia. In the new dialectic, this project of "Socratic" definition is taken over by the principle of *per se* predication. But the new notion of connection between forms will be developed in a much broader range of conceptual relations, as reflected in a wide diversity of *per aliud* predications, both positive and negative. It is this new conceptual landscape that is presented here in a dazzling system of logical relations between concepts, where the account of any given form will specify its relation to other forms.[15]

We may note that Plato has here systematically varied his term for the connection between forms. He begins with the expression "sharing in Being" (*metechein tēs ousias*), which was used repeatedly in the *Parmenides*. But that terminology is also replaced by others (*proskoinōnein, summeixis*, etc.), some of which (like *metechein*) may be logically asymmetric, while others (like *summeignusthai*) are apparently symmetrical. Plato seems to have left the terminology for connections deliberately open. Thus, he is free to insist that Motion and Rest share in Being, whereas Being shares *per se* in neither of them.

3.12   Five great Forms and the definition of Not-Being

It turns out that the notion of Being is so fundamental for Plato, so logically primitive, that it can be explicated only by a set of examples. These will be introduced as the "greatest kinds" (*megista genē*), beginning with Being, Motion, and Rest.

The Stranger's critique of the older Platonic theory in section 6 concluded with the argument that knowledge and understanding (*nous*) require

---

[15] A full account of any given form might in principle specify its relation to all other forms. A radical view of this kind seems to have been developed by Speusippus.

that "being and the universe" include both what is in motion and what is unmoved (249d). That conclusion gives us three of the five great forms as basic objects for knowledge: Being, Motion, and Rest. It is then shown that these three are distinct from one another (250b–c). We later note that Motion and Rest are not only different but that each is the same as itself (254d14). This conclusion adds the forms of Same and Different and so completes our list of the five greatest kinds. Plato has presented a sort of "proof of being" for all five, by displaying them either as subject or predicate or direct object in a true statement about the objects of knowledge. What we have, in effect, is a list of fundamental concepts required for any rational account of the natural world, that is to say, of a world admitting change.

Once again, as throughout the *Sophist*, we recognize Plato's realist commitment to interpreting logico-linguistic connections in ontological terms. For Plato, fundamental truths about rational language must reflect truths about being. The underlying premise for this conclusion is formulated later in the motto that rational discourse (*logos*) is given to us by the weaving-together of forms with one another (259e5). Thus it is the underlying rational structure of the world that makes it possible for us as human beings to have both rational language and rational thought.

It is this fundamental structure of the world that is illustrated now by an elaborate exercise with these five greatest forms: Being, Same, Different, Motion, and Rest, an exercise that will conclude with the definition of Not-Being as a sixth form. For clarity, I divide this argument into five subsections.

3.12.1 Proof that the five kinds are different from one another (254b–255e)

Being had previously been distinguished from Motion and Rest (250a–c). A brief proof of non-identity by substitution establishes that the three forms are different from one another, but that each is the same as itself. As we have seen, this argument introduces the two other basic forms, the Same and the Different. We now prove that these two forms are not identical with any of the three previous kinds.

The argument to show their non-identity with Motion and Rest is straightforward. Since Motion and Rest are opposites to one another, any attribute common to both of them (as Same and Different are) cannot be identical with either one. The test is again substitutability: "Motion is the same (as itself)" is true, but "Motion rests" is false. Similarly, substituting Motion for Same, "Rest is the same (as itself)" is true but "Rest moves" is false (255a). The same test establishes that Same is not identical with Being, since Motion and Rest both *are*, but they are obviously not the same thing (255c1).[16]

The moment of central significance here is the proof that Being and Different are not a single kind. This proof, which might seem superfluous, serves to call attention to a fundamental contrast between the two ways of being that I refer to as *per se* and *per aliud* predication, a distinction between two uses of "is" that was encountered earlier in this dialogue and more frequently in the *Parmenides*: *tōn ontōn ta men auta kath' hauta ta de pros allo aei legesthai* "of beings, some are said by themselves, others are always said in relation to something other" (255c12). (This is the distinction first identified by Michael Frede under the title of "*is*₁" and "*is*₂".)

The relevant point here is that, whereas Being is said in both these ways, the Different is always and only said *per aliud*. Being different is always being different *from something else*: there is no intrinsic, self-referential way of being different. By contrast, Being comes in both modes. Ordinary predications express being *per aliud*, where the subject is characterized by an attribute that introduces a distinct form or nature. In being *per se*, on the other hand, the predicate directly expresses the being of the subject itself, its essence or nature as specified in response to the Socratic *What is F?* question. Thus, self-predication ("The F is F") is the default form of *per se* predication.

Since the Different is always predicated *per aliud*, whereas Being is predicated in both ways, the Different must constitute a form distinct from Being. There might have been simpler ways of establishing this non-identity, for example by substitution. Plato has chosen this occasion to draw attention to the fundamental distinction between two modes of predication, the distinction corresponding to the difference between *being a form* and *having a form as attribute* by way of participation. The distinction has been carefully prepared, both here and in the *Parmenides*.[17] What is added here is a formal characterization of this distinction in terms of the two modes of being. This distinction will now be repeatedly illustrated by resolving the apparent contradiction between the pairs of assertions that follow. This entire analysis aims precisely to resolve the problems of Not-Being by the systematic

---

[16] The conclusion seems obvious, but the argument is problematic, since Being and Motion are after all each the same with itself, only different from one another. (That is the distributive sense given to "being the same" at 256a7: Motion was the same διὰ τὸ μετέχειν πάντ' αὐτοῦ, "because everything shares in it," namely, in the Same.) On the other hand, the argument at 255c1 construes "both being the same thing" as "both being the same with one another."

[17] There was a first hint at 244c1. Then at 245b–c, a clear distinction was drawn between being the same as the One (having One as its nature or φύσις) and having One as an attribute (πάθος). For examples of this distinction in the *Parmenides*, see above, p. 25.

distinction between these two modes of predication. And this analysis can also be seen as Plato's final answer to the challenge posed by the notorious Third Man objection to the theory of Forms.

3.12.2 Examples of "X is not F" interpreted as "X is different from F" (255e–56c)

Given the recognition of these five distinct Forms, the argument now proceeds to develop apparent contradictions for each of the Forms. Taking Motion as his subject, the Stranger shows first that Motion both is and is not the same, and then that it both is and is not different. These apparently contradictory conclusions are explained as follows. Motion is the same because it shares (*metechei*) in the Same in relation to itself. Motion is not the same "because of its communion with the Different, through which it is separated from the Same and is not that but different" (256b, trans. after Brown). The negative member of this pair ("not the same") – which we moderns might construe in terms of non-identity – is thus explained by a positive connection with the Different. The same explanation applies in the second case. Motion is different from other forms, including the Different (as was proved earlier, at 255b); hence it is not (the) Different, since it is different from the Different (256c5). Here, we have two examples of not-being expressed by the negation of *per se* predications, examples that a modern reader might construe as denials of identity between forms ("Motion is not the Same" and "Motion is not the Different"). In both cases, the negation is reinterpreted as a positive assertion of difference. These examples serve to anticipate the general definition of Not-Being in terms of the Different.

A full analysis would specify that Motion is different from *what is the same*, where *is the same* is further specified as *is per se the same*, i.e. is the form of the Same. For Motion is, of course, not different from whatever is *per aliud* the same: every form is *per aliud* the same as itself, by participating in the form of the Same.[18]

3.12.3 "X is not F" for F=Being, and also for X=Being (256c–57a)

So far the apparent contradictions do not include any mention of Not-Being among the opposite predications. The opposites were simply "the

---

[18] My typographical distinction here between "different" with and without a capital "D" corresponds to nothing in the Greek text (and similarly for the distinction between "same" and "Same"). For the sake of clarity, I introduce a capital letter wherever the text seems to refer to the form as an entity, and not only as an attribute or predicate.

same and not the same" and "different and not different." Plato's strategy is first to display and resolve these apparent contradictions without confronting the special problem of negation for Being, and then to show that negation for Being can be resolved in the same way.

The Stranger will now produce apparent contradictions for the predicate *being*. Since Motion is different from Being, it is not Being; whereas it also is (a) being, because it shares in the form of Being. Here, again the apparent contradiction is eliminated by the distinction between two ways of *being F*. "Some beings are said to be by themselves (*auta kath' auta*); some are always said to be by reference to other things (*pros alla*)" (255c12). Motion is being *per aliud*, by sharing in the form of Being. But Motion is not being *per se*, because it is different from the form of Being. There is only one form of Being in play here, and hence only one predicate, but two ways of being that form. Hence, with ironic veridical emphasis, the Stranger concludes: "clearly, Motion is truly (*ontōs*) not Being (*ouk on*), and also being, since it shares in Being" (256d8).

Thus far, the parallel to the earlier cases is clear and the argument straightforward. What follows is a generalization and reversal of the prior claim. The generalization consists in applying this result to all the kinds, not just to the five forms directly in play. The reversal consists in taking both Being and Not-Being as subjects for predication rather than attributes:

> Then, necessarily, it is possible for Not-Being (*to mē on*) to be, in the case of Motion and for all the kinds (*genē*). For all of them the nature (*phusis*) of the different, by rendering each one of them different from Being, makes it not-being. Concerning each of the forms (*eidē*), then, being is many and not-being is unlimited in number. (256d–e, trans. after Brown)

On the one hand, the Stranger has established the reality of Not-Being as an attribute for all of the kinds, representing their difference from the kind Being, corresponding to the modern notion of non-identity between two forms. On the other hand, he has also pointed to a reversal of predication, taking Being and Not-Being not only as attributes for other kinds but also as subjects for "being many" or "being unlimited" *in regard to each of the kinds* (*peri hekaston tōn eidōn*, 256e5). This remark introduces the new and crucial notion of converse predication, expressed as *Kind X is many concerning Y*, or, more simply, *X is concerning Y*, meaning that X is instantiated in the case of Y. This converse form corresponds in truth value to the direct form of predication *Y is X*.

Converse predication will play an important role in what follows, above all in the final formula defining true and false statement (below, section 14).[19] But the immediate conclusion here is formulated in terms of direct predication. Taking "Being itself" as the subject, the Stranger points out that *Being is not* in as many cases as there are other forms, since for all of them *Being is not them.* "It is itself one, while it is not an unlimited number of things" (257a4–6). Corresponding to our notion of non-identity, the negation of *per se* predication relates every form to every other form. Thus, Being is not Rest (although it will share in Rest), because it is different from what is *per se* Rest – from what is the form or nature of Rest. Hence, Not-Being (construed as being different from others) is an attribute of Being itself, just as it is an attribute of all other forms, in their distinction from one another.

3.12.4   First definition of Not-Being (257b–58c)

Coming now to the climax of his analysis, the Stranger will take Not-Being as a subject, and establish the form of Not-Being as a part of the form of Different.

Up to this point the notion of Not-Being has been presented in examples that we can interpret as cases of non-identity between forms (although that is not Plato's interpretation). The statement that Motion is not Rest, interpreted as the claim that Motion is different from (the form of) Rest, is a typical example. But for Plato's project in the *Sophist* we need a more general account of sentence negation, not limited to denials of identity. Specifically, for the explanation to be given of falsehood we will need an interpretation of "Theaetetus flies" that shows how this is a case of "saying of *what-is-not* that it is" (269b9). "Theaetetus flies" will be an example of what-is-not because the attribute of flying does not belong to Theaetetus. But to express that negative claim in terms of the Different will require us to assert that Theaetetus is not simply different from the form of Flying (which would be true but irrelevant) but rather that he is different from *everything that flies.* We need somehow to introduce the universal quantifier into the expression for *what x is different from.* Only then can Plato's account of Not-Being in terms of difference apply to negative predication in general, while including the difference between two forms as a special case.

---

[19] Converse predication may be alluded to in the summary at 259b4–6: "Being is not thousands of things; and all the other forms, taken singly and together, are in many ways and in many ways are not." It plays no role in the argument, however, until we reach the formula for truth and falsity at 263b.

Plato begins to take account of the need for this more general formula of negation in his discussion of the *not-large* and the *not-beautiful* (at 257a6 and d10). The immediate point of these examples is to show that the negation of a term does not mean its opposite. (Hence, Not-Being will not mean the opposite of Being. This is a crucial point. Such an opposite would introduce the incoherent notion of unqualified Not-Being that we have dismissed as unintelligible, in section 4.) But these examples, which now introduce forms other than the initial five kinds, are also designed to show that our account of negation will apply to descriptive terms generally, and not only to cases of difference that can be construed as examples of non-identity. We need, for example, an interpretation of "not large" that applies not only to the Small or to other forms, but to anything that is not large – anything different not only from the form of Largeness but different *from all large things*. Plato's problem here is to introduce the equivalent of a universal quantifier.

It is in response to this problem that Michael Frede proposed that we understand "different from large" in this context as "different from what is large," so that not only the Large itself but all large things will be included in *what is large*. They will be distinguished precisely as "what is *per se* large" for the Form, and as "what is *per aliud* large" for everything else. In the case of Largeness itself, of course, being large will be a case of self-predication. As we have noted, self-predication is the default form of *per se* predication.

Following Frede, then, the universal quantifier will be introduced by the formula "what is large," understood as "whatever is large." Besides its generality, Frede's formula "what is large" has the advantage of suggesting that every form must be construed both (1) as a way of *being* (as expressed in "what is"), and also (2) as being something definite, in this case *large*. This double construal does justice to the fact that for Plato, as for Aristotle, to be is to be something or other – to be something definite.

Plato's definition of Not-Being in terms of the different is prepared by the observation that "the nature of the Different is broken up into parts, like knowledge" (257c7). Just as knowledge is a unity divided into a plurality whose parts are named after their object (e.g. "biology" as study of life, "sociology" as study of society), so the Different is a unity divided into parts that are identified by what they are different *from*. The not-beautiful is the part of the Different that is set over against the nature of the Beautiful: whatever is not beautiful (and also not the Beautiful). And similarly for the not-large and the not-just. And since the nature of the Different has itself been recognized as a being, something-that-is, its parts (such as the Not-Beautiful and the Not-Large) are no less beings (*onta*) in turn (258a7–9). This brings us to the general definition of Not-Being as a specific part of the Different, the part identified by reference to Being itself:If the nature of a part of the Different is set over against the nature of Being, the contraposition (*antithesis*) of these to one another is, if one is allowed to say so, no less a being than Being itself. This contraposition signifies not an opposite to Being but only something different from it. (258a11–b3)

    I resist the temptation to insert *moriou (tou ontos)* in 258b1 for "part of Being," as some translators have done, and thus to read the initial clause as "if a part of the Different is set over against *a part of* Being" rather than "over against Being itself." No such alteration of the text is needed. At this point in the exposition, it is not a part of Being but the whole form that is in play. We identify the parts of the Different by specifying a particular form that each part is different *from*. Hence, in defining Not-Being as a part of the Different, we specify the relevant part by relating it to a particular form, namely, to Being (just as the Not-Large is related to the Large, or the Not-Beautiful to the Beautiful).

    The temptation to avoid this straightforward translation is understandable, however. If we follow Frede's reading for the universal quantifier, there would seem to be a problem here. If the Not-Large is understood as the kind or *genos* of things different from *whatever is large*, then Not-Being should be the *genos* of things different from *whatever is or has being*. But can there be such a *genos*? Doesn't this drag us back to the *mēdamōs on*, the impossible sort of thing that has no being at all?

    The solution seems again to be provided here by the distinction between two modes of "is," inserted in the formula "different from what *is* being." For this will give us two readings of the definition just sketched and two different versions of Not-Being. Being different from what is *per se* being would mean being different from the form Being. This part of the Different will define a *genos* that includes all forms other than Being itself. Being different from what is *per aliud* being, on the other hand, will mean being different from whatever-is-F, where F designates a particular part of Being, that is, a particular form other than Being itself. Hence being different from what is *per aliud* being will designate a *genos* that includes everything that is not F, for a particular value of F, where F is any form other than Being itself. Thus the parts of Not-Being *per aliud* would be just the particular negative forms, such as the Not-Beautiful (including whatever is not beautiful), the Not-Large, and so forth.

    The import of this first definition has to be unravelled in what follows. But the close connection with Plato's distinction between *per se* and *per aliud* predication is indicated by the prominence of self-predications in the Stranger's very next remark:

> Should we now confidently pronounce that Not-Being firmly *is*, with its own nature, just as the large was large and the beautiful was beautiful, and the not-large was not large and the not-beautiful not beautiful, so also Not-Being, in just the same way, was and is not being, to be counted as one form among the many that there are?" (258b9–c3, trans. Brown).

3.12.5   *Second definition and summary of results (258c–59e)*

In drawing conclusions now from the definition of Not-Being, the Stranger shows that we have in effect provided an ontological basis for negative predication, at least in cases where the subject of negative predication is a form.[20]

To mark with a kind of ring composition that the preceding analysis constitutes the final rejection of Parmenides' attack on Not-Being, this section begins with a repetition of the two verses of Parmenides that were cited to introduce the discussion of Not-Being at 237a, 20 Stephanus pages earlier. Against Parmenides we have not only shown that "not beings are" (*mē onta einai*); we have established Not-Being as a genuine form:

> We have demonstrated the nature of the Different, showing that it is, and that it is parceled out over all the beings, set against one other; and the part of it set against each being – that very thing is what we've dared to say really *is* not-being (*estin ontōs to mē on*). (258d7–e3, trans. after Brown)

This second definition of Not-Being differs from the first in distinguishing the parts of Not-Being from one another. In the preceding definition Not-Being was defined as a whole, as a single form; namely, as difference from the form of Being. There was no need in that first definition to mention other parts of the Different. The point of that definition was quite limited: to separate the notion of Not-Being from the confused notion of an *opposite* to Being; from the notion of *what is not in any way* or what is nothing at all. By identifying Not-Being as difference, the first definition establishes Not-Being as one of the five "greatest forms," and thus as an entity (*ousia*) no less real than Being itself.

---

[20] We note again that no account has been given of the "is and is not" formula that served in *Republic* V to define a lower level of reality for things that change. Predication is analyzed in the *Sophist* only as a relation between forms. On the other hand, in the definition of true and false statement that follows in section 15, predication will be illustrated for individual subjects such as Theaetetus. Since the theory is not fully stated, we cannot say with confidence how predication should be analyzed for such individual subjects.

It was left for the second definition to distinguish the *parts* of the Different from one another. What identifies each part (and hence the corresponding part of Not-Being) is the specific part of Being that each one is different *from*. The Different, we recall, is always *per aliud* (255c–e). Accordingly, Not-Being too must always be relative to another form.[21]

This conceptual dependence on a positive form was emphasized in the intervening paragraph, where the Stranger mentioned the Large next to the Not-Large, and the Beautiful next to the Not-Beautiful (258c). Hence, in the second statement of the definition at 258d–e, the Different is now "parceled out to all the beings, set over against one another," so that "the part of it set against each being" – against each form – is the corresponding Not-Being. For any F, the corresponding part of Not-Being is not being F. The not-large and the not-beautiful have been mentioned as specimen parts of Not-Being, just as the corresponding positive forms will be parts of Being. (The negative forms in turn can also be counted as (second-order) parts of Being, since they are parts of the Different, and Difference itself is a being. There can be no form that is not a being.)

In a second example of ring-composition, the Stranger closes the discussion of Not-Being with a reassertion of the case against the Late-learners. Their attempt to separate everything from everything constitutes a mortal threat to philosophy, since it would mean the disappearance of all rational discourse. "For *logos* has been given to us by the weaving-together of the forms with one another" (259e). This is the summary conclusion to Plato's account of Being and Not-Being. The ontological basis for *logos* – for rational discourse – has been revealed as a network of positive and negative relations between forms, illustrated in these connections between the five greatest forms. It is one of these forms, namely, the Different, that provides the basis for a coherent account of Not-Being, covering both non-identity and negative predication, although (from what we have seen so far) only in relations between forms.

3.13   Analysis of *logos* as propositional structure (260a–262e)

This elucidation of Not-Being has cleared the way for the treatment of falsehood that was required for the definition of the *Sophist*. It will now be possible to give an account of false statement (*logos*) and false judgment or

---

[21] As being is always being X, so not being is always not being X. What distinguishes the case of the Different is that the same form cannot be both subject and attribute: for Not-Being there is no *per se* predication.

belief (*doxa*). The Eleatic Stranger will first analyze the notion of *logos* and then show how it can combine with Not-Being to produce false statement. The final move from false statement to false belief will follow easily, from the analysis of *doxa* given in the *Theaetetus*, where thought was defined as the silent dialogue of the soul with itself (189e). A judgment is a silent assertion or statement to oneself (*Soph.* 264a). Since the logical structure of judgment is therefore that of statement, the problem of false *doxa* will be automatically resolved by Plato's solution to the problem of false statement.

We begin then with a general account of *logos*. The existence of *logos* as one form among the things-that-there-are (*ta onta*) may be taken as given. Its possibility has been established by the "weaving-together of forms with one another"; its actuality is confirmed by the fact that we can and do carry on this discussion (260a9). What is called for now is an understanding of what *logos* is, as a form or kind, and how it can combine with Not-Being.

The Stranger relies here on a familiar conception of falsehood as "saying what-is-not" (*ta mē onta legein*). A formula of this sort lies at the root of all the sophistical puzzles that had made the concept of Not-Being, and hence the concept of falsehood, seem so problematic. The analysis of Not-Being in terms of difference has freed us from these puzzles. What is required now is an account of *logos* that shows how it can blend with the form of Not-Being.

It is at this point that the Stranger offers his analysis of *logos* as propositional structure. In historical terms, this is the central achievement of the dialogue and Plato's major contribution to the philosophy of language. In the *Cratylus* Plato's treatment of linguistic meaning was still dominated by the archaic model of naming, as a one-to-one relationship between words and what they designate or signify. Although there were earlier hints of a richer model, it is only now, in the *Sophist*, that Plato offers a full account of *logos* in which naming is only part of the story.[22]

The missing factor makes its appearance here in a new sense given to the term *rhēma*, which had been previously used to refer to anything said: a saying, phrase, or expression.[23] Here, for the first time Plato assigns to *rhēma* the sense of "verb," in contrast to the sense of "noun" for *onoma*. These new meanings for *onoma* and *rhēma* are now specified by two sets of examples at

---

[22] For anticipations of the subject-predicate distinction in *Euthydemus*, *Cratylus*, and *Theaetetus*, see above, p. 68.

[23] So always in the *Cratylus*, and both earlier (257b7) and later (265c5) in the *Sophist*. The conjunction ὀνόματα καὶ ῥήματα for "words and phrases" was a standard formula, already in *Apology* 17c. The revolutionary nature of Plato's innovation here has been frequently obscured by an erroneous translation of ῥῆμα as "verb" in earlier texts, for example in the *Cratylus*. The distinction between nouns and verbs turns out to be equivalent to the discovery of propositional structure.

262b. Plato's new terminology, taken up by Aristotle in the *De Interpretatione* (and transferred into Latin as *nomen* and *verbum*), will thus became the standard expression for the noun-verb distinction in the Western tradition.[24]

The morphological distinction between nouns and verbs is easy to make in Greek but (as far as we know) no one before Plato had made it. *Sophist* 262a is the first passage in extant Greek literature where *rhēma* appears in the sense of "verb." But Plato's interests are not simply grammatical. He has invented here the noun-verb distinction between word-classes (identified in our text by his examples) in order to display the subject-predicate structure of elementary sentences, such as *Theaetetus sits* and *Theaetetus flies*. It is this insight into propositional structure that provides the key to Plato's account of the distinction between truth and falsehood.[25]

The Eleatic Stranger thus draws what is both a morphological distinction between word-types and a syntactical analysis of sentence structure, but only as a device for identifying the semantic distinction between subject and predicate; that is, between what the sentence is talking *about*, and what it *says* about that subject.

Our modern use of the terms "subject" and "predicate" for parts of the sentence tends to confuse the syntactic distinction with its semantic interpretation. In Plato's text, however, there is no confusion. Syntactically, he recognizes nouns and verbs as parts of the sentence or proposition (*logos*). But the semantic distinction is drawn not between nouns and verbs but between agents (*prattontes*) and actions (*praxeis*). The crucial achievement here is not only to see that a *logos* is a complex, a "weaving-together," but that its complexity functions at two levels, both syntactic and semantic. This duality is clearly recognized: "a *logos* puts together a thing (*pragma*) with an action (*praxis*), by means of a noun and a verb" (262e12). By *logos* here, Plato refers to the grammatical sentence, but he has in view its assertive content, so that "proposition" or "thesis" would be an appropriate translation. Similarly, nouns and verbs are identified here not by their morphological features but by their semantic function: a verb signifies an action or a state of being (*ousia*); a noun designates an agent or subject of being (*on*) (262a–c).

In the *Theaetetus* Socrates had defined a *logos* as "a weaving-together of words" (*onomatōn sumplokē*, 202b5). But the Eleatic Stranger goes a step

---

[24] The new terminology of the *Sophist* is reflected in Plato's *Seventh Letter* 342b6: λόγος δ' αὐτοῦ τὸ δεύτερον, ἐξ ὀνομάτων καὶ ῥημάτων συγκείμενος.

[25] I am repeating here some observations from Kahn (2007) 43 ff.

further. He points out that if these words are all nouns (like "lion," "stag," "horse"), stringing them together will produce no blending and hence no *logos*. The simplest *logos* must combine a noun with a verb, as in Plato's first example: *anthropos manthanei*, "(a) man learns":

> [When someone says this] he indicates something about the things that are or are coming to be, or that have been or will be, and he does not name them only but achieves something (*ti perainei*) by interweaving verbs with nouns. And that is why we described him as not only naming but saying (*legein*), and in fact we bestowed on that combination the name "statement" (*logos*). (262d2–6, trans. after Brown)

Thus, Plato has finally succeeded in liberating the theory of meaning from the model of naming by identifying both the linguistic form and the logical structure of a proposition. And he has achieved this by recognizing the elementary union of a noun and a verb in a sentence, where these are understood as the subject and predicate of a proposition (*logos*). What remains to be seen is how this propositional *sumplokē* is to be related to the ontological "weaving-together of the forms with one another" that was described earlier as making *logos* possible.

It is probably no accident that in Plato's first example, *anthrōpos manthanei* "(a) human being learns," the subject expression can be understood as referring to the form or nature of human being. The weaving-together of the two forms Human Being and Learning is a necessary condition for the truth of any claim that a particular person is learning. It is more difficult to identify such a blending between forms in the next examples, where the subject is Theaetetus.

3.14   Definition of true and false *logos* (262e–263d)

Plato has formulated these preliminary distinctions with an elegant economy of examples. He is even briefer now in deriving the consequences. We need to look closely at the text to see how his definition of truth and falsehood makes use of the preceding account of Not-Being.

The Eleatic Stranger begins his account of true and false statement by recognizing three conditions.

(1) The *logos* must have an extra-linguistic subject: it must be about someone or of something (*tinos*). "If it were not of someone, it would not be a *logos* at all; we have made clear that it is impossible for there to be a *logos* that is not the *logos* of anyone [or anything]" (263c9, referring to 262c5).

(2) It must have a truth quality (*poios*); it must make a truth claim that is either valid or invalid.

(3) To satisfy these two conditions, the *logos* must have a subject-predicate structure: it must combine an agent or thing (*pragma*) with an action (*praxis*) (262e).

On this basis, the Stranger offers two simple sentences, one true (*Theaetetus is sitting*) and one false (*Theaetetus is flying*). In Greek these are both two-word sentences, combining a noun (which in this case is also a name) with a verb. The Stranger's first move is to get Theaetetus to recognize that both statements are "about me" (263a). He thus succeeds in separating the function of identifying the subject from what is said about it. This is the decisive moment of success in Plato's project of distinguishing reference from predication, and thus overcoming the archaic confusion between naming and describing. In these two sample statements, the subject named is the same: Theaetetus. But one assertion is true and the other false.

How is this difference in truth-value to be construed in terms of the preceding account of Not-Being? It is here that Plato finally makes use of the converse form of predication: *being about* a subject. "The true *logos* says about you the things-that-are, that they are (*legei ... ta onta hōs estin peri sou*)" (263b4).[26]

The false statement, on the other hand, "says things different from the things that are (*hetera tōn ontōn*) ... It says of things-that-are-not (*ta mē onta*) that they are (*hōs onta*) ... <It says> things-that-are (i.e. genuine beings) but things different from the things-that-are about you."

In these three paraphrases for the false statement, Plato draws on his preceding account of Not-Being as difference, while at the same time alluding to the Protagorean formula for truth quoted in the *Theaetetus* (152a): to say of what-is that it is, and of what-is-not that it is not.

Thus, we see that, in Plato's analysis here, the notion of Being enters at three levels.

(a) There is in the first place *ta onta*, "the things that are," understood as what is the case concerning Theaetetus (namely, sitting). This use of being represents the true attribute, to be interpreted in terms of sharing in the appropriate form or kind.

---

[26] It is also possible to construe this clause as "says about you the things-that-are as they are (ὡς ἔστιν)." But that construal would be unsatisfactory, given the parallel ὡς ὄντα in the formula for falsehood at 263b9. So also Frede (1992) 418, who adds the parallel at 263d2.

(b) Then there is *ta mē onta* "the things that are not" about Theaetetus (namely, flying), interpreted as *hetera tōn ontōn* "things different from what is the case" concerning Theaetetus. It is at this point that a universal quantifier is required for an adequate account: flying is different from everything that is the case concerning Theaetetus, different from all true predicates. Of course, flying by itself is also a being, a genuine kind – instantiated, for example, by birds. Only it is not a being *about Theaetetus*, not a kind to which Theaetetus belongs, not a form in which he shares.[27]

(c) Finally, there is being as truth claim, the being-so that is asserted in each of the two *sentences*: "that it is the case" (*hōs estin* at b4, *hōs onta* at b9 and d2).

Notice that in addition to this truth claim, we also have Being asserted for both the subject and the predicate, distinguished respectively as what the statement is about (namely, Theaetetus), and what is said about it (namely, sitting and flying). Thus, we can see how Plato's analysis of propositional structure covers the three semantic values for the verb that I have identified as presupposed in the Platonic-Parmenidean concept of Being: existence for the subject, instantiation for the predicate, and truth claim for the complex of the two. (See above, section 2.) The subject is of course Theaetetus, a person in the dialogue, not his name in a sentence. If there is no subject, there is no statement, as the Stranger points out at 263c9. Instantiation of a predicate is represented as "sharing (*metechein*) in a form" and, more explicitly, in reverse predication as "being about Theaetetus." Both predication and truth claim ("that it is") are reflected in Plato's remark that the speaker of a sentence *says* something (*legei*) and does not merely name things (262d5). It is for this reason that the statement as a whole has the quality (*poios tis*) of being true or false (262e8, 263a1–b3).

Plato concludes his analysis of true and false statement with a return to the notion of reverse predication: "For we have said that, concerning each thing (*peri hekaston*), there are many things that are <the case>, many that are not" (263b11).[28]

Reverse predication makes transparent the semantic structure of a *logos*: saying something *about* someone (or about something), where what is said may be either the case (*onta*) or not the case (*ouk onta*).

---

[27] This notion of sharing in a form (μετέχειν) for an individual subject like Theaetetus is not explicated by the theory as presented in the *Sophist*, but obviously required for a general account of predication.

[28] This was said for each form at 256e5, generalized at 259b5.

Plato's account of truth and falsehood is now complete. One issue left unresolved is just what connection is intended between the weaving-together of nouns (subjects) and verbs (predicates) in these two sample sentences and the larger claim that *logos* is given to us by the objective weaving-together of *forms*. We do not immediately recognize a weaving of forms in the truth of *Theaetetus sits*, or a separation of Forms in the falsity of *Theaetetus flies*. On the other hand, although Theaetetus is not a form, he is certainly an instance of the form of Human Being.[29]

The blending of Human Being with the form of Sitting is a necessary condition for the truth of *Theaetetus sits*, as the failure of Human Being to connect with the form of Flying is a sufficient condition for the falsehood of *Theaetetus flies*. Although there is no clear indication of these connections in the text, I offer this as my best guess at what sort of weaving-together of forms Plato must have had in mind as background for these two sample sentences. As it stands, the *Sophist* account is simply incomplete on this point.

3.15   Conclusion (263d–268d)

Since falsehood has now been defined for the case of statement, and thinking was earlier understood as silent speech, it is easy to extend this analysis to false judgment (*doxa*). So the long series of paradoxes about false judgment will now be resolved, and the path is clear for a final definition of the sophist as a source of false judgment and appearance. We thus return to the "divisions according to kinds (*eidē*)" of the earlier sections of the dialogue (264c referring back to 236b–c). The relevant kind (*genos*) for the sophist will be an art of imitation, a subdivision of the art of making or production (*poiētikē*). The concept of the maker is further analyzed by two separate cross-divisions: divine versus human making, and making of things as distinguished from making of their images. The sophist is classified as a human maker of images, an imitator of wisdom, and the producer of deceptive appearance and false belief.

Of special interest in this final definition is the Eleatic Stranger's mention in passing of a divine maker: a Maker whose products include things such as "us and the other animals and the sources out of which they are naturally produced, such as fire and water and their siblings," together with the natural images of these things in dreams, shadows, and reflections (266b–c). Since only the human makers were needed for the definition of

[29] Such a form is explicitly mentioned in *Philebus* 15a and implied here in "man learns" at 262c9.

the sophist, Plato's reference here to a divine Maker suggests that he has other connections in mind. There have been earlier Platonic references to a divine demiurge, notably in *Republic* VI, where such a figure was said to be responsible for the intricate apparatus of vision (507c). The concept of a Maker for the world of nature will become an increasingly important theme in later dialogues, beginning with the *Statesman* (270a, 273b–d) and culminating in the cosmic craftsman of the *Timaeus*. The mention of a divine Maker here, in the concluding pages of the *Sophist*, seems to point to things to come.

CHAPTER 4

The new dialectic: from the Phaedrus *to the* Philebus

4.1 Introduction

The *Sophist* and *Statesman* are presented as a pair of dialogues, reporting two conversations occurring on the same day with scarcely a break between them.[1] (A third conversation, on the Philosopher, is promised but apparently never written.) Both dialogues begin by referring back to the conversation reported in the *Theaetetus*, said to have taken place on the preceding day. Hence these two dialogues are presented as a pair, as a sequel to the *Theaetetus*. On the other hand, there are marked changes of style in both the *Sophist* and *Statesman* which suggest that a considerable lapse of time may have occurred since Plato's writing of the *Theaetetus*.[2] The stylistic shift between the *Theaetetus* and the *Sophist-Statesman* is reinforced by other changes in both literary form and philosophical content. From the literary point of view the *Sophist* and the *Statesman* represent a new project. Instead of separate dialogues, each of which has the autonomy of a single work, Plato now composes a pair of dialogues with the promise of a third, all said to continue a conversation recorded in an earlier work, the *Theaetetus*. We thus have a projected series of four connected dialogues, only three of which were actually written. There is no parallel to this in Plato's earlier writing. (There will be a parallel later in the *Timaeus-Critias*, again a project left incomplete. The *Timaeus* itself begins with a backward reference to the *Republic*.) In the *Sophist-Statesman* this formal contrast with Plato's earlier writing is reinforced by the replacement of Socrates by an anonymous

---

[1] There are three explicit cross-references from the *Statesman* to the *Sophist* (i) *States.* 266d5: ἐν τῇ περὶ τὸν σοφιστὴν ζητήσει; (ii) 284b7–8: καθάπερ ἐν τῷ σοφιστῇ προσηναγκάσαμεν εἶναι τὸ μὴ ὄν; (iii) 286b10 (τὴν μακρολογίαν) τὴν τοῦ σοφιστοῦ πέρι τῆς τοῦ μὴ ὄντος οὐσίας. There may be another implicit reference in the imperfect tense of ἤστην at 282b7, which could refer back to *Soph.* 226c8. I see no reason to doubt that the words ὁ σοφιστής in passages 2 and 3 refer to that dialogue by name.
[2] It is tempting to speculate on an explanation for this apparent time gap between the *Theaetetus* and the *Sophist*. Was Plato away from Athens in Syracuse around 370 BC, trying to influence Dionysius II?

visitor from Elea. (In the *Timaeus-Critias*, of course, Socrates will again be replaced.)

With this new protagonist and this new plan for a continuing series, Plato marks a clear departure from his earlier work. We should take note of a corresponding innovation in philosophical method, in the shift from definition in the Socratic mode (pursued still in the *Theaetetus*) in favor of the dialectic of Division and Collection. This new conception of method, proposed earlier in the *Phaedrus*, will be deployed systematically in these two "dialectical" dialogues; and the same method will be pursued again in the *Philebus*. Before proceeding with these later dialogues, I pause here to survey the treatment of dialectical method throughout Plato's work. We begin by looking back to the presentation of the method in earlier dialogues. We will conclude by looking beyond the *Sophist-Statesman* to the last account of dialectic in the *Philebus*.

4.2   Dialectic before the *Phaedrus*[3]

The term *dialektikē* was apparently invented by Plato. Its original meaning is the art of philosophical conversation (*dialegesthai*) as practiced by Socrates. The term was formed by opposition with *rhētorikē*: dialectic is the art of philosophical conversation, by way of question and answer, in contrast to rhetoric as the art of public speeches. From the *Meno* on, however, dialectic is also characterized by the opposition to *eristic*, the sophistic pursuit of refutation without regard to truth.[4] Even in later dialogues, where dialectic has acquired a special status as the official method for philosophy, the technique of question and answer preserves the original format. The first full discussion of the topic is in the *Republic*, where dialectic is presented as the coping-stone of the sciences. There it takes the Forms as its object and rises above mathematics, of which it will critically investigate the foundations (*Rep.* VI, 511b–c).

This close relationship with mathematics and the method of deduction, as developed in *Republic* VI, turns out to be only one moment in Plato's presentation of dialectic. In his classic study Richard Robinson complained "that the term 'dialectic' has a strong tendency in Plato to mean the ideal

---

[3] I here summarize and extend the account given in Kahn (1996) 303–9.

[4] The adjectival form διαλεκτική is relatively rare (see e.g. ἡ διαλεκτικὴ μέθοδος at *Rep.* VII, 533c7; cf. the alternative form διαλέκτῳ (versus ἔρις) at V, 454a8). In earlier contexts the verb διαλέγεσθαι is more common, e.g. in *Gorgias* 448d10. The contrast with eristic probably originated in polemic with Isocrates, who used the term "eristic" against Plato. Plato preserved this contrast as a permanent mark of dialectic; cf. *Phil.* 17a.

method, *whatever that may be.*"[5] But this is an exaggeration. Robinson himself recognized that both the format of question and answer and the concern for unchanging essences ("what a thing is") were constant features of dialectic throughout Plato's work. And we will find other marks of continuity. But Robinson is right to emphasize the diversity in Plato's account. Thus, in dialogues prior to the *Republic* (i.e. in the *Meno* and *Phaedo*), the method of hypothesis is developed as a separate topic, independently of an account of dialectic. It is only in the *Republic* (and by implication in the *Parmenides*) that the notion of dialectic is taken to include the method of hypothesis.[6]

In the *Cratylus*, on the other hand, references to dialectic point in a different direction, since dialectic appears here in the context of a theory of naming. As an expert in asking and answering questions, the *dialektikos* is presented as a user of language who is specially qualified to judge the correctness of names. It is in virtue of his access to "the name by nature" (*Crat.* 389d4, 390e3) or the form of name (*to tou onomatos eidos*, 390a5), that the dialectician can judge how successful the name-giver has been in his work of putting the form of name into the letters and syllables of the language. What is referred to here as the form of name will turn out to be the essence (*ousia*) of the thing named. Thus, in a later passage of the *Cratylus* the art of naming is described as imitating, in letters and syllables, the essence of things, "what each thing is," as distinct from its color or shape (423e–424b2). In a reference to the alphabet that will become paradigmatic for later dialogues, the art of naming is said to proceed by division (*dihairesis*, 424b7), first distinguishing (*dielesthai*) the letters and then the syllables, just as those who study meters in poetry have first distinguished the lengths of letters and then that of syllables. Hence, in order to name things correctly we must first distinguish the vowels, the kinds (*eidē*) of vowels, and the kinds of consonants. Similarly, we will distinguish the things to be named, identifying their elements and kinds. Finally, we can assign names to things according to a principle of similarity (424b–d). A name will be correctly given if it faithfully represents the essence of the thing named.

Such is the account of dialectic in the *Cratylus*. The first mention of this term in the *Republic* takes up this notion of dialectic as a method of

---

[5] Robinson (1953) 70.

[6] There is perhaps a hint of this connection in the *Meno*, where Socrates insists that for a speaker to respond "more dialectically" (διαλεκτικώτερον) is "not only to answer truly but by means of what the interlocutor agrees that he knows" (75d). This remark seems to imply a deductive connection between premises and conclusion that would correspond to the method of hypothesis introduced at *Phaedo* 100b and more fully developed in *Republic* VI.

"dividing things according to kinds" (*kat'eidē diaireisthai*, *Rep.* V, 454a6). There is at first no reference either to the method of hypothesis or to the theory of Forms. (That theory will be introduced later, at the end of Book V; hypothesis enters only in Book VI.) The first *eidē* to be distinguished are the distinct natures of men and women, and then different types of sameness and difference (454c9). The term *eidos* is used here in the idiomatic, non-technical sense of "kind" or "type," as in the phrase *kat' eidē dielesthai*, "dividing by kinds" in the *Cratylus*.[7]

In these passages from the *Cratylus* and *Republic* V we meet a new feature that will characterize dialectic throughout Plato's later work: the notion of dividing things according to kinds. If we add this to the contrast with merely verbal argument or eristic, and to the two constant features recognized by Robinson (question-and-answer and the pursuit of essences), we obtain a rather full description of dialectic, one that will remain independent of the specific link to mathematics and the method of hypothesis that is characteristic of dialectic in the central books of the *Republic*. On the other hand, what is introduced in these central books that is essentially new is Plato's view of dialectic as the highest form of knowledge, taking as its object the highest form of being. In effect, *Republic* VI–VII will redefine dialectic in terms of the theory of Forms.

We may summarize as follows the presentation of dialectic in these earlier dialogues, from the *Gorgias* to the *Republic*. As a method of question and answer, dialectic is distinguished from unscrupulous refutation (i.e. eristic) by its benevolent attitude to the interlocutor and by its constructive concern with truth rather than refutation. In terms of content, the distinctive feature of dialectic is (as Robinson pointed out) the pursuit of definitions and the investigations of essences, or *what a thing is*. It is this concern with essences that connects dialectic with the metaphysics of Forms in the *Republic*. Even in the *Cratylus*, where the topic is not definition but the meaning of names, the object of dialectic will turn out to be essences. So in the *Republic*, the dialectician is distinguished from the mathematician by his capacity to investigate *what each thing itself is* (532a7, 533b2; cf. *Euthydemus* 290c). There is a partial parallel in the *Gorgias*. Polus was asked by Socrates to say *what rhetoric is*; but instead he praises its quality, answering *poion* rather than *ti*, because he has studied speech-making rather than *dialegesthai*

---

[7] Also characteristic of this passage in *Republic* V is the opposition between dialectic and eristic, as in the *Meno* text. The eristic critic of Plato's thesis is accused here of misusing the true principle of "different natures, different tasks" by rejecting the equality of women guardians on the basis of a verbal quibble about "different natures," without making the necessary distinction between relevant and irrelevant differences (454d).

(448d9). This passage of the *Gorgias* is probably the earliest occurrence of the term in any dialogue. And here dialectic is already concerned with finding out *what a thing (essentially) is.* What is new and decisive in the central books of the *Republic* is that such essences are now located within the metaphysics of unchanging Being, understood as the highest object of knowledge.[8]

4.3 Dialectic in the *Phaedrus*

We thus find a consistent core in Plato's conception of dialectic from the *Gorgias* and *Meno* to the *Republic* and beyond. The original notion of *dialektikē* as the art of conversation by question and answer is enriched to include the pursuit of essential definition and finally, from the *Republic* on, to constitute the privileged mode of access to unchanging reality. In later dialogues, beginning with the *Phaedrus*, dialectic will reappear as the art of arts, the general method of scientific thought, again understood as knowledge of stable reality. But we must take note here of a possible conflict between this more general description and the earlier more specific conception of dialectic: between dialectic as a formal method of research, identifying unities and pluralities in any subject matter, and, on the other hand, dialectic as directed to a privileged object, the knowledge of eternal reality. We will meet both conceptions in the *Philebus*. In the *Phaedrus*, however, it is the more general conception of rational method that prevails, with little or no reference to the privileged ontology of its object.

Dialectic enters the *Phaedrus* in the context of a discussion of rhetoric. The background here reflects not the *Republic* so much as an earlier passage in the *Gorgias*, where Socrates treated rhetoric with contempt as a crude substitute for philosophy. In the *Phaedrus*, by contrast, rhetoric is presented in favorable terms, as a special application of the method of philosophy to the technique of persuasion. The discussion of dialectic opens with a reminder of the hostile portrayal of Polus in the earlier dialogue. It is because such orators were ignorant of dialectic that they (unlike Socrates) were "unable to define what rhetoric is" (*Phaedrus* 269b6). In this new view, rhetoric is presented as a scientific art, the genuine *technē* of persuasion that traditional rhetoric lacks. By relying on the notion of rhetoric as an "art of discourse" (*hē tōn logōn technē*), Plato can combine in a single concept the new philosophical rhetoric to be outlined here by Socrates together with the professional speech-technique practiced by the orators and described in

---

[8] For dialectic in the *Republic*, see passages beginning at VI, 511B and VII, 532A.

their handbooks. But their version is in no sense a genuine art. It is merely an empirical skill – the artless knack described in the *Gorgias* – or at best a training in the prerequisites of the art (269b8). What Socrates presents as the true art of rhetoric, the art of enchanting the soul by means of discourse (*technē psychagōgia dia logōn*, 261a7), is an application of the general method of rational knowledge. Thus, the best version of rhetoric is simply dialectic, as applied to the task of persuasion.

Rhetoric and persuasion are here understood generously to include all communication by language, whether spoken or written. But what makes this art of discourse into a genuine *technē* is its component of rational science or philosophy, what the *Gorgias* had described as the capacity "to give an account" of its procedures (501a2). A key feature of the new art remains the concern with definition. It is by an initial definition of their topic that Socrates' two speeches in the *Phaedrus* distinguish themselves from the artless discourse of Lysias. Just as Socrates in the *Gorgias* argues against Polus on the basis of a systematic definition of rhetoric, so Socrates in the *Phaedrus* begins both of his speeches by a careful definition of *erōs*, different in each case but equally paradigmatic for the method of division. Thus, Socrates' first speech defined *erōs* as a species of excess (*hubris*), in which rational judgment for good is overcome by the desire for pleasure in a beautiful body (238c). The second speech gave a more favorable account of love as a species of divine madness. In each case the genus (excess, madness) is presented as a unity embracing a plurality of parts or subdivisions. Thus, *hubris*, in the first definition, is *polumeles kai polumeres*, "of many members and many parts" (238a3; the different parts are called *ideai*).

In reflecting later on both speeches, Socrates will combine the two definitions into a single scheme, unified by the general concept of madness or derangement (*mania*), subdivided into two kinds (*eidē*) of disorder, human and divine, with the corresponding evil and beneficial subsections compared to the left and right sections of the body (265a–266a). Thus Socrates' two definitions of love are gathered together in a complex system of examples (*paradeigmata*) illustrating the method of collection and division. Socrates says he is a lover of such divisions and collections, which he needs in order to be competent in speaking and thinking (*legein te kai phronein*, 266b4).

In its new incarnation as Division and Collection, dialectic in the *Phaedrus* is characterized as a general method of inquiry, the art of rational thinking, to be carefully formulated in precise language. This wider conception of dialectic, presented here for the first time, will be dominant throughout Plato's later work.

This new formulation of dialectic in terms of a system of interconnections will have major implications for Plato's metaphysics. The earlier notion of essence, or *what each thing is*, was associated with the concept of naming and naming-after (eponymy): the Form was the *one* after which the *many* were named. Thus, objects recognized as beautiful are so named after the Beautiful itself. In this conception Forms or essences were naturally conceived as individual items or separate "nameables" (in Ryle's phrase). The connection of dialectic with mathematics did not by itself alter this conception, since definition in mathematics can also be thought of as applying to individual terms. By contrast, the conception of dialectic in the *Phaedrus* introduces a fundamentally new framework for interpreting essences. An essence as target of definition will now appear not as a separate item but as a point of intersection between a plurality of concepts or Forms. The system of Forms will unfold into a network of conceptual relations disclosed by the logic of division and collection.[9]

The metaphysical implications of this new conception of essence are scarcely mentioned in the *Phaedrus*. In that dialogue the Forms are presented in the mythical context of Socrates' second speech, as individual objects of vision for disembodied souls in their chariot ride beyond the heavens. For an appropriate ontology corresponding to this new conception of dialectic, we must wait for the *Sophist* with its conception of *sumplokē eidōn*, the interweaving of Forms. But there are some hints of this notion in the *Phaedrus*. When Socrates speaks here of "cutting things apart into *eidē* according to the natural joints" (265e1), he seems to have in view something like the genus-species inclusion and exclusion, the overlap and separation between kinds that will be articulated in the *Sophist*. But the status of such "kinds" is left without further explanation.

We can detect some connection between the new dialectic and the old Forms in Socrates' final comment on rhetoric in the *Phaedrus*, before turning to the specific issue of writing. One will never become an expert in the art of discourse (*technikos logōn peri*), he says, without investigating things according to the method described here; and that is an enormous task. A wise man, says Socrates, should undertake this task "not for the sake of speaking and acting with regard to human beings, but in order to be able as far as possible to speak and act in a way pleasing to the gods." Scientific rhetoric thus turns out to be a form of piety. If the road is a long one, that should be no surprise; it is "for the sake of great things" (*megalōn heneka*) that this task is to be pursued (273e–274a). This mysterious comment

---

[9] We have recognized the general sketch of such a network in the *Sophist*; see above, p. 112.

points to a link between the logic of dialectic and the transcendental suggestions of the myth, but without telling us how this link is to be understood.

If the *Phaedrus* is silent on the metaphysical implications of the new dialectic, it is more outspoken on the application to natural philosophy. Whereas Socrates in the *Phaedo* had presented the art of *logoi* as an alternative to the investigation of nature pursued by Anaxagoras, the Socrates of the *Phaedrus* takes a more positive view of the philosophy of his predecessors. It is primarily the study of nature that Socrates has in mind in his warning that "if Phaedrus does not adequately pursue philosophy, he will not be an adequate speaker on any topic" (261a). That is because "all the great arts require idle speculation and the study of natural philosophy" (*adoleschia kai meteōrologia physeōs peri*, 270a1). It was through his contact with Anaxagoras and the doctrine of cosmic Mind that Pericles became a great orator. The method of investigating nature is common to scientific rhetoric and Hippocratic medicine (270b1). Both must be capable of studying natures generally, analyzing the nature of the body (for medicine) and that of the soul (for rhetoric). "But do you suppose that it is possible to understand adequately the nature of the soul without the nature of the whole universe?" (270c1).[10]

Is this nature simple, or complex with several types (*eidē*)? What is the natural capacity (*dunamis*) of each type to act on what, and to be acted on by what? These are the questions to be answered in an account of the essential nature (*hē ousia tēs physeōs*) of anything, and specifically in the account of the nature of soul to be pursued in scientific rhetoric (270d–e). We note here that this conception of nature and essence in terms of the capacity (*dunamis*) to act and be acted upon is a precise anticipation of the definition of Being that will be accepted by the moderate materialists in the *Sophist*; namely, the natural capacity to act on anything or to be acted upon (*Soph.* 247e1).[11] Studying the nature of the soul, which is required for the art of persuasion, is only a special case of studying nature itself. As the general method of rational inquiry, dialectic in the *Phaedrus* thus points to a movement in

---

[10] Despite the hesitation of some editors, in this context (following the emphasis on Anaxagoras and μετεωρολογία) the requirement to study τῆς τοῦ ὅλου φύσεως at 270c2 must refer to the nature of the universe as a whole. The same cosmological concern is expressed in the following sentence as τῆς μεθόδου ταύτης, namely, μετεωρολογία. According to Plato, it is the view of Hippocrates that the doctor cannot understand the body without some knowledge of natural philosophy (270c3). For the Hippocratic expression of a similar view, see *Airs, Waters, Places* 1–2.

[11] See above, p. 105.

the direction of natural philosophy, a movement absent from the *Republic* but increasingly prominent in Plato's later work.

4.4   Dialectic in the *Sophist* and the *Statesman*

The dramatic shift in speaker and methodology between the *Theaetetus* and the *Sophist-Statesman* tends to mask an underlying continuity of theme. In particular, the concept of knowledge, which was the explicit subject of the *Theaetetus*, reappears as starting-point for each of the following dialogues, as the topic subjected to analysis and division. This initial subject is identified as *technē* in the *Sophist* and *epistēmē* in the *Statesman*; but these terms are clearly treated as equivalent in both dialogues. (So also in the *Theaetetus*, e.g. 146d1–2.) What is new and different in these two dialogues is that each one treats the concept of knowledge by focusing on a particular model of expertise: the sophist in the first instance, the statesman in the second (and, by implication, the philosopher in the missing third dialogue).

This change points to a new conception of method. Instead of attempting a single formula of definition in the Socratic manner, as in the *Theaetetus*, these two "dialectical" dialogues approach the concept of knowledge as a complex unity to be analyzed by revealing its structured plurality. In the contrast between these two different accounts of expert cognition (as well as in the diversity of definitions offered for the sophist in the first dialogue) these works suggest that the unity of a general concept like knowledge or sophistry is fully grasped only when one can identify and distinguish the systematic plurality of its constituents.

This interconnection between unity and plurality in the task of conceptual understanding will be most fully articulated in the *Philebus*. In the *Sophist-Statesman* it is often difficult to see the philosophical implications of these intricate systems of dichotomy. We might compare these two displays of definition-by-division to examples in a logic textbook, interpreting them as pedagogical exercises designed to train the mind in reflection and analysis. On the other hand, we also recognize that, in a subject like biology, such tree-like classifications can be of major scientific importance. As a matter of historical fact, we learn from the mockery of such definitions in surviving quotations from contemporary comedy that classifications of this kind were actually carried out in Plato's Academy. And in Aristotle's own work in zoology we can recognize a critical reflection on systems of division that are not unlike those illustrated here in the definition of the angler.

4.4.1   Divisions in the Sophist

The *Sophist* presents the most systematic exhibit of the new methodology. Beginning with the modest example (*paradeigma*) of a definition for the fisherman or angler, Plato proceeds to display his technical versatility in seven successive definitions of the sophist. The formal cunning of this procedure may not be immediately obvious. We need to take notice that the preliminary account of the angler provides the outline for six of the following seven definitions. Each of the first five definitions of the sophist takes its point of departure from a previously recognized but typically discarded alternative formulation, which in turn reflects the initial dichotomies presented in the definition of the angler. Thus, the first definition of the sophist, as hunter of rich and distinguished young men, starts from the notion of "hunter on land" at 221e, which refers back to 220a8, where the angler was separated off as hunter on water. The second, third, and fourth definitions of the sophist as a commercial salesman all reflect the earlier alternative "acquisition by exchange" that was previously rejected for the angler (*allaktikon* at 223c7, referring back to *metablētikon*, which was discarded at 219d5). The fifth definition of the sophist as money-making eristic, which concludes at 226a, begins with the notion of "acquisition by combat or competition" (*agōnistikē* at 225a2), applied earlier to the angler (at 219e1). Thus, the first five definitions of the sophist are all prepared by forms of acquisition identified within the initial dichotomous scheme or tree diagram provided for the sample definition of the angler.[12]

Things are significantly different for the sixth definition, "the sophist noble in kind (*genos*)." This type has always been recognized as problematic, since it looks like a description of Socrates himself as presented in the aporetic dialogues. The Stranger is understandably reluctant to count this practitioner of Socratic *elenchos* among the sophists (at 231a). This discrepancy is reflected formally in the fact that the initial *genos* for this set of divisions does not fall within the tree diagram provided for the preceding definitions. For the sophist of noble lineage a new collection is required, to identify a new unity as starting-point for the relevant dichotomies. Hence, we need the collection of "household names" for filtering, straining, winnowing, and the like at 226b, which furnishes the general concept of separation and purification (*katharsis*) that serves as basis for the sixth definition. Although our Eleatic Stranger has somehow construed

---

[12]   There seems to be some confusion in Plato's numbering. The fifth definition in the summary at 231d11 is apparently counted as fourth at 225e4.

Socrates as a kind of sophist, we see nevertheless that, under the title of "purifiers," this sixth classification has drawn a careful distinction between this type and the previous tribe of commercial hunters and salesmen.

The methodology of division becomes even more complex in the seventh, final definition, which seeks to identify a fundamental unity underlying the multiplicity of definitions so far proposed. This search for a unifying definition serves in fact to shift the focus of discussion from the logic of definition to substantive issues of truth and knowledge. It achieves this effect by introducing the topics of appearance, falsehood, and not-being that will occupy the rest of the dialogue. It is only now that the reader begins to understand why the *Sophist* is presented as a sequel to the *Theaetetus*.

The seventh, final definition of the sophist that eventually emerges, and will be summarized at the end of the dialogue, is related in a new way to the dichotomies of the first five definitions. As we have seen, the sixth case (the noble sophist) has no place within the original scheme outlined by the sample definition of the angler. But by introducing the notion of "maker of images," this seventh account returns to an even earlier division between two kinds of knowledge: between the productive (*poiētikē*) and the acquisitive (*ktētikē*), recognized in the very first dichotomy proposed in the preliminary definition of the angler (219a–d). The first five definitions all fall under the acquisitive rather than the productive branch of cognition. But by focusing on the notion of image-making, the seventh definition reverts to this alternative concept of *poiēsis* or production that had been discarded in the opening dichotomy of knowledge. Thus, the final definition of the sophist returns us to the original point of departure in the concept of knowledge, the point from which the entire discussion began. And it is precisely this topic of image-making that introduces here the fundamental problems of appearance and not-being that were being discussed in our preceding chapter on the *Sophist*.

4.4.2 Divisions in the Statesman

Continuing now in the *Statesman* with the project of definition, we begin with an initial *dihairesis* that is significantly different from the starting point in the *Sophist*, but still directed to the concept of knowledge. Plato seems to be acknowledging here the complexity of this concept by dividing up the same cognitive territory in two different ways. In each case division is preceded by collection. Starting with the notion of knowledge or skill, a few examples are cited in each case to illustrate the first dichotomy. The *Sophist* began by distinguishing between cognition that does and does not bring into existence what was not there before: the former was productive (*poiētikē)*, the latter acquisitive (*ktētikē)*. Examples of the first were farming, manufacturing and image-making; examples of the second were all forms of mathematics together with skill in money-making, competition for prizes, and hunting (219a–c). (The streak of humor in the methodology of divisions makes its first appearance here, with the selection of activities bundled together in this first dichotomy.)

The initial division emphasized the creation of a product as distinct from mere acquisition. Now, the *Statesman* begins by dividing knowledge differently, but with some of the same examples. Arithmetic and the kindred arts appear again, but this time as "devoid of actions (*praxeis*) and providing only knowledge" (258d5). Carpentry and handicraft, by contrast, "have knowledge naturally embedded in actions and they contribute to the completion of bodies that previously did not exist." This contrast recalls the first dichotomy of the *Sophist*, but the nomenclature points in a new direction. Instead of productive, one group is called "active" (*praktikē*), and instead of acquisitive the others are "cognitive" (*gnōstikē*). It would be tempting but incorrect to identify this new dichotomy with the Aristotelian distinction between practical and theoretical knowledge. For Plato all knowledge is practical, since it has consequences for action. Hence, the skill of the statesman will fall under *gnōstikē*, not under *praktikē*. Political rule is not "active" in the relevant sense, because it does not require the work of the hands or the use of the body. Something more like our theory/practice distinction will appear later, in the next dichotomy of cognitive expertise into judgmental (*kritikē*) and directive (*epitaktikē*) at 259d–260c. Both of these forms of knowledge presuppose theoretical understanding (*gnōsis*). But the cognition called "judgmental" (for example, in mathematics) is that of an observer (*theatēs*), whereas directive knowledge implies the authority to give orders and control action.

Having displayed his formal mastery of the dihairetic technique in the first five definitions of the *Sophist*, Plato in the *Statesman* is content to offer a simpler series of continuous dichotomies, leading from directive knowledge in general to rule over human societies in particular. This analysis concludes with two deliberately obscure statements of the definition of political expertise (*politikē*) as care or nurture of a flock of featherless bipeds (266a–267b). We may wonder why this conclusion is so perversely formulated. Thus, the distinction between two-footed and four-footed animals is expressed in terms of "the diagonal on the diagonal" of a one-foot square (266a–b)!

What follows, however, is a criticism of this definition for philosophical rather than stylistic reasons. First of all, the definition of the statesman as shepherding the human flock is rejected for failing to distinguish human from divine rulers. A second criticism is that the proposed definition gives an inadequate account of rule as nurture (*trophē*) or care for the human community. The Eleatic Stranger then briefly notes the needed corrections: first, to divide human rulers from divine shepherds (276d–5), and then to distinguish kings from tyrants (276e).

The first defect, the failure to distinguish human rulers, is corrected by the fantastic myth that serves to draw the line between two cosmological cycles: the age of Kronos with gods as the shepherds of mankind, and the age of Zeus where human beings rule over civic life in the polis. It turns out that the model of a shepherd for the human flock applies only to the previous cycle, where the rulers are gods, nature is bountiful, and there is no need to organize human life in cities.[13]

The second defect, the failure to specify the manner (*tropos*) of human rule, is corrected not by a myth but by the extended analysis of political rule that occupies the rest of the dialogue. Thus, at 276d–1 the term *trophē* (nourishing) for the shepherd's role is replaced by *epimeleia* (caring) as the term for political rule, and caring is then divided into "voluntary" and "involuntary" in order to distinguish the king from the tyrant (276e). The original *dihairesis* for human (as distinct from divine) rule is apparently not carried beyond this last division, although it remains as point of reference (for example, in the distinction between *aitia* and *sunaitia* at 287b.) The Stranger never returns to the systematic process of division that would be needed to perfect his original definition.

Thus, unlike the *Sophist*, the *Statesman* does not end with a formal conclusion, the completed and corrected version of an earlier definition. The original model of shepherding simply disappears from view, and the Stranger bases his new application of the method on the *paradeigma* of weaving (279a–b). The rest of the dialogue, including the final theory of civic virtue, is built around this model of weaving. Weaving itself is defined by a brief series of dichotomies (279c–280a), and then separated from allied and subordinate practices such as spinning and carding (280b–281b). The discussion of weaving introduces the basic distinction between causes (*aitia*) and co-causes or necessary conditions (*sunaitia*) at 281c–e; and it is this distinction that will separate statesmanship from the other arts needed for the care and functioning of the city. Finally, weaving will serve one last time as model for the statesman's role in blending different temperaments together in the concluding fabric of civic virtue.

---

[13] See the Epilogue below, on the Myth of the *Statesman*.

Before leaving this survey of methodology, we need to take note of the comic elements in Plato's treatment of method in the *Sophist* and *Statesman*. There were some points of satire here from the beginning, in the description of the sophist as hunter of handsome young men and salesman of virtue in the early definitions of the first dialogue. But in the *Statesman* these notes of humor become more outrageous. The Stranger himself refers to jokes and laughter in connection with his definition of the statesman as the shepherd of a flock of wingless bipeds (*States.* 266b10, c10). But the dialogue reaches its comic climax when human beings are grouped with pigs, and the latter are described as "the most noble and also most easy-going of beings" (266c5).

We can only guess at the intention of Plato's humor here. The Stranger justifies these pleasantries by recalling his defense of similar examples in the *Sophist* (266d, referring to *Soph.* 227a–c). If we bear in mind Plato's concern in the *Phaedrus* for the distorting power of the written word, we may wonder whether he is not here satirizing his own pedantry in the mechanical (and occasionally ridiculous) application of the method of division. Although this method may genuinely represent the procedure of rational thought, its literary depiction can easily lend itself to caricature.[14] Plato's decision to abandon the project of a third dialogue on the Philosopher may reflect his own impatience with such labored illustrations of the method of division.

4.4.3   *Ontological basis for dialectic in the* Sophist-Statesman

For a realist like Plato, the method of Division and Collection can be the method of scientific knowledge only if it somehow reflects the structure of reality itself. The clearest statement of this will come in the *Philebus*, where the method of dialectic is said to be grounded in the structure of the cosmos (*Phil.* 16c9-d2). But a similar assumption is reflected in the methodological principles of our two dialogues. That is why care is needed to make divisions that reflect the nature of things rather than the idiosyncrasies of language and habit. Thus the Eleatic Stranger scolds Young Socrates for dividing humans from beasts, instead of selecting a more fundamental genus of living things or animals. This is a warning against what we might call terminological naiveté: the assumption that any group designated by a familiar term corresponds to a natural kind. The divisions of ordinary language do not always cut nature at the joints. The general lesson is that every kind (*eidos*) is

---

[14] Compare the comic fragment on defining a melon in the Academy (Epicrates, 11 Kock).

a part (*meros*), but not every part is a kind (*States.* 263b7). Dividing humans from beasts is like dividing Greeks from barbarians, or separating a myriad (10,000) from all other numbers. In general it will be safer to cut in the middle, for that is where we are more likely to encounter genuine kinds (*ideai* 262b6). But not every unity divides naturally in two. Thus, when the Stranger seeks to enumerate the kinds of expertise that are "co-causes" (*sunaitioi*) of civic rule, he is obliged to identify a larger number, ultimately eight or more classes of necessary conditions for life in the city. "Then let's divide them limb by limb (*kata melē*) like a sacrificial animal, since we can't cut them in two. For we must always cut to the nearest number possible" (287c, trans. after Rowe).

The results of good cutting will be a definition, a statement of *what a thing is*. Both the *Sophist* and *Statesman* set out to answer this question for their respective topic, just as in the *Republic* dialectic aimed (not altogether successfully) to answer the question *what is the Good?* (*Soph.* 217b3, 218c1, 6–7; cf. *Rep.* VII, 532a7, 533b2). The new dialectic, like the old, is a search for essences. And the terminology for these objects is the same as in the classical theory: *eidos, idea, genos*.[15]

But this appearance of continuity may be misleading. After the *Parmenides* attack on the classical theory, it remains an open question how far the kinds and forms of the new dialectic are meant to preserve the metaphysical status of their homonyms in the earlier theory. As we have seen, in the *Theaetetus* Platonic metaphysics was deliberately bracketed – "put on hold." It will only gradually re-emerge in later dialogues, in a modified form. We can see the first signs of this in the *Sophist* and *Statesman*.

The positive ontology of the *Sophist* can be identified in the description given of the objects of dialectic. The dialogue offers three brief, converging accounts. Dialectical expertise is described as "dividing according to kinds (*genē*) and judging neither the same form (*eidos*) as different nor a different form as the same" (*Soph.* 253d1). It is also knowing "which kinds accord with one another and which do not admit one another" (253b11). More generally, dialectic is the mastery of "the weaving-together of forms with one another" (*allēlōn tōn eidōn sumplokē*, 259e5). But, as we have seen, the dialogue tells us little about the status or nature of these forms, except for their identity as modes of stable Being.

---

[15] The terms εἶδος and ἰδέα for the Forms are familiar from the *Phaedo* and *Republic*; the term γένος was added in the *Parmenides*.

We can draw some conclusions from the larger context. The description of dialectic just cited follows the long passage on theories of being discussed in the previous chapter, including the doctrine of the Late-learners who would limit predication to something like a theory of proper names. It is instructive that the doctrine of the Late-learners, which to a modern reader might seem to be a theory of language or linguistic meaning, is included in this survey of "everyone who has had anything whatsoever to say about being" (*peri ousias*, 251d1) – a survey that began with thinkers who tried "to determine the things that are, how many they are and of what sort" (*ta onta, posa te kai poia estin*, 242c4). Thus, what might seem to be a thesis about language is treated by Plato as raising the same kind of question as claims about the nature of things made by Parmenides, Heraclitus, and the cosmologists. In the context of the *Sophist*, problems of *logos* and linguistic meaning, on the one hand, and problems of knowledge and reality, on the other hand, come together in the analysis of true statement and true belief (*doxa*). The preceding chapter has shown that the entire survey of theories of being leads up to the definition of true and false *logos*, presented as a key to clarifying these issues concerning being and not-being.

This larger, ontological context of Plato's argument helps to specify the status here of the terms *genos* and *eidos*. As classificatory concepts or universal terms, *genos* and *eidos* will represent the constituents of true and false statements; but they also stand for the corresponding constituents of the world, as types or kinds of things – as genus and species. In effect, the objective fact of agreement and disagreement between these forms will be reflected in true combinations of the corresponding terms.

Such connections do not fully determine the ontological status of *eidos* and *genos*. On metaphysical issues, the Eleatic Stranger steers a neutral course. Thus, we find no theory of Becoming in the *Sophist*, and no contrast between knowledge and sense perception of the kind presented in the classical theory. More generally, there is no positive account of the world of nature, change, and sensory phenomena, and hence no indication of how the forms of the *Sophist* are related to this world.

Plato will confront these questions only when he is ready to develop his own cosmology, in the *Philebus* and *Timaeus*. The Eleatic Stranger is not a cosmologist. He does, however, take a position on two fundamental issues. On the one hand, he insists that rational understanding requires psyche and life, and that these in turn entail motion and change. If everything were unchanging, there would be no life and no rational understanding (*nous*). Hence, it is incoherent for a rational thinker to deny the reality of change. (Our speaker is no orthodox Eleatic.) On the other hand, knowledge requires a stable, unchanging object, just as in the classical theory (249b12: the speaker is an Eleatic after all). If everything were undergoing change, there would be nothing to know. Hence the famous conclusion: being and the universe (*to pan*, including the world of nature) must include both what changes and what is unchanging (249d).

This does tell us something about *genos* and *eidos* as objects of dialectic. If dialectic is a form of knowledge and understanding, these *genē* and *eidē* must be unchanging. In their stability the kinds of the *Sophist* will resemble the Forms of the classical theory, whose names they bear. Beyond that point, this dialogue does not take us. Since it does not defend a position either on change or on participation, it has nothing to say about the relation between these forms and the phenomenal world. But since one of the Greatest Kinds is *kinēsis*, the very form of motion and change, we are reminded after all of the challenge of the natural world, as a problem that remains to be dealt with.

4.4.4   *Function of dialectic in the* Sophist-Statesman

Dialectic in the *Republic* has a strong protreptic function: its role is to gently draw the eye of the soul from the sensory slough in which it lies buried, upwards to the intellectual realm and to the vision of the Forms (*Rep.* 533d ff.). Now neither the *Sophist* nor the *Statesman* is explicitly committed to the Being-Becoming/noetic-sensory dualism that underlies this account. However, several passages, both here and in the *Phaedrus*, suggest a similar pedagogical role for dialectic. It is in virtue of his command of dialectic that the philosopher is described in the *Sophist* as "always adhering to the form (*idea*) of Being by his reasoning, a form that is difficult to see because of the brilliance of the place." The "form of Being" here suggests, but does not directly entail, the doctrine of noetic Forms. The metaphor of light in this text recalls our situation in the cave: "for most of us cannot bear to keep the eyes of the soul fixed firmly on the divine" (*Soph.* 254a–b, trans. after L. Brown). In the *Phaedrus* there is a similar aura of divinity surrounding the practice of dialectic. Investigating things according to the method of division and collection turns out to be an enormous task. Hence, as we have seen, Socrates insists that we should undertake this task "not for the sake of speaking and acting with regard to human beings, but in order to be able as far as possible to speak and act in a way pleasing to the gods." As we have seen, it is "for the sake of great things (*megalōn heneka*)" that this task is to be pursued (*Phaedrus* 273e–274a). A similar quasi-religious conception of dialectic is developed in the *Statesman*, when the Eleatic Stranger explains the function of definition by dichotomy. He insists that no one with any intelligence would seek a definition of weaving for its own sake, and that even the definition of the Statesman by this method, which occupies the entire dialogue, is not pursued for its own sake but "for the sake of becoming better at dialectic (*dialektikōteros*) on all matters" (285d6).[16]

This is explained as follows:

> Some beings (*onta*) have by nature perceivable similarities that are easy to grasp ... By contrast, the greatest and most valuable beings have no image (*eidōlon*) clearly generated for mankind ... fitted to one of the senses ... Therefore one must practice being able to give and receive an account (*logos*) of each thing. For incorporeal things, which are the greatest and finest (*ta asōmata, kallista onta kai megista*), are clearly indicated only by a rational account (*logos*) and by nothing else. It is for the sake of these (*toutōn heneka*) that all our present discourse is carried out. (*States.* 285e–286a).

In this passage the goal of dialectic is described not in terms of pleasing the gods, as in the *Phaedrus*, but in access to incorporeal entities that have no adequate sensible image. Thus, the point of view expressed in the *Phaedrus* in the language of mythopoetry is reformulated in the *Statesman* in terms of Platonic epistemology. The denial of clear sensible images for incorporeals recalls the passage from *Phaedrus* 250b–d, where Beauty is said to be an exception to this very rule, that Forms do not have clear sensible images. This second parallel establishes a kind of epistemic continuity between the incorporeals of the *Statesman* and the Forms of the classical theory, as reflected in the *Phaedrus* myth. What incorporeals and Forms have in common is that neither of them can be reached by way of sense perception.

This passage from the *Statesman* is the only explicit statement in these two dialogues of a cognitive-ontological dualism like that of the classical theory of Forms – a dualism that will reappear in the *Philebus* and *Timaeus*. Together with the vaguer parallels in the *Sophist*, these texts testify to a certain continuity in metaphysical language. But they leave open the question how much of the classical theory has been retained. No answer to this question can be provided until Plato is ready to give an account of the world of change and sense perception.

4.5 Dialectic in the *Philebus*

To complete this survey of dialectic, we look beyond the *Sophist-Statesman* to the last and fullest treatment of the topic in the *Philebus*. Here, dialectic

---

[16] Compare *Soph.* 227a10: "for the sake of acquiring understanding (νοῦς) our method tries to discern the points of affinity and difference in all the arts" (trans. after L. Brown).

appears once again as a method of collection and division, the method introduced in the *Phaedrus* and deployed at length in the *Sophist* and *Statesman*. But unlike the *Phaedrus*, the *Philebus* now presents dialectic in a context heavily charged with metaphysical doctrine. The *Philebus* conceives the objects of dialectic in a framework not unlike that of the *Sophist*: as a network of being, in which a system of forms is woven together in various combinations and oppositions. But the *Philebus* is less concerned with the structure of this system than with its application to sensible examples such as pleasure and speech, and ultimately to cosmology.

The discussion of method in the *Philebus* opens with a verbal echo of the *Phaedrus*: "This is the procedure of which I have always been a lover, although it has often escaped and left me helpless and bereft."[17] This method will now be invoked in response to a series of one-many problems, arising in the dispute between pleasure and knowledge concerning the nature of the good. The question is initially posed in terms of genus-species diversity: how can all pleasures be one, qua pleasure, but also different and opposite, so that some pleasures may be good and others bad? (*Phil.* 12c)

Socrates illustrates this one-many problem by two examples from the *Meno* (*Phil.* 12e, echoing *Meno* 74b–75a): color, where white and black are not only different but opposite, and figure, where straight and curved are also opposites. Thus, color and figure are each a single kind (*genos*), but with parts (*merē*) that are different and opposed. The original point of these examples in the *Meno* was that, although all of these notions are generic, unities such as color and figure are more abstract and "intelligible." Unlike specific colors, the notion of color as such, like the notion of figure, can be indicated "only by a *logos*," since (in contrast to individual colors or figures) "they have no image . . . fitted to the senses" (to quote from *Statesman* 285e). We can draw circles or squares, but we cannot draw *figure* without deciding which kind. (And similarly for colors.) In this passage of the *Meno* Plato has cunningly prepared the way for the distinction between sensible and intelligible items that will later play a central role in the classical theory of Forms.

In the *Philebus* these same examples are cited in connection with a wider question, raised here for pleasure and knowledge: the question of generic

---

[17] *Philebus* 16b6, echoing *Phaedrus* 266b4, where the term "lover" (ἐραστής) reflected the theme of the dialogue. Since Plato is thinking here of dialectic as a method of definition, the mention of cases where it has left Socrates "helpless and bereft" presumably refers to his unsuccessful pursuit of definition in earlier dialogues, such as the *Theaetetus*. The *Phaedrus* is recalled again at *Philebus* 18b7 when Theuth is mentioned as the inventor of writing.

unity for a diversity of kinds. This question is posed as a principle of plurality causing trouble to everyone, namely, that the many are one and the one is many (14c). Described in poetic terms as "the immortal and unaging condition of discourse (*logoi*) itself among us" (15d7), this principle is illustrated by two examples, one of them repeated from the *Parmenides*: a single human being with many limbs, one subject with contrasting properties (*Phil.* 14d–e, echoing *Parm.* 129c). But these two examples are dismissed here as trivial. By contrast, it is a third problem (again from the *Parmenides*) that is now presented as the fundamental paradox concerning unity and plurality. The passage that follows (15a–b) is difficult, and its interpretation is so controversial that my commentary will be deferred to the next chapter. What is clear, however, is that the one-many paradox serves here to introduce the central problem for any theory of Forms: the problem of participation, or how Forms are represented in the sensible world.

In order to proceed in the debate between pleasure and knowledge, Socrates appeals here to his beloved method of dialectic (16b). The familiar procedure of collecting individual examples into conceptual unities, and dividing larger unities into kinds, is described as the general form of rational inquiry: "everything ever discovered in the domain of science (*technē*) has come to light through this road" (15c2). This is the way given to us by the gods, enabling us "to inquire, to learn (or understand, *manthanein*), and to teach" (16e3). This familiar method is now, for the first time, applied to the order of the physical world. In effect, the cosmology of the *Philebus* will be presented here as an outline for this new conception of dialectic. We return to this cosmic application in the next chapter. Here we are concerned with the account of method.

The method of dialectic is said to have been tossed down to our ancestors, together with fire, by a Prometheus figure generally identified with Pythagoras. A reference here to Pythagoras is suggested by the fundamental role assigned to *peras* and *apeiria*, a pair familiar from the system of Philolaus. (Philolaus is the only Pythagorean known to have composed a written cosmology in the period before Plato.)[18] The Pythagorean flavor of this cosmology is confirmed by the interpretation of *peras* in terms of mathematical ratios. On the other hand, we know that Plato likes to exaggerate his debt to his predecessors, both mythical and historical. Despite the Pythagorean color of this cosmology, there is every reason to believe that the theory presented here is Plato's own.

---

[18]   See Huffman (1993).

The god-given method is introduced by a dense passage that I call the Announcement:

> The ancients, our superiors who lived closer to the gods, handed down to us this message, that all of the things that are ever said to be (*ta aei legomena einai*) take their being from one and from many (*ex henos kai pollōn onta*), having limit and unlimitedness inherent in their nature (*peras kai apeirian en autois sumphuton echousin*). Because these things are cosmically structured in this way (*toutōn houtō diakekosmēmenōn*), we should inquire concerning every subject by positing a single concept (*idea*) in each case – for we will find that such a unity is present. (16c9–d2).

Socrates' account is illustrated by three examples, the most fully developed of which is the alphabet. But first comes a summary statement of the method, which tells us to begin by positing a single form or concept (*idea*) as subject of inquiry, to be supported by the implied cosmology: "for we will find that such a unity is present":

> When we have grasped this [unity], we must inquire if there are two <subdivisions>; if not, then three or some other number. <We must do> the same again for each of these ones, until we see that the original one is not only one and many and unlimited in number (*apeira*) but also how many it is (*hoposa*). We do not assign the property of unlimited (*hē tou apeirou idea*) to the plurality until we have discerned the entire number between one and unlimited. Then, finally, we let all the ones go each into the unlimited (*eis to apeiron*) and say goodbye to them. As I have said, this is the way the gods have given us to inquire, to understand [or learn, *manthanein*], and to instruct one another. (16d–e)

A little later, Socrates adds a description of the reverse procedure: "When we are forced first to grasp the unlimited plurality (*to apeiron*), we should not look immediately for the one but discern some number determining each plurality, and conclude by passing from all of them to one" (18a9-b3).

4.5.1 *General description of the method*

This brief and enigmatic text constitutes Plato's fullest account of the method of division. We begin by explicating the central concept of *apeiron*. The underlying metaphor implied by this term is one of unlimited spatial extension. The alpha-privative in the adjective *apeiros* serves to negate the verbal root of *peraō, perainō*, "to move forward," "come to the end."[19] Thus, the basic meaning is "intraversible," not allowing passage to the end. In

---

[19] See my discussion in Kahn (1960) 232–33.

Homer the earth and sea are *apeirōn*, "boundless," not because they lack a *peras* (for the epic also speaks also of "the ends of the earth," *peirata gaiēs*) but boundless in the sense of stretching off endlessly into the distance, no end in sight. This spatial metaphor carries with it a quantitative connotation: the earth is intraversible because it is so large. Thus, in poetry the adjective *apeiros* can mean simply "enormous," unlimited in size or number. It is only when Zeno and the mathematicians introduce the concept of the infinite that the meaning of *apeiron* as "without limit" begins to be taken literally.

This quantitative meaning of *apeiron* remains primary for Plato, but there is a second, epistemic sense of the term. Whatever is unlimited in multitude is also indefinite, indeterminate, hard to grasp. This secondary idea is brought out in the wordplay at 17e3. "In each and every case, an unlimited multitude (*to apeiron plēthos*) makes you unacquainted with understanding (*apeiros tou phronein*)"; that is to say, an unlimited plurality deprives you of knowledge. The ignorance in question operates at two levels. In the beginning we confront the *apeiron* as a confused, unnumbered plurality. Later, after definite units have been recognized, we conclude by letting each unit go into an equally uncounted multitude of instances.

Such is the quantitative-epistemic sense of *apeiron* in our text. This method is described throughout in terms of multitude and number. There is no mention of genus and species, of universals or particulars, and thus no allusion to the technical problems of participation. In the Announcement the object of the method was similarly described in quantitative terms as one and many, limit and unlimitedness (*peras kai apeiria*, 16c10). There is no reference to particulars, except as unnumbered instances of each unit; and also no contrast between what is intelligible and what is sensible. Going *eis to apeiron* means simply going where things are unnumbered, where one loses count.

If now we proceed methodically, we will fill the logical space between an unanalyzed unity and an unlimited plurality with a definite number (*arithmos*) of subdivisions, the units or ones. (These will turn out to be specific forms or kinds.) Only after these intermediate divisions have been marked is it appropriate to describe the total multitude of (sensible) instances or exemplifications as unlimited, by applying the *idea tou apeirou*, the concept of the unlimited many (16d7). At that point each individual unit (or form) may be allowed to dissolve *eis to apeiron*, to melt into the indefinite plurality of instances and exemplifications, beyond the reach of analysis.

4.5.2   *Two examples: the alphabet; musical notes and scales*

More light is thrown on this formal structure by the examples of the alphabet and music. The discussion of the alphabet is the most complete. Since it has been interpreted as Plato's solution to the participation problem as posed in the *Parmenides*, we need to look closely at this text.

The discussion recalls passages in other dialogues where the alphabet figures as a model for scientific knowledge.[20] The special charm of the alphabet is that it constitutes a body of knowledge familiar to every educated Greek, while at the same time presenting the analysis of a structured domain of reality: the sound system of the language divided into its elemental forms, the *stoicheia*. The alphabet is considered here as a nested unity with a well-defined internal structure, involving not only plurality but levels of plurality, with the whole system unified by its serial order and constituting the object of a single art or science (*grammatikē*).

To invent the alphabet means matching a series of written symbols with a series of basic sounds or phonemes, in such a way that all the words of the language can be represented. Hence, when Socrates speaks here of "letters" (*grammata*), we understand him to mean not only the graphic signs but also the corresponding sounds of the language. This ambiguity is harmless, since the double reference to sounds and written symbols is an essential feature of the alphabet. Potentially more confusing is Plato's notion of *grammatikē* as a science, since the term covers both mere literacy (the capacity to read and write) and also a specialized competence in the analysis of language, like phonology. It is only this special knowledge that divides the letters into vowels and consonants, and subdivides the consonants into mutes and semi-vowels or sonants. So it is only from the point of view of a specialty like phonology that *grammatikē* serves to illustrate a nested system of division and collection. In effect, Plato presents the professional knowledge of the *grammatikos* as differing only in degree from that of his pupils learning to read and write. But even as mere literacy, *grammatikē* does imply the mastery of a unified structure, where knowledge of the separate parts – the individual letters – is of no use without a knowledge of the other parts and their mutual combinations.

The invention of the alphabet by Theuth (following the myth introduced earlier by Plato in the *Phaedrus*) is presented in the *Philebus* as a general paradigm for scientific discovery. The mythical inventor begins with an indefinite object, speech, or "sound (*phōnē*) coming through the mouth"

---

[20] See *Cratylus* 422a (and *passim*); *Theaetetus* 20e ff.; *Sophist* 252b; *Statesman* 277e–278e.

(17b3). The term *phōnē* means both speech and voice, and thus covers the two distinct examples of language and music.[21]

This double application is surely intentional. It shows how insecure an initial grasp of unity will be until one proceeds to the analysis into kinds (*kat' eidē dihairesthai*). The genus itself is well defined only by the structure of its logical parts; we do not have a definite *one* until we can identify the many that it contains.

Theuth begins by recognizing speech not as one but as *apeiros*, indefinitely many (18b6). The sounds of a language are "unlimited in multitude (*apeiros plēthei*) for all of us and for each" (*pantōn te kai hekastou*, 17b4). This is the first example of a plurality that counts as an *apeiron*. Both the individual speaker (*hekastos*) and the whole speech community (*pantes*) produce an unlimited number of different sounds. But in the unanalyzed unity of a spoken language – whether for speaker or for community – no line can be drawn between the unlimited diversity of *kinds* of sounds and the unlimited number of particular sounds. Until the relevant kinds have been identified, the inchoate *apeiron* will contain both. (It will also include vocal noises that do not belong to the language at all, such as the imitation of cows or sheep.) In the indiscriminate flow of speech, every new utterance is potentially a new kind. So we must distinguish the content of the *apeiron* before and after the recognition of kinds.

Once the sounds of the alphabet have been enumerated, grouped into definite pluralities, and ordered in a series, there are no more basic units for this science to investigate. As elements, the final result of division, letters are also the *infimae species*, the ultimate kinds. Hence, *after* the recognition of the letters (i.e. phonemes), the remaining *apeiron* will contain instances of these kinds, together with noises that are not classified by the system. But there is no scientific interest in individual utterances, any more than in particular inscriptions. (The unlimited plurality cannot contribute to understanding, 17e.) It is only the limited number of kinds that is an object for scientific knowledge. Particular occurrences of a sound or letter can be dismissed *eis to apeiron*, into the unlimited plurality of coming-to-be and perishing, the unnumbered many that lie beyond the ken of science. Thus before the invention of the alphabet, the initial *apeiron* of vocal sound represents an indefinite domain, the potential genus for a science (or in this case for two sciences, grammar and music). But once the alphabet is defined as the object of *grammatikē*, the unlimited contains only those items that lie

---

[21] Compare *Cratylus* 423b4–d4, where voice (φωνή) applies first to language and then also (καὶ τότε, 423d2) to music.

outside or below the system of division and collection. The units recognized in the system (whether by dialectic or by the alphabet) do not include sensible individuals, things that come to be and perish. The lowest level of unity in the system is a particular letter (or a particular musical note), that is to say, a type not a token. Plato's account of *grammatikē* clearly applies to what linguists call *langue*, not to *parole*. Except as examples of a type, individual utterances do not come under consideration here. (In the cosmology also, the term *apeiron* will not refer to individuals, but to the general multitude as designated by pairs of opposite properties – by qualities such as hot and cold, dry and wet.)[22]

The structure is similar for the more summary account of music that serves here as second illustration of the method of division. Once the analysis into notes and scales is completed, the method of division will not seek to describe particular poems or songs, much less particular performances.[23] But the example of music brings out a feature that is less conspicuous in the case of speech. Music, more than speech, illustrates the role of number and ratio in structuring an indefinite domain. That is true both for the meters and rhythm of the dance and for the scales and modes (*harmoniai*) of vocal and instrumental music (17d). Socrates' brief account of music thus foreshadows the role of number and ratio that will operate in the cosmology as the principle of *peras* (25a7–b2).

If this account of the method of division-collection is correct, there is no sense in which the example of the alphabet can be regarded as an answer to the problem of participation, as has been proposed.[24] For that problem concerns the way that Forms (represented here by the letters of the alphabet and their subdivision into kinds) can remain one and the same while becoming present in the unlimited multitude of things that come to be and perish (*en tois gignomenois and apeirois*, 15b5). In terms of the alphabet

---

[22] It is significant that in this context the term "sensible" is not used to distinguish the things identified as "many and unlimited" (*polla kai apeira*) or as "coming-to-be and passing-away" (*gignomena kai apollumena*). The relevant distinction is ontological rather than epistemic, since the kinds of speech and music are also sensible in principle. In the context of natural philosophy, the intelligible-sensible distinction no longer draws the right line, since Plato is dealing here with forms for natural and artistic kinds. Correspondingly, there will be no reference to *aisthēsis* in the distinction drawn between dialectic and cosmology at *Phil.* 59–61.

[23] But a word of clarification is needed for music and literature. Particular performances are, of course, not covered by the method of division. But particular poems or compositions can be included here if these are understood as collections of phonemes or notes – as types rather than tokens. The contrast is between Shakespeare's *Hamlet*, as a timeless text, and particular printings and presentations; or between Beethoven's Fifth Symphony and its many recordings and performances. The former are, the latter are not, candidates for the method of division.

[24] See Striker (1970) 17–24.

example, the question concerns the relationship between the letter Delta as a type and particular utterances or inscriptions of this letter. But the method described in the *Philebus* and illustrated in the alphabet example has nothing whatsoever to say about sensible particulars – about particular utterances or particular inscriptions. They can be dismissed *eis to apeiron*, because the lowest unit of numerical analysis – the lowest *one* – is the individual letter: the type not the token. And the same is true for notes and scales, meters and rhythms, in the musical examples. The method of division operates only at the level of forms or types; it has nothing to say about the sensible instances of these types, except to admit their existence and dispatch them into the *apeiron*. (In the terminology of linguistics, the dialectical analysis operates only at the level of *langue*, not that of *parole*.)

Hence, the method tossed down by the gods makes no contribution to solving the metaphysical problem of participation, the problem of the relationship between the one unchanging Form and its many perishable homonyms. On the other hand, there is a close and reciprocal connection between this method and the cosmology that follows. Since dialectic is presented here as the general method of rational inquiry (16c2), the study of cosmology will automatically count as an exercise in dialectic. This poses a problem already mentioned, namely: how can dialectic (with its divisions of *genos* and *idea*) be applied to cosmology and the realm of Becoming without ceasing to take unchanging Being as its proper object. This is a problem to which we will return in the next chapter.

CHAPTER 5

The Philebus *and the movement to cosmology*

5.1   Plato's return to the subject matter of the Presocratics

As described in the *Sophist*, dialectic takes as its object a conceptual system of forms or kinds with no immediate application to the world of nature and change. By contrast, the object of dialectic in the *Philebus* is described as a cosmic order in which the principles of Limit and Unlimited are blended to constitute a changing world (16c–17a, 23c–27b). In this new account of dialectic, Plato signals his return to the cosmological questions that concerned the Presocratics – questions that he has surveyed but not answered in the *Theaetetus* and *Sophist*.

This new description of dialectic presents us with a problem: how is it related to the account of dialectic in the *Sophist*? Is the cosmology of the *Philebus* to be understood as a fuller description of the same subject, or is this a more limited application of that scheme to the natural world? Or is this a special case, adapted for the analysis of Becoming? The relation between these two separate accounts of dialectic poses a question to which we must return. But first we deal with the connections between dialectic and cosmology within the *Philebus* itself.

This dialogue marks a decisive step in Plato's move towards natural philosophy – a move that we find adumbrated in the *Phaedrus*, initiated in *Parmenides*, *Theaetetus*, and *Sophist*, and fully developed in the *Timaeus*, with a sort of postscript in *Laws* X.[1] It will be convenient here to treat the *Philebus* before the *Timaeus*. That seems the more likely order of composition; but nothing essential depends on this chronology.

In discussing the *Phaedrus* we noted a sharp contrast with the *Phaedo* in the attitude towards physics. Whereas in the *Phaedo* Socrates describes himself as turning away from the study of nature to pursue his own version

[1] An earlier tendency in this direction can be recognized in the discussion of Heraclitean flux in the *Cratylus*.

157

of philosophy in the investigation of *logoi*, the Socrates of the *Phaedrus* re-establishes the link to Anaxagoras and natural science (identified here as *meteōrologia*) which is now presented as an essential training for philosophical rhetoric.[2] It is not that Plato in the meantime had lost interest in physics and cosmology. But in both the *Phaedo* and *Republic* his cosmological vision is presented above all in the form of myth. At no point did Plato indicate in any detail how the classical theory of Forms was to be applied to the natural world. That theory is regularly illustrated by what we may call the normative trio: the three Forms for the Just, the Beautiful (or Noble, *to kalon*), and the Good. The *Phaedo* also includes mathematical Forms such as the Equal. But it was never made clear how this classical theory was to be extended beyond ethics and mathematics into physics. This uncertainty is dramatized in the embarrassment of Young Socrates in the *Parmenides*, who is at a loss when asked whether his theory applies to natural kinds such as Human Being, Fire, and Water (130c). There Plato himself calls attention to the fact that his theory was not originally designed with such problems in view.

We have seen how, after Parmenides' attack on the classical theory of Forms, the second part of the *Parmenides* does offer a sketch for the outlines of a cosmology.[3] But this suggestion is left implicit in the text. The *Theaetetus* deals at length with problems of change and perception, but without presenting any positive theory. In the *Sophist* a new attitude towards the study of nature can be recognized in the insistence that Being must include what changes as well as what is unchanging. And the *Sophist* deals at length with problems of natural philosophy in its survey of monists, cosmologists, and corporealists. In this context Plato makes clear that he counts not only Anaxagoras but also Heraclitus, Parmenides, and Empedocles among his predecessors. But if we look for Plato's positive theory of the natural world, we cannot find it in the *Theaetetus* or the *Sophist*. We must turn to the *Philebus*, the *Timaeus*, and the tenth book of the *Laws*.[4] It is in these texts that Plato finally undertakes the task of reclaiming the subject matter of the Presocratics and incorporating it into his own philosophical vision.

This more constructive approach to the philosophy of nature is accompanied by a basic change in the conception of mathematics. Whereas in the *Republic* the study of mathematics was designed to turn the soul upwards, to

---

[2] See above, p. 138.   [3] See above, p. 42.
[4] We can find at least one anticipation of this later theory in the *Phaedrus*, in the account of the soul as a principle of motion (ἀρχὴ κινήσεως), a view to be more fully developed in *Laws* X. There are other anticipations in the *Cratylus*, e.g. in the etymology of ψυχή at 399d.

liberate it from the darkness of Becoming and direct it toward the intelligible realm of Forms, in later dialogues the aim of mathematics is rather directed downwards, to identify structure in the realm of nature and change.

This new function for mathematics was first announced in the *Statesman*, where the Eleatic Stranger draws a distinction between two arts of measurement, two forms of *metrikē*, one of which measures quantities and dimensions relative to one another, as in ordinary mathematics. But the second art of measurement evaluates these quantities by reference to "the necessary being of Becoming" (*kata tēn tēs geneseōs anankaian ousian*, 283d–8). This mysterious phrase is explicated by reference to measuring the large and the small relative to "what is moderate" (*to metrion*), or more fully to "what is fitting (*prepon*) and timely (*kairon*) and needed (*deon*), and everything that is transferred from the extremes to the middle" (284e). In this obscure burst of normative terminology we may recognize not only Plato's plan for a mathematical cosmology but also the immediate ancestor for Aristotle's doctrine of virtue as a mean between extremes. However, the Eleatic Stranger is not talking about moral virtue but about excellence in the arts and crafts. In this context the concept of "the moderate" is not explained further, although its importance is emphasized. All the arts and sciences (*technai*) are said to depend upon their ability to measure the greater and the lesser not only relative to one another but also relative to the "coming-into-being of the moderate" (*pros tēn tou metriou genesin*, 284d–6).

This intriguing reference to normative mathematics and its connection with coming-to-be (and hence with the natural world) is left without further explanation in the *Statesman*. For more information on this new conception of mathematics we turn to the *Philebus* and *Timaeus*. In this connection it is noteworthy that measure and harmony both top the list of ingredients of the Good at the end of the *Philebus*. Numerical ratios play a central role in the order of nature according to both dialogues. Thus, the normative mathematics described in the *Statesman* as basis for the arts and crafts will reappear in the *Philebus* as the principle of Limit in cosmology, and in the *Timaeus* as the instrument by which the cosmic artisan gives structure to the world.

5.2   The world as a work of art

The underlying theme of the *Timaeus* is the idea of nature as a work of art; but it is in the *Philebus* that this idea is most explicitly formulated. There are, of course, earlier references to a divine maker or demiurge, in the *Republic* and elsewhere, including passages in the writings of Xenophon.

Such texts suggest that the notion of a cosmic craftsman or creator was already a familiar concept in the late fifth century; and Xenophon ascribes the idea to Socrates himself.[5] However, pre-Platonic documentation for such a view is hard to find. In texts earlier than Plato, Greek notions of creation tend to be biological and sexual rather than technological.

Of course, it is a basic assumption of Greek piety that the gods are responsible for everything important, whether good or bad. Thus, in Hesiod's story of the Myth of Metals, both Zeus and the gods generally are said to "make" (*poiein*) the successive races of mankind (*Works and Days*, vv. 109–58). But when Hesiod comes to describe the origins of the world in his *Theogony*, he speaks of Earth and Heaven as being born (*genesthai*) rather than being made. Gaia and Ouranos arise by spontaneous generation and parthenogenesis, respectively. Once this first cosmic couple is available, it is *erōs* who functions as explanatory principle for almost everything else. Thus, the narrative pattern of the *Theogony* is firmly biological rather than technological.

Under the influence of Hesiod, the Greek tradition remains slow to adopt the scheme of artistic creation that was popular in the Near East – the model presupposed in the Biblical presentation of God as Maker of heaven and earth. This artisan model is represented, for example, in the Babylonian epic of creation, *Enuma Elish*, where the gods build the world like a house, by craft activity modeled on carpentry. There are a few parallel stories of artistic creation in Greece, but not for the world itself. Hephaistus as craftsman god is responsible for shaping Pandora; but her production presupposes the existence of earth and water (*Erga* 61). There are very few early Greece examples of technological cosmogony. (The term "cosmogony" itself points in a different direction.) One example from the sixth century shows how weak this tradition is. In the prose creation story invented by Pherecydes as a rival to Hesiod's account, Zeus produces a great cloth on which Earth and Ocean are embroidered.[6] In his cosmology from the mid-fifth century, Empedocles occasionally depicts the creative work of Aphrodite with images borrowed from the crafts.[7] But the earliest evidence for a systematic attempt to represent the world as the product of divine art seems to be a lost work of Antisthenes from the late fifth century.[8] Whether due to Antisthenes or to someone else, the conception of a cosmic

---

[5] *Rep.* 507c5, 530a; cf. 597d2; Xenophon *Memorabilia* I.iv.7; cf. IV.vii.6. I am less inclined than Sedley (2007) 82 to accept as historical Xenophon's attribution of divine creation to Socrates.

[6] Kirk, Raven, and Schofield (1983) nos. 49 and 53.   [7] Diels-Kranz 31B. 86–87.

[8] See Caizzi-Decleva (1966).

craftsman is certainly familiar to Plato, and at first invoked by him without further explanation.[9] In the *Philebus*, however, Plato presents this conception as an explicit philosophical thesis, in which divine causation is interpreted as making:

> It is necessary that everything that comes-to-be come to be through some cause (*aitia*) ... But the nature of a doer or maker (*to poioun*) differs only in name from a cause, so that the doer/maker and the cause can rightly be said to be one ... And again the thing that is done/made (*to poioumenon*) and what comes to be (*to gignomenon*) differ only in name. (*Phil.* 26e–27a)

The identification of causation with making is justified in this text by a word play on the double meaning of *poiein* ("to do" and "to make"). But this wordplay serves only to articulate the philosophical thesis asserted by Socrates in the *Phaedo* and developed here in the *Philebus*: in order to be rational, a causal account must take the form of an action explanation, an account that shows how the agent aims at a good outcome. This reflects the distinction, drawn in the *Phaedo* and reformulated in the *Timaeus*, between an explanatory cause (*aition*) and a necessary condition (*sunaition*): between a rational explanation of some end to be achieved, and the instrumental account of a needed mechanism.[10]

This identification of causing with making in the *Philebus* offers the explicit justification for what is taken for granted as the starting point of the *Timaeus*, namely, that the principle of causality implies the action of a maker or demiurge as source of cosmic order (*Tim.* 28a). This is no trivial assumption. It is just this reinterpretation of the cosmic *nous* of Anaxagoras in terms of artistic making that makes possible the explanatory scheme of the *Timaeus*, enabling Plato finally to satisfy the demand for a teleological account of nature that remained unsatisfied in the *Phaedo*. We return to this topic in the next chapter.

5.3 Introduction of the world soul

Another innovation developed in the *Philebus* but taken for granted in the *Timaeus* is the conception of a world soul, an *anima mundi*. Now, some conception of the universe as *empsychon* – alive and ensouled – was generally presupposed in Presocratic speculation, as in Hesiod, and expressed, for example, in microcosm-macrocosm analogies. Thus, from Anaximander on, the world is described as being born, like an organism gradually taking

---

[9] See e.g. *Rep.* 507c6 ὁ τῶν αἰσθήσεων δημιουργός.   [10] See *Phaedo* 98c–99c and *Timaeus* 46c–e.

shape. But what is implicit in the Presocratic tradition becomes an explicit doctrine only here in the *Philebus*, where Socrates argues (1) that our psyche must be derived from a world soul, just as the elements of our body are derived from the elements of the cosmos, and (2) that the causal action of *nous* in the cosmos could not take place without a cosmic soul (30a–c).[11] The second argument (which has a partial parallel at *Timaeus* 30b) links the notion of world soul directly to the teleological interpretation of nature, and hence to the cosmic function of *nous*.

The conception that there must be an intelligent principle responsible for the world order is at least as old as Anaxagoras. (An earlier version can probably be found in Xenophanes fr. 25, and perhaps even in Anaximander, if he said that the Boundless "steers all things.") What is new here is the necessary connection between psyche and *nous*. That connection will serve later as the basis for Plato's argument in *Laws* X, which presents psyche as source of motion (*archē kinēseōs*) and hence as the organizing principle of the cosmos.

As later in *Laws* X, the world soul of the *Philebus* (which includes the action of *nous*) can be seen as replacing the functions of the demiurge as the source of cosmic order. On this point the *Timaeus* goes its own way, retaining the notion of a divine Maker as distinct from the world psyche which is its product. We might be tempted to see this distinction between the world soul and its creator as an artifact produced by the literary form of the creation story in the *Timaeus*. But the role of the demiurge cannot be so easily dismissed. There are good philosophical reasons for Plato to draw a sharp distinction between the world soul, as an immanent principle directly engaged in cosmic self-motion, and the demiurge as a transcendent cause free of motion and change. There is no room for such a distinction in the brief cosmological sketch of the *Philebus*, nor in the minimalist cosmology of *Laws* X.[12]

The brevity of this cosmic text in the *Philebus* must be borne in mind in any comparison with the *Timaeus*. We do not have here two alternative theories designed to cover the same ground. Whereas the cosmology of the *Timaeus* fills an entire dialogue (66 Stephanus pages out of 76, omitting only the proem), the cosmological section of the *Philebus* constitutes but a small fraction of the whole work (8 Stephanus pages out of 56). This contrast in scale reflects a fundamental difference in function. Whereas

[11] For the standard view in Plato that νοῦς does not exist without a psyche see the parallels cited below, p. 179 n. 4.
[12] On *Laws* X see below, in the Epilogue.

the cosmological narrative of the *Timaeus* is a self-standing work – Plato's contribution to *peri physeōs historia*, "the investigation of nature" – the corresponding section of the *Philebus* serves only as means towards a larger end. Cosmology is formally subordinate here to its role in a macrocosm-microcosm analogy. The cosmic blending of Limit and Unlimited is designed to provide a large-scale parallel for the mixture of knowledge and pleasure in a good human life.

5.4 Cosmology in the *Philebus*: the Announcement

We turn, then, to the cosmology, introduced by the text cited in our previous chapter as the Announcement. Compressed and enigmatic, this passage poses many problems for the interpreter:

> All of the things that are ever said to be (*ta aei legomena einai*) take their being from one and from many (*ex henos kai pollōn onta*), having Limit and Unlimitedness inherent in their nature (*peras kai apeirian en autois sumphuton echousin*). Because these things are cosmically structured in this way (*toutōn houtō diakekosmēmenōn*), we should inquire concerning every subject by positing a single form or concept (*idea*) in each case; for we will find that such a unity is present.[13]

The first problem raised by this text is: What are the beings that are said to be derived from one and many? On the most natural reading of the text (taking *aei* as modifying *legomena*), these are all the beings that there are or can be, all the things that can ever be truly said *to be*. Hence, the beings in question will include some version of Platonic Forms or monads, although (for reasons that will be seen in a moment) Forms are not the center of attention here.

There is an alternative, more difficult construal of the text that would limit the reference to eternal beings, i.e. Forms (taking *aei* with *onta*): "the things which are said to be forever."[14] On textual grounds alone this reading seems forced, and it has not been generally followed. In addition to linguistic considerations, there is a strong philosophical reason not to

---

[13] 16c9–d2. In the initial reference to τῶν ἀεὶ λεγομένων εἶναι the adverb ἀεί "always" is most naturally taken as a generalizing modifier with λεγόμενα: "what is said in every case," thus echoing the earlier expression τῶν λεγομένων ἀεί, καὶ πάλαι καὶ νῦν "what is ever said, both previously and now" (15d5). The addition here of εἶναι does not change the meaning of λεγόμενα, since what is said is always a case of being. The verb εἶναι is added to echo the preceding clause: ἐξ ἑνὸς μὲν καὶ πολλῶν ὄντων. For a parallel to the phrase "what is ever said to be," see *Cratylus* 423e4 "all things that deserve this title of being" (ὅσα ἠξίωται ταύτης τῆς προσρήσεως, τοῦ εἶναι).

[14] See Striker's (1970) defense of this reading.

restrict the reference of "beings" here to Forms. For this text announces a cosmology based on Limit and Unlimited, to be further described in what follows. (The reference to cosmology is explicit in *houtōs diakekosmēmenōn* at 16d1.) But the study of the cosmos will be carefully distinguished from knowledge concerning beings that are eternally the same and unchanging. Cosmology is about Becoming, that is to say, about "things that come to be and will come to be and have come to be" (59a7). Hence, if the Announcement is about a cosmology, it is not about beings that are "eternally the same and do not admit coming to be and perishing" (15b3). A reference to eternal Forms may be included in the Announcement (since it refers to beings generally), but they are not the focus of attention. The cosmology is about the world of nature and change. Hence, the beings in question in the Announcement may include Forms, but they also include whatever else there is.[15]

The next question is: What are the One and Many from which all beings are derived? This is the most fundamental case of one-many polarity. Now, One and Many in this sense, as basic principles of ontology, are scarcely mentioned again in this dialogue or in any other part of Plato's written work. (The only exception might be an implicit reference in the discussions of the One and the Others in *Parmenides*, Part Two). But a similar pair plays a central role in the so-called Unwritten Doctrines ascribed to Plato by Aristotle and the later tradition; and such a pair appears also in the metaphysics of Speusippus.[16]

According to Aristotle's account of Plato's oral teaching, the One and the Indeterminate Dyad (called "the Many" by Speusippus and by the so-called Pythagoreans) were the most fundamental principles of all, from which even the Forms were derived, by the action of the One in structuring the indeterminate plurality of the Dyad. It is possible, then, that in the phrase "beings from one and many" Socrates is referring to something like this unwritten *Prinzipienlehre*, "the doctrine of principles" much discussed in some modern literature on Plato. Even the Forms, then, would be derived from these two fundamental principles of unity and plurality. On this view, the conjunction of the one and the many will be not only an immortal feature of discourse (*logoi*), but also a fundamental principle in ontology, inherent in the composition of all beings.

[15] Compare the reference at 23c4 to "all the beings now present in the world" (πάντα τὰ νῦν ὄντα ἐν τῷ παντί) as the realm of πέρας and ἄπειρον.
[16] See also ἕν and πλῆθος in the Pythagorean table of opposites cited by Aristotle *Met.* A. 5, 986a24. But this list may not be older than Speusippus and the *Philebus*.

The second clause of the Announcement indicates that this universal one-many structure finds expression in the immanent principles of Limit and Unlimitedness (*peras kai apeiria en autois sumphuton echousin*). Does this claim apply to Forms as well as to other beings? The cosmology will tell us in some detail how Limit and Unlimited belong to the nature of perishable things. But for eternal Forms we are told nothing, and can only speculate. How could Limit and Unlimited belong to Forms? These do not seem to represent intrinsic properties of Forms. (In what sense would the nature of a Form be deprived of limit?) It seems more likely that Limit and Unlimited can belong to Forms only in their relation to perishable homonyms. On the one hand, Limit may belong to perishable things by virtue of their relation to Forms, whereas the Unlimited will belong to Forms as source of structure for the perishable phenomena of nature. This is speculation on my part. But it may explain Plato's cryptic reference to Limit and Unlimited as intrinsic to the nature (*sumphuton*) of whatever is said to be.

5.5   Limit and Unlimited in the structure of the cosmos

Unlike One and Many or Same and Different, which belong to the most universal system of concepts, Limit and Unlimited refer more narrowly to the structure of the natural world. As we have seen, Plato may have borrowed these terms from the system of Philolaus, where they represent principles of Presocratic cosmology interpreted from a Pythagorean perspective. Since Anaximander, the Unlimited (*apeiron*) had been recognized as the universal source of cosmic coming-to-be. The corresponding notion of Limit (*peras*) plays a central role in the poem of Parmenides, where it denotes the symmetrical structure and stability of Being, illustrated by the comparison to a geometric sphere (fr. 8, 42; cf. verses 26, 31, and 49). In historical terms, then, the mixture of Limit and Unlimited points to a blend between Parmenides and Anaximander, and more generally to a union between Being and Becoming. Ultimately, it will be this sort of mixed ontology that Plato has in mind, adding an intermediate blend to the simple dualism of the classical theory of Forms. In the immediate context, however, Limit points to a typically Pythagorean concern with number and ratio. For it is precisely by means of such mathematical concepts that Plato will forge this union between Being and Becoming.

In the original Milesian conception, the *apeiron* seems to have served not only as the boundless material source from which the world comes into being, but also as the active, governing principle of cosmic order.[17] In the cosmology of Anaxagoras, on the other hand, the active and passive principles are sharply distinguished. According to Anaxagoras, the *apeiron* begins as an original mass of "all things together, unlimited (*apeira*) both in multitude and in smallness," a disorderly mixture that must then be separated out and organized by the active power of Mind.[18]

Plato's scheme in the *Philebus* can be seen as a refinement on this Anaxagorean dualism, with the Unlimited retaining its original Milesian role as material world-source, while the dynamic principle is now divided between Limit, as the immanent structure of the world, and the more active causal factor of *nous*, identified here with the world soul. Nothing further is said in the *Philebus* about this second causal principle, beyond its recognition as soul and intelligence, together with its allegorical representation as the highest form of divinity: "in the nature of Zeus there is the soul of a king (*basilikē psuchē*) as well as a king's reason (*basilikos nous*), in virtue of this power displayed by the cause" (30d, trans. D. Frede). The *Philebus* offers no further information about this relation between psyche and *nous*, and no mention of any separate demiurgic principle.

In this context only the notion of the Unlimited is analyzed in any detail (24a–25c). As Socrates himself points out (25d7), no corresponding account is provided for the Limit; it is only described as equality, duality, and "every relation of number to number or measure to measure" (25a7–b1). Its role (as the instrument by which the causal principle imposes order on the Unlimited) is to "put an end to the quarrel between opposites [in the *apeiron*], making them commensurate and harmonious (*summetra kai sumphōna*) by the imposition of number" (25d11–e2).

If we look for a point of comparison in the fuller cosmology of the *Timaeus*, we see that what corresponds to Limit is not the Forms as a model for creation (for in the *Timaeus* these lie outside the realm of Becoming and do not enter into phenomenal blends) but rather the role of normative mathematics, as the instrument by which the demiurge imposes order on the Receptacle. It is this mathematical principle of order that appears as ratios in the construction of the world soul and as triangles in the construction of the world body. In the *Timaeus* it will be these mathematical structures, and not the transcendental Forms, that serve like Limit as a principle of immanent form, organizing the passive matter of the

---

[17] Aristotle *Phys.* 203b4–15: πάντα κυβερνᾶν, as interpreted in Kahn (1960) 238.
[18] Anaxagoras fr. 12: πάντα διεκόσμησε νοῦς.

Receptacle. In both dialogues, then, it is mathematics that provides the tools by which the supreme causal power is able to organize the world.

The raw material to be organized is represented in the *Philebus* by the principle of the Unlimited. In earlier cosmologies this material factor had been conceived in two different ways: first, as a set of opposing powers, such as hot and cold, wet and dry, light and dark; but also as a set of cosmic masses such as fire, earth, and sea. In response to Parmenides' attack on coming-to-be, natural change was regularly explained (by Anaxagoras and Empedocles, and also by the atomists) in terms of the mixing and separation of imperishable elements.[19] These elementary forms were identified in different ways in the competing cosmologies of the fifth century. The most successful solution was the system proposed by Empedocles, in which the two older notions of opposites and cosmic masses were combined in his doctrine of the four elements. It was of course this Empedoclean scheme that is taken over by Plato and given its classical form by Aristotle.

These four elementary forms (earth, water, air, and fire) do not figure prominently in the *Philebus*, since it offers no general physical theory. (The four elements do appear as constituents of the human body, and hence of the cosmos, in the argument for the existence of a world soul at 29a.) Instead, the contents of the *apeiron* are described in terms of the traditional opposites, including at least two pairs familiar from Presocratic cosmology: the hot and the cold at 24b, the dry and the wet at 25c. What is distinctive of the *Philebus* account, however, is that these opposites are presented in comparative form, as hotter and colder, drier and wetter. And these two opposites introduce a more general set of opposing pairs, governed by the comparative pattern of more and less: the intense (*sphodra*) and the mild (*ērema*), the more numerous and fewer (*pleon, elatton*, 24c), the faster and slower, larger and smaller (25c), and even the high and the low in musical sound (26a).

Plato offers no general characterization of the system of opposites constituting the *apeiron*, other than the criterion of *more-and-less*. Some of these opposites do correspond to sensory qualities (hot-cold, dry-wet, high-low in sound); and the criterion of *more-and-less* is suggestive of the Aristotelian

---

[19] It is because of the traditional symmetry between mixing and separation in Presocratic physics that the interlocutor asks Socrates if he does not need a fifth principle for separation (διάκρισις) after a fourth has been introduced as cause of mixing (σύμμειξις at 23d7). (Compare διακρίσεις καὶ συγκρίσεις as a pair in the cosmological summary at *Soph.* 243b5.) But in the *Philebus* the notion of a blend between Limit and Unlimited is quite different from a physical mixture of elementary bodies, and it does not require a reciprocal principle of separation. Hence, there is in fact no fifth principle to be added here to the cosmology.

category of Quality.[20] But some of these pairs are clearly quantitative (larger/smaller, more numerous/fewer); and other examples do not belong to any one category. In fact, the principle of more-and-less defines a fluctuating scale of comparison that excludes any definite quantity. It is by focusing on this denial of precise quantity that Socrates manages to bring these diverse pairs of opposites together into a unified "collection" (*sunagein eis hen*, 25d6):

> Whenever these opposites are present, they do not allow a definite quantity or amount (*poson*) to exist … If they did not exclude definite quantity but allowed it and the moderate (*to metrion*) to come to be in the seat of the more-and-less and stronger-and-milder, these opposites would themselves vanish from the place where they had been present … For the hotter is always moving on and not standing still, and the colder likewise; whereas the definite quantity (*to poson*) comes to a halt and stops the movement forward. And it is on this account (*logos*) that the hotter and its opposite are both unlimited. (24c3–d7)

The contrast here between motion and rest – between moving forward and standing still – serves to unify all these comparative pairs of the Unlimited within a framework of Heraclitean flux. Thus, the notion that the opposites vanish when confronted with definite quantity and measure is expressed in Heraclitean terms as "flowing" (*errei* at 24d2). Taken in isolation, the Unlimited would constitute an unstructured chaos without definite properties, like the elemental flux that Plato has rejected in the *Cratylus* and *Theaetetus*. In these two earlier dialogues Plato had demonstrated that the principle of unrestricted change does not allow for a coherent account of anything. A parallel conclusion was drawn in the *Sophist*: there can be no knowledge or understanding without some element of stability in the object (249b–c). What was missing in these earlier depictions of unlimited flux is precisely what is provided here by the Eleatic-Pythagorean principle of Limit. It is this principle that introduces structure into the flux of opposites by "imposing number," that is, by importing the system of normative mathematics that we encountered in the *Statesman* as *metrikē*, the art of measurement. This mathematical notion of Limit is here specified by the concepts of definite quantity (*poson*) and moderate measure (*to metrion*). Just as the Receptacle in the *Timaeus* will inherit the role of the Unlimited as passive source of motion and qualitative flux, so the triangles and ratios introduced by the Demiurge will represent the role of normative mathematics performed here by Limit in the briefer

---

[20] Compare Arist. *Categories* 10b26.

sketch of the *Philebus*. It seems natural to regard this blend of Limit and Unlimited in the *Philebus* as a preliminary move on Plato's part to tame the image of Heraclitean flux and reshape it as part of his own constructive theory of Becoming.

5.6 Comparison with the *Timaeus*

At a certain level of generality, then, there are clear parallels between the cosmologies of the *Philebus* and *Timaeus*. Both theories take as their explanandum the realm of nature or Becoming, and both offer an explanation in terms of a pair of fundamental principles (Unlimited and Limit in the *Philebus*, Receptacle and Forms for the *Timaeus*), plus the agency of a rational cause. To this extent both schemes provide a precedent for the Aristotelian analysis of nature in terms of material, formal, and efficient causes. But the differences between these two Platonic schemes are as striking as the similarities. In particular, we have noted the basic discrepancy between the immanent principle of Limit in the *Philebus* and the transcendent Forms of the *Timaeus*, which lie outside the created cosmos.

As the simpler version, the *Philebus* is in some respects the more explicit, for example in the introduction of the world soul. In general the *Philebus* is more attentive to the problem of combining Being with Becoming, that is, to the challenge of extending the framework of Platonic ontology to include the principle of regularity in the phenomena of nature and change, an extension that is taken for granted in the *Timaeus*. In discussing the *Statesman* we took note of the paradoxical expression connecting Being with Becoming: *hē tēs geneseōs anankaia ousia*, "the necessary being of coming-to-be" (above, p. 159). Similar formulae recur in the *Philebus*. The joint offspring of Limit and Unlimited is described first as a "becoming into being (*genesis eis ousian*) from the measures (*metra*) produced with the Limit" (26d8), and later as a "mixed and generated being (*mēktē kai gegenēmenē ousia*)" (27b8). The blending of Limit and Unlimited is thus presented in the *Philebus* as a nature (*phusis*) in which Being is mixed with Becoming.[21]

In the outcome of such a mixture we recognize Plato's anticipation of the Aristotelian concept of form as a stable nature within the realm of change. What is distinctively Platonic here is the conception of this nature in strictly mathematical terms. In the *Philebus* this principle of Limit is barely

---

[21] For φύσις in this context see *Phil.* 31d5, 8, 32a2–3, 8, b1; other references to γένεσις/γίγνεσθαι 26e3, 27a9 and *passim*.

sketched, but it represents a stable structure imposed on the flux of opposites by means of numbers and measures. A full statement of this mathematical conception of form is given only in the *Timaeus*.

The cosmology of the *Philebus* is not only briefer, but also more selective. The union of Limit and Unlimited is presented not as a general account of phenomena but as a pattern for successful blends, for positive outcomes like health, virtue, and harmony (25e–26b, 31e). The strongly normative slant given here to the notion of mixture reflects the rhetorical function of this cosmology as a paradigm for the successful blend of knowledge and pleasure in a good life. Hence, what the *Philebus* has to offer is not a general theory of coming-to-be but a partial account of successful mixtures, designed to serve this normative function. At the same time, by introducing mathematical concepts as the key for extending the notion of Being in a new direction, to penetrate the domain of sensory flux and Becoming, this partial account points the way for the larger enterprise of the *Timaeus*.

5.7 Relation between cosmology and dialectic

In one respect the *Philebus* confronts problems that the *Timaeus* can avoid. With its mythical framework and its insistence on the status of a "likely story," the cosmology of the *Timaeus* has no need to define its relationship to the method of dialectic. The *Philebus*, on the other hand, cannot avoid this problem, since it offers a detailed account of dialectic and also insists on a cosmological basis for this method (16d1–2). In fact, it makes use of the technical vocabulary of division and collection in the very statement of the cosmology.[22] Since dialectic has been presented both here and elsewhere as the general method of rational inquiry, it seems inevitable that the study of cosmology must also take the form of an exercise in dialectic.

However, the connection between dialectic and cosmology cannot be so straightforward. As we have seen, dialectic was regularly conceived as the search for essences or *what a thing is*. Furthermore, these essences were assimilated to the Forms of the classical theory, as eternal objects immune from change. So we expect that here too the object of dialectic will represent either unchanging Forms or their revised equivalents, like the eternal monads of *Philebus* 15a–b. (These unities were identified precisely as the

---

[22] κατ᾽ εἴδη διιστὰς καὶ συναριθμούμενος 23d2; διελόμενοι 23e3; συναγαγόντες e5 and 25a3. Cf. ἐσχισμένον, διεσπασμένον 23e4–5, 25a3, etc. The emphasis placed (at 23c–e, and again at 27b) on Socrates' counting and miscounting the number of factors needed in the cosmology (two, three, or more) reflects the importance of definite number for the method of division.

subject of debate "accompanying division," *meta diairesiōs*, 15a7, i.e. as implying dialectic.) Does it follow that the blending of *peras* and *apeiron* in the object of cosmology is to be understood in terms of the weaving-together of Platonic essences or Forms?

We cannot simply identify the objects of cosmology and dialectic. To begin with, the cosmic principles of Limit and Unlimited do not fall in the same category as eternal monads like Man, Ox, the Beautiful, and the Good (precisely those items mentioned in *Philebus* 15a that recall the Forms of the classical theory). Unlike such forms, Limit and Unlimited do not represent first-order concepts, defining a class of sensible homonyms in the realm of Becoming. The principles of Limit and Unlimited are more abstract and general, more like the "greatest forms" of the *Sophist* (Being, Same, Different, Motion, and Rest). As objects of dialectic, such terms define a wider domain of conceptual knowledge, not limited to the natural world of change and coming-to-be.

This formal gap between the subjects of cosmology and dialectic is reinforced in a later passage in the *Philebus*, where Plato draws a sharp ontological distinction between dialectic, which takes as its object eternal, unchanging entities, and cosmology, which is concerned with matters of change and becoming (57e–58a):

> Even someone who claims to be investigating the nature of things (*peri phuseōs*) is, as you know, spending his life in the study of this world order (*kosmos*), how it came into being, what it does and what it suffers . . . Such a person has chosen to work not about eternal beings (*ta onta aei*) but about things that come into being, that will come to be, and that have come to be. (59a)

But this leaves us with a problem. How are we to reconcile this clear contrast between the objects of dialectic and those of natural philosophy with the earlier introduction of cosmology as an application of the dialectical method (16c–d)? Does Plato present two incompatible notions of dialectic in the *Philebus*, one purely methodological and applicable to any subject matter, and another dialectic that takes as its object only eternal entities?[23]

A similar ambiguity arises concerning the reference of the terms *eidos*, *idea*, and *genos*, which appear both in the account of dialectic (*idea* 16b1, 7; *eidos* 18c2) and in the statement of the cosmology (*eidos* 23c12–e 2; *genos* 25a1, 26d1, d2, 27a12; *genna* 25d3; *idea* 25b6). These are, of course, the same terms

---

[23] Compare the discussion of this question by D. Frede (1993) x–xiii.

used for the classical doctrine of Forms as subjected to criticism in the *Parmenides*, and again for the object of dialectic in the *Sophist* (*Parm.* 135c2; *Soph.* 253d–e). Are the terms *eidos* and *idea* being used here to refer to two different kinds of entities, corresponding to two different conceptions of dialectic, only one of which entails Plato's metaphysical commitment to eternal objects exempt from change? Or how can dialectic, when applied to cosmology, remain a concern with unchanging objects?

If Plato is to have a consistent conception of dialectic, we must provide him here with a distinction that is at best implicit in the texts. There must be a sense in which, insofar as dialectic is an exercise of *nous*, its objects are all *noēta* – intelligible through and through. It is the function of *nous* to see things *sub specie aeternitatis*, as pure concepts. So in this respect the objects of dialectic are all eternal entities that exist unchanging in logical space, in the *noētos topos* of *Republic* VI. For the *Philebus* (by implication), as for the *Republic* and the *Timaeus*, it is the inhabitants of this space that are the *ontōs onta*, the true realities.

On the other hand, many (and perhaps all) of the objects of dialectic also admit a reference to their changing and perishable homonyms. In this respect, the terms of *eidos* and *genos* are essentially ambiguous. Gisela Striker has pointed out that, in the perspective of post-Fregean logic, terms like *genos* operate both as concepts and as classes: as classes they contain perishable individuals as members; but unlike classes, they are not defined in terms of their perishable extension.[24] Terms like *genos* and *eidos* properly refer to the rational form or kind in question, as a timeless object of cognition. But the same term may also be taken distributively, to refer to perishable instances of this kind. Thus, the word *anthrōpos* can designate the concept of human nature (man as such, or "Man itself"), but it can also apply to the perishable homonyms, individual human beings. It is in this latter regard that cosmology takes as its object things that come to be and perish. According to the narrative of the *Timaeus*, the cosmos itself is an individual *zōon*, a sensible living thing that has come into existence and in principle might perish. On the other hand, the components of cosmological theory such as the One and the Many, the Different and the Same (as studied, for example, in the dialectical arguments of *Parmenides* Part Two), exist as stable concepts in the logical space of the intellect. Thus, any particular *genos* may be construed either as an unchanging noetic unit, the *ousia* formulated in a definition, or as the range of sensible individuals answering to this definition.

---

[24] Striker (1970) 36–37.

We can recognize a similar referential duality in Plato's favorite example of the alphabet. Thus, the *eidos* of mutes (*aphōna*) may denote either this phonetic group, as a timeless component of linguistic science (*grammatikē*), or the corresponding class of sounds uttered by actual speakers in real time. Let us distinguish these two denotations as the intentional and the extensional interpretations of an *eidos*. It is clear that *eidos* in the intentional sense represents a timeless concept – the mutes as an object of linguistic theory, whereas *eidos* construed extensionally refers to all the individual sounds of this kind that ever have been or will be uttered. Part of Plato's fascination with the alphabet may be traced to this dual status of the letters as simultaneously noetic and sensible, objects for both dialectic and physics. A given letter (or phoneme) is the same whether visible or audible, but intrinsically neither. It is essentially a unique position in an abstract series of signs.

I suggest that this distinction between two ways of construing the objects of dialectic will enable us to see how Plato can, on the one hand, regard cosmological theory as a systematic application of the method of dialectic, while at the same time drawing a sharp ontological distinction between the objects of dialectic as eternal beings, as components of cosmological theory (reflected, for example, in the abstract dialectic of the *Parmenides*), and, on the other hand, as the extensional reference of these same terms to entities that come to be and perish.

5.8 A sketch of cosmology as object of dialectic

It may help to make clear the view of Plato's cosmological theory that I am proposing if we sketch here the outline of such a theory. In what follows I present a conceptual scheme of dialectic along the lines suggested by some passages in *Parmenides* and *Philebus*, as well as in Aristotle's report of the Unwritten Doctrines. According to the system of double reference that I have just described, cosmology understood as a description of the world of nature and change will then appear as the sensible projection or external point of reference for a theoretical structure that itself consists only of immutable noetic entities.

We may conceive this purely noetic structure as a hierarchy of intelligible items or concepts, stretching from the sheer unity of the One at the uppermost point, down to the unlimited plurality of the Indefinite Dyad at the lowest. Within this total vertical space we recognize descending levels of generality, beginning with the Greatest Forms of the *Sophist*, and ending with natural kinds such as Man, Ox, Fire, and Water. In between will come mathematical structures of the kind suggested by the principles of *peras* and *apeiria* in the *Philebus*.

I omit from this diagram any reference to the normative trio of the Good, the Beautiful, and the Just. They do not represent a distinct level in the hierarchy but rather a different dimension of the system as a whole – an alternative way of conceiving the objects of dialectic, namely, as the targets of rational desire and as norms for human action.

The following diagram is intended, then, to suggest different levels in the system of intelligible forms that constitutes the rational structure of the world.

The noetic cosmos (realm of Being)

The One (as principle and source of unity)
Unity (One as an attribute), Being, Same, and Different
Limit and Unlimited, Motion and Rest
Number theory and geometry (the Forms of Equal, Greater, Lesser, and the numbers; circle, triangle, and square)
Mathematics of change (space and time)
Forms as natural kinds, each one defining a class of sensible homonyms (Man, Ox; Fire, Water, etc.)
The Many (as principle of plurality)

Comment: Just as the One appears twice at the top, first as the general principle of unity and again as an attribute of each Form, so at the bottom the Many appears not only as the principle of plurality for Forms taken generally but also as the potential plurality of instances for each Form. But this potential plurality of sensible instances lies not in the noetic domain but in the visible cosmos, and hence below the line that follows here to divide Being from Becoming.

****

The visible cosmos (realm of Becoming)

"This world," the world of nature and change, as organized by the Demiurge and the lesser gods in the *Timaeus*.
This represents the Many at the level of sense perception, including heavenly bodies and the four elements, together with instances of natural kinds and other homonyms of the Forms.

The scheme presented here is of course partial and designed only to be suggestive. Besides the omission of normative concepts such as the Good and the Just, I have left out the World Soul and the psyche in general, since its position in this hierarchy is not well defined. As a product of creation and as an entity in motion, the soul of the *Phaedrus, Timaeus,* and *Laws* X would seem to lie below the line that separates Being from Becoming in the diagram presented above. On the other hand, the soul is not an object for sense perception. Hence, epistemically the soul belongs rather with the entities that lie above this line. (See *Phaedo* 79e.) This mixed status for soul makes clear that Plato's system is not a simple dualism.

For similar reasons, there is no place for *nous* in my diagram. In all relevant texts, *nous* is closely connected with (and apparently dependent on) soul.

For a different reason I have omitted any mention of artifacts. As types for sensible objects, these should belong on the same level as natural kinds. Several passages in *Cratylus* and *Republic* IX assume Forms for man-made objects such as Shuttle and Bed, just as for works of nature. However, in revising his theory after the *Parmenides* with the philosophy of nature in view, Plato seems to have abandoned (or at least neglected) the notion of eternal Forms for artifacts.

If we bear in mind the double system of reference for *eidos* and *genos* (described above in section 7) we see that the network of Forms in the noetic space above the Being/Becoming line also serves to define the structure of the phenomenal world, which is its sensible image. But of course these are not two distinct worlds. Since the noetic system of Forms, as studied by dialectic, is stable and unchanging, it cannot be physically present *in* the world of change and sense perception. But although this formal structure is not properly located in the sensible world, it is also not present somewhere else. It is not located in any place at all. Only in this privative sense is it "separate" from the natural world, whose structure it defines. Hence, the cosmologist, as a student *peri phuseōs*, investigates the Forms not in themselves (as the dialectician does), that is, not as eternal inhabitants of noetic space, but as defining the structure for the world of change and appearance, determining the natural kinds, and thus defining the types of phenomena that come into being and perish. It is in this sense that cosmology is a special application of the method of dialectic, namely, its application to the world of Becoming, by way of this intermediate study of "Becoming into Being" that constitutes Plato's return to natural philosophy.

CHAPTER 6

The Timaeus *and the completion of the project: the recovery of the natural world*

6.1 The myth of creation

Turning to the *Timaeus*, we hope to find answers to old questions concerning the application of the doctrine of Forms to the natural world. Here, finally, we see Plato returning to a full-scale treatment of nature, the terrain cultivated by the Presocratics that he (speaking through the voice of Socrates) had dramatically abandoned in the concluding pages of the *Phaedo*. Of course, both the *Sophist* and the *Philebus* can be seen as preparing for this return. But it is only in the *Timaeus* that the project is actually carried out. Hence, it is only here that we might hope to find an answer to the problem of participation, that is, the problem of applying the theory of Forms to an explanation of the natural world. This problem was vividly recalled in the *Philebus*, and it will now be reformulated in terms of images and imitation. How can a single Form, such as Justice or Humanity, while remaining one and changeless, nevertheless determine many images of itself in particular actions and individual human beings? In addition to this general problem for Plato's theory, there is a more specific issue to be addressed in the *Timaeus*. How can a doctrine of immutable Forms, designed for a different purpose, be adapted to provide an account of the natural world?

Before pursuing these substantive issues, we need to take account of a radical change in literary form. Insofar as Plato offers any solution to these problems in the *Timaeus*, he does so within the format of a creation story. The cosmic narrative of the *Timaeus*, like its fragmentary sequel in the *Critias*, is located within the familiar framework of a dialogue between Socrates and his interlocutors. But the cosmogony itself is presented not in dialogue form but as one continuous speech. In effect, Timaeus' monologue constitutes a self-standing treatise in physics, an exercise in the traditional form of *peri phuseōs historia*: "an investigation into the nature of things." Plato has appropriated not only the content but also the narrative form of a

Presocratic treatise, "beginning from the coming-into-being of the world and ending with the nature of human beings" (27a5).

The disappearance here of any dialogue with interlocutors (after one brief encouragement from Socrates at 29d) reflects a shift in philosophical method as well as in literary form. For abandoning the mode of Socratic dialogue marks a double deviation. On the one hand, the flexibility of the dialogue form allows a certain variety of philosophical perspectives reflecting the diversity of interlocutors and occasions; on the other hand, and paradoxically, the same form can aspire to a higher level of intellectual rigor, marked in the later dialogues by the method of dialectic. (A different kind of rigor is represented in the earlier dialogues by the technique of *elenchus*: challenging an interlocutor on the basis of an inference from premises that he accepts.) Both aspects of the dialogue form – both the diversity and the rigor – are excluded from the didactic prose of a Presocratic treatise. Here, there is no room for debate or diversity, and also no dialectical method. There is only a continuous exposition of unchallenged doctrine.

This shift in literary form points to an important epistemic change. Instead of attempting to clarify the conceptual relations between Forms, as in the *Sophist*, or criticizing various definitions of knowledge, as in the *Theaetetus*, Plato embarks here on a constructive account of phenomena within the field of perception and change, where in place of dialectical method we must rely on something more like *doxa*: doctrine or opinion. Since, as Timaeus tells us, the natural world is only an image of changeless reality, we must be satisfied with a correspondingly lower level of clarity and precision. We will need to remember this warning when some aspects of the cosmological theory turn out to be less than perfectly clear and consistent.

Plato has prepared this new enterprise by his survey of change and perception in the *Theaetetus*, as well as by the vision of a network of intelligible Forms in the *Sophist*. But in neither dialogue did he attempt to relate these two realms to one another. The *Theaetetus* ignores the reality of the Forms, as the *Sophist* offers no positive account of the world of change. In the *Philebus* we are finally given the principle of a union between the two domains in the blending of *apeiron* and *peras*. But it is left for the *Timaeus* to show in detail how such a mixture might be carried out, and to give an account of the changing world of nature within the framework of a theory of unchanging Forms.

As literary vehicle Plato has chosen the form of a creation myth. If we bear in mind the distinction between the choice of this literary device and the goal of Plato's philosophical project, we may be able to avoid some familiar paradoxes of interpretation. For example, there has been much discussion of the creation of time. How could the demiurge create the world at a particular moment, but also create time on the same occasion? I think this posing of the problem reflects a confusion between literary fiction and philosophical intent. The narrative form that Plato has chosen requires that creation be represented as a temporal event. But for the philosophical interpretation Augustine was surely right: *non in tempore sed cum tempore creavit Deus mundum*; "not in time but together with time did God create the world." It is incoherent to suppose that time itself was created at a moment of time. Yet that, in effect, is implied by Plato's narrative of creation, if this story is taken literally. So read, the narrative is strictly incompatible with the claim it makes, namely, that time itself is a product of creation (37d–38c). Of course, Timaeus begins by admitting that his story will not be free of contradiction (29c–d), and he may well have in mind this conspicuous incongruity. For it is precisely this ambiguity between creation as a temporal event and Becoming as an ontological category that is exploited in the dubious argument claiming to prove that, because the world is visible and bodily, it must not only constitute a realm of becoming but be itself an object that has come into being. This argument is, I think, a transparent fallacy, playing in 28b–c on two distinct notions of becoming. But such an argument is *required* to make the narrative form seem compatible with the philosophical interpretation. For Plato, whatever is bodily and perceptible will necessarily belong in the ontological category of Becoming, as distinct from unchanging Being (28b4–c2). But although the world of nature must belong in this category, it does not follow that there was a moment at which it came into being for the first time. (It was and will be forever in the process of changing.) In order to preserve the narrative form of the creation story, Timaeus must deliberately slide from correctly classifying the world in the category of Becoming to falsely inferring that it is itself a product that has come to be.[1]

I see no need to provide Plato with the dubious notion of a chronological ordering of before-and-after in which nothing definite happens before the creation of time, in order to make his literal narrative seem compatible with his philosophical notion of time as co-extensive with the created world.[2]

---

[1] The philosophical argument shows that the contents of the world are presently γιγνόμενα (28c1), in process of coming-to-be, but not that the world as a whole is γενόμενος (c2), the result of previous coming-to-be. The shift from present to aorist is prepared here by the perfect γέγονεν (28b6 and c2), which (like γεννητά at c2) is chronologically ambiguous between past and present.

[2] The classical attempt to make the literal narrative compatible with the philosophical thesis is that of Gregory Vlastos. See especially Vlastos (1996) 265–79.

We have already explored Plato's reasons for choosing the form of a creation narrative. It was essential for him to insist on the rational and teleological structure of the world order, in contrast to the mechanistic tendencies of earlier cosmology and, above all, in opposition to the atomist attempt to explain the world as the product of chance collisions between lifeless bodies. The concept of a divine Craftsman producing the world as a work of art provided Plato with the ideal device for his interpretation of the order of nature as a rational plan, the object of teleological design.

Despite the utility of this device, it is not easy to provide a clear philosophical interpretation for all aspects of the narrative, and in particular for the divine agent, the Demiurge himself. It is tempting to interpret this figure as a super-cosmic Mind, a personified version of Anaxagorean *nous*.[3] But Plato insists that he is not ready to offer us an account of the nature of the Demiurge (*Timaeus* 28c). And there is a serious obstacle to any attempt to identify this figure as a representative of *nous*. Here as elsewhere, Plato insists that *nous* can be found only in a psyche.[4] But since the world soul is said to be created by the Demiurge, it can scarcely be identified with its maker. On the other hand, I will suggest below that the uncreated model might include both a psyche and a *nous*. Perhaps that is where the Demiurge is hiding: in the uncreated *nous* of an uncreated psyche? But then he appears again as an item in his own model for creation? Or is this simply one more inconcinnity in the cosmogonic narrative? I am afraid we must be resigned to leave these questions unresolved.

What is clear on any reading is that, as an intentional agent, the Demiurge serves as a paradigm for artistic making and hence for teleological causation.[5] As we have seen, this underlying principle of explanation was most clearly formulated in the *Philebus*, where the notion of causation is spelled out in terms of rational action and artistic production, by reliance on the two senses of *poiein* as doing and making.[6] The allegorical role of the Demiurge as rational agent and maker is thus clear and fundamental, even if his position within Plato's metaphysical scheme must remain obscure.

The mythic form of the creation story was chosen not for this reason only – to present nature as a work of art – but also because it represents a

---

[3] For an interpretation along these lines see Menn (1995) who cites Hackforth and Cherniss as his predecessors.

[4] *Timaeus* 30b, 37c, 46d; *Soph.* 249a; *Phil.* 30c.

[5] Compare the minimalist interpretation of the Demiurge by Johansen (2004) 86 as "the art personified," the principle of craftsmanship as such. For the full philosophical significance of the conception of the creator as an artist, as a response to the problem posed for *nous* in the *Phaedo*, see Lennox (2001) 280–303.

[6] See above, p. 161 on *Philebus* 26e–27a.

lower level of scientific rigor. As Timaeus says, in describing the world of change and becoming we are dealing only with an image of the truth, not with the full reality of unchanging Being. And the method here must be proportionate to the subject matter. "As Being stands to Becoming, so truth stands to conviction or belief (*pistis*)" (29c3). Hence, it is only belief or opinion that is expected for the creation narrative. We cannot ask for the rigor of dialectic in dealing with the phenomena of Becoming. The notion of the natural world as an image serves precisely to direct our attention to this relationship between Being and Becoming – between the system of Forms and the world of change and perception. As we have seen, the nature of that relationship was never discussed in either the *Theaetetus* or the *Sophist*; and in the *Philebus* it is mentioned only as a problem. In deciding now to confront this problem directly, Plato in the *Timaeus* is obliged to resort to a different mode of discourse, one that makes weaker claims of clarity and precision.

6.2   The Forms as the model for creation

By presenting the sensible world as an image of reality, Plato reintroduces the framework of ontological dualism that was typical of his classical theory of Forms. But that framework must now be updated. Both parts of the dualist scheme need to be reformulated in a way that takes into account not only the objections of Parmenides but also the intervening discussion of perceptual flux and the blending of Forms. What is needed is a fresh view of the Forms as a complex, dynamic network to be imitated by the creator. And we also need a new account of the being and cognitive status of perceptible things. Above all, we need to understand the connection between these two categories: the relationship between copy and model that was earlier called participation and is now described in terms of image and imitation.

The Forms are introduced here by familiar formulae: "being forever, having no coming-to-be ... grasped by intellection together with rational discourse (*meta logou*)" (27e–28a); what is stable, self-identical, and unchanging (*monimon kai bebaion*, 29b6). It is this eternal being that is said to serve as model (*paradeigma*) for creation. Phenomenal properties appear as its imitations or likenesses (*mimēmata*, 50c5, b6; *aphomoiōmata*, 51a2). So much is familiar Platonic doctrine. But which exactly are these Forms presented in the new model, to be imitated now in the creation of the natural world? We need to consider three or four texts that offer partial accounts of the model.

First, we briefly review the population of the Forms according to the classical theory. Beginning with the *Symposium*, and continuing with the *Phaedo* and *Republic*, the primary exemplars of the theory are what I call the normative trio: the Beautiful (*kalon*), the Just, and the Good. The *Phaedo* adds the Equal, the Greater and Smaller, and other mathematical notions such as the numbers.[7] In reviewing this theory for criticism, Parmenides can take for granted the ethical domain represented by the normative trio (the Beautiful, Just, and Good), together with logical-mathematical Forms such a Similarity, One, and Many. But the Young Socrates hesitates to accept Forms for natural kinds such as Man, Fire, and Water (*Parmenides* 130b–c). Socrates' reluctance is significant. It is precisely this extension of the theory, beyond ethics and mathematics to the phenomena of nature, that is recognized here as problematic. On the other hand, such Socratic hesitation is overcome, at least in principle, in the *Philebus*, where Man and Ox are named next to the Beautiful and the Good as examples of eternal unities (*henads*), free from generation and corruption (15a).

Once Forms are recognized for natural kinds, the way is open for a cosmology on Platonic principles. Thus in the *Timaeus* the realm of Forms will be expanded to include the natures of Fire, Water, and the other elements. It is here, for the first time, that the theory of Forms will be fully extended to apply to the world of nature.

However, that is not where the *Timaeus* begins. The model for creation is not introduced by reference to physical elements or natural kinds, nor even by ethical or mathematical concepts, but instead as a fully formed exemplar of life: a *noēton zōon*. The Forms constitute a living being that is *noēton* in two senses, both intelligible and intelligent (*ennous*, like its image the world at 30b). This is a strikingly new conception of the realm of Forms, and it is not immediately clear which Forms are to be included in this new model. Before discussing the cosmology itself, we must try to get a clear view of its pre-cosmic model. Since the interpretation here will be controversial, we begin with a close view of the texts.

6.3 The extension of Forms in the model

Text 1 (30a–b): {Finding everything visible in confused motion, the Demiurge led it from disorder to order.}

---

[7] In a more poetic mode, the myth of the *Phaedrus* introduces a list of virtues as Forms, beginning with justice (*dikaiosunē*) but adding *sōphrosunē, epistēmē* (247d6), and *phronēsis* (250d4). I take this to be a stylistic variation on the normative trio, tailored to the demands of the *Phaedrus* myth.

Reasoning that, among things visible by nature, anything with intellect (*nous*) was better than anything without it, but that it was impossible to possess intellect without soul (*psuchē*), as a result of this reasoning the god composed the whole by fashioning intellect in soul and soul in body ... Thus according to the plausible account (*ho logos ho eikōs*), we must declare that this world (*kosmos*) is a living being possessing soul and intellect (*zōon empsychon ennoun te*).[8]

{Since the Demiurge wanted his work to be as fine (*kalon*) as possible, he took as his model the most complete *zōon*.}

Let us assume that the world is most like the Living Being that has all other Living Beings as its parts, both individually and by kinds (*genē*). For it [the model] contains in itself all the intelligible Living Beings (*noēta zōa*), just as this world comprises us and all the other visible creatures. (30c)

Although the text is not explicit on this point, it seems natural to assume that the model is also noetic in both respects, both as intelligent (being *ennous*, like the created world at 30b8) and also as an intelligible object of *nous*: *nooumenon*, like all other Forms.

It is less clear whether other intelligible Forms are also noetic in the active sense, as possessing *nous*. The parallel to the visible animals may suggest that it is only the passive sense "intelligible" (not the active sense "intelligent") that applies to all the Forms. However, the text does not draw a clear distinction between broader and narrower readings of "intelligent." See the discussion below.

Text 1A (39e): Since the intellect can recognize four kinds (*ideai*) as present in the Form of Living Thing (*to ho estin zōon*), the Demiurge will produce visible images of all four, corresponding to the four elements. These four kinds include (1) the heavenly race of visible gods, namely, the fiery celestial bodies; (2) the birds of the air; (3) the fish of the sea; and (4) the animals that walk on earth.[9]

Among visible bodies, active intelligence (possessing *nous*) is ascribed to the Earth and the heavenly bodies, in addition to human beings and to the world as a whole. Such active possession of *nous* (being intelligent) will presumably apply also to the corresponding parts of the noetic model (i.e. parts corresponding to Earth, to heavenly bodies, and to human souls.)

Texts 1 and 1A present the model for creation as a quasi-biological entity, the complete noetic Living Being or Form of Animal, whose parts are the

---

[8] The cautious formulation at 30b ("among things visible by nature") leaves open the possibility that, among invisible things like Forms, the beings possessing mind (e.g. divine souls or knowers) need not be better than the (presumably mindless) Forms that are objects of knowledge.

[9] The sun, moon, and stars, recognized here as visible gods, will reappear as the celestial gods of *Laws* X.

kinds of living beings. Some commentators, following Cornford, have taken these two texts to constitute a complete description of the model, which accordingly includes living Forms only.[10]

On this view, the *noēton zōon* that serves as model for creation by the demiurge, although said to be "the finest of intelligible beings and in every respect complete" (30d2), is only one Form, or group of Forms, among many. Its completeness consists in its containing every kind and variety of living thing. But it does not contain, for example, the Forms for Fire and the other elements that are mentioned later in the text. Let us call this the narrow reading of the model.

Although this narrow reading has been widely accepted, it raises many problems. In principle, every basic property of the visible world should be derived from the model, by imitation. In particular, since the model is a noetic *zōon*, it should have a noetic psyche and a noetic body, of which the created psyche and body of the world are images. Furthermore, the created psyche is said to include among its components three of the "greatest forms" from the *Sophist*. (See below, Text 2.) Surely these Forms must be present in the noetic model as well as in its generated image? Similarly, the created body will include the four elements; and Timaeus in fact specifies that there must be four corresponding Forms (in Text 3, below). If these Forms were absent from the model, why would their images appear as fundamental constituents of the created world? How could the model be complete (*teleos*) if it fails to include these elemental Forms? The argument for inclusion in the model is particularly clear in this case, since the existence of these four Forms is asserted later in the text. But the same argument applies generally to any fundamental feature of the natural world. Why would the Demiurge introduce a feature in his product if the corresponding Form were not present in the model?

One possible response might be that the model itself need not include all these Forms, since other features will be logically entailed by the fact that the world is a living thing. A *zōon* must have a body, a body must have the four elements, the elements will be *different* from one another, etc. But of course this argument applies equally well to the entailment of Forms in the model.

We might still distinguish between those Forms that are directly contained in the model or present in it as parts (like the four kinds of animals),

---

[10] Cornford (1937) 41: "We have no warrant for identifying it [the model] with the entire system of Forms, or with the Form of the Good . . . or even [with] the Forms of the four primary bodies, whose existence is specially affirmed at 51b ff."

on the one hand, and, on the other hand, the wider class of Forms that are logically entailed by the specified parts. It is this wider class that would include the whole network of Forms.

It is not clear that any such distinction is actually drawn or implied by Plato's text. Nevertheless, we might invoke it here in order to explain why, at 39c, Timaeus mentions only the kinds of animals as parts of the Animal Itself. For a more vivid presentation, Plato can at first ignore the wider connection between his model and the whole range of Forms, and instead focus the reader's attention on the four kinds of life that the model immediately contains. This narrow reading is all we need for Timaeus' initial description of the model.

However, I think it would be a mistake to limit our interpretation of the model to this narrow reading. The model for creation will have to contain the whole system of Forms sketched in the *Sophist* and recalled here in Timaeus' opening statement of ontological dualism. What is new here is not a different, more limited set of Forms but the conception of this set as a unified organism, as a Living Being. This view comes as a surprise, but it is not difficult to see why Plato has been led to it. Since (as the *Philebus* has argued) the natural world is itself a living being, unified and controlled by a world soul, its noetic model must have the same unity and vitality. It is this "vitalist," quasi-biological aspect of Plato's model in the *Timaeus* that has made commentators like Cornford unwilling to identify this model with the entire system of Forms. But I can see no philosophical reason for Plato to exclude any Form from his model. On the contrary, the noetic animal created by the Demiurge is "complete in every way" precisely by containing among its parts an image for every item in Plato's noetic system – the system for which we proposed a partial sketch at the end of Chapter 5. The organic unity of this system is a new thought in the *Timaeus*, the reason for which is spelled out in the text. The model is designed to explain the presence of *nous* in the world, and hence (since *nous* can be present only in a psyche), the model must contain the Form for psyche as well as the Form for life (if these two are distinct).[11]

From the point of view of Plato's invention or discovery of the theory, it is his analysis of the visible world that reveals its noetic structure. And it is this revealed structure that specifies what is required of the model, if the model is to play its assigned role in the creation story. I can see no reason for Plato to exclude from his model any essential feature of the world to be

---

[11] We recall that a Form of Life was mentioned in the *Phaedo* at 106d. But this need not be different from the Form for Soul.

created – except, of course, for those features that derive from its categorial status as an image, as a world of change accessible to the senses. Every other basic feature of the world, including its unity, its beauty, and its motion, must be a homonym, that is, a feature named and derived from a corresponding Form.[12]

This interpretation of the model as containing the whole system of Forms seems to be confirmed by the following texts.

Text 2 (34c–35b): {The created world soul is composed from a blend of Being, Same, and Different (together with their corresponding phenomenal images); and likewise for our souls.}

These created souls thus contain as parts three of the "greatest Forms" presented in the *Sophist*. Since the noetic model is itself a *zōon*, this model will presumably have its own uncreated psyche; and this paradigm psyche should contain the same three "greatest Forms" as parts.

Text 3 (51b–52): In connection with the transformation of fire, water, and the other elements into one another, Timaeus raises the following question: Is there a noetic Form (*eidos*) for each of these, or is there only what we perceive through the senses? On the basis of a distinction between *nous* and true opinion (*doxa*), he concludes that there must be an immutable *eidos*, which is ungenerated and indestructible, whose perceptible homonym and likeness comes to be in a place and disappears again from that place (52a). The argument directly concerns only the Forms for the four elements, but the logic of the argument applies equally to all basic properties appearing in the Receptacle. Hence, every such property will be explained as the image of one or more noetic Forms.[13] Here we have Plato's affirmative answer to Parmenides' question whether there are Forms for natural kinds, the same answer that was implied in *Philebus* 15a by the mention of Ox and Human Being as *henads*, next to the Beautiful and the Good.

Thus, the evidence from Texts 2 and 3 confirms my general argument in favor of a broad rather than a narrow reading of the model for creation.

6.4 Status of Becoming and the problem of flux

In Plato's classical theory, the phenomena of the world of nature are defined by two fundamental contrasts with the ontology of Forms: they are subject

---

[12] See in this connection the critique of Plato's argument by Keyt (1971) 230–35, with answer in Lennox (2001) 295.

[13] For the recognition that not every word corresponds to a genuine property, the homonym of a Form, see *Statesman* 263b, cited above, p. 145.

to change and hence belong to the category of Becoming rather than unchanging Being; and they are objects of sense perception and opinion (*doxa*) rather than intellect (*nous*) and knowledge. The second, epistemic contrast remains unaltered in Plato's later writing, including the *Timaeus*.

A caveat is in place here. All Forms are noetic as objects of dialectic, but some Forms are by nature also related to the senses, such as Sound (*phonē*). Thus, the Form of Sound is, on the one hand, represented by a mathematical ratio; but it is also essentially related to acts of hearing. The ontological principle of contrast becomes more complex, once the notion of Being is itself divided into unchanging being and being that changes.[14] The recognition that moving as well as immobile entities must be included in Being is announced dramatically at *Sophist* 249d, as if it were a new discovery. As we have seen, this insight is reflected in the *Philebus* by the paradoxical terminology of "becoming into being" and "being that has come to be."[15] This new notion of a cross-blend between Being and Becoming is designed to make room for something missing, or at least never fully articulated, in the classical theory. This is the notion of a regular nature or essence embedded in the world of phenomenal change, an immanent, recurrent structure distinct from (but dependent on) the eternal essence of the Forms. It is this recognition of the category of changing Being, associated with the turn towards natural philosophy, that leads Plato in later dialogues to make occasional use of the redundant expression *ontōs onta* ("true beings" or "really real") in order to distinguish the transcendent Forms from these new immanent essences.

In this notion of "being that has become" we have the immediate ancestor for Aristotle's concept of enmattered form, as the structural basis for regularity in nature. But Plato has his own way of conceiving this principle. Unlike Aristotle, Plato's version of immanent form will be fundamentally mathematical. Thus, in the *Philebus*, where the order of the cosmos is conceived as a form-matter blend between *peras* and *apeiria*, the formal cause of *peras* is described solely in terms of numerical proportion.[16] The corresponding passive or material principle of *apeiria* will be

---

[14] This wider notion of being, including things that change, was implicit in a few earlier texts, for example, in *Phaedo* 79a6: "we posit two kinds of beings (εἴδη τῶν ὄντων), one visible, one invisible." But in the classical theory visible objects are normally counted with Becoming.

[15] Above, p. 169.

[16] James Lennox reminds me that this mathematical conception of form in the *Philebus* is faithfully reflected in Aristotle's introduction of the formal cause in *Physics* II.3, where Aristotle's formula for essence is as follows: (ὁ λόγος ὁ τοῦ τί ἦν εἶναι) "the cause of an octave is the ratio of two to one, and more generally number" (194b28). This is one of many echoes of the *Philebus* in Aristotle's physical writings.

responsible for the fluctuating, qualitative content of the phenomenal world. The blending of these two principles in the *Philebus* points the way to the work of the Demiurge, who will impose mathematical structure on the formless material of the Receptacle.

The introduction of the Receptacle is the most fundamental innovation of the *Timaeus*. It lays the foundation for Plato's new positive account of the world of change by providing the framework needed in order to connect the world of nature to his Parmenidean ontology of Forms. In the classical theory, Plato had rejected Parmenides' denial of truth for the phenomenal world and had admitted instead a mixed reality for Becoming, as what-is-F and also not-F. (Thus, only the Form of Beauty is unqualifiedly beautiful; a beautiful face or body is in some respects also not-beautiful.) Some coherent notion for the negation of being was indispensable for this mixed ontology of the world of appearance, where things appear to be what they really *are not* – are not, that is, fully and forever whatever they are. That is why Plato in the *Sophist* saw himself obliged to salvage the concept of Not-Being from Parmenides' attack. But to account for this partial reality of the phenomenal world, the old notions of participation and imaging provide only weak and potentially misleading metaphors.

The Forms were identified by the names of their homonyms; thus, the Beautiful is the model and source for all things beautiful. But what does it mean for a beautiful face to be derivatively (temporarily, imperfectly) beautiful? Inseparable from this problem of participation is the question of a nature for homonyms or non-Forms, such as a beautiful face or a beautiful person. What kind of *being* can be possessed by these items in sensible Becoming? That is the question posed in the *Philebus* by that paradoxical notion of "becoming into being" or "being that has come-to-be," a question posed both for individual phenomena and for the corresponding sortals or natural kinds. Thus, the problem of Becoming turns out to be the problem of applying the theory of Forms to the natural world. The key to Plato's solution is his theory of the Receptacle.

Plato's doctrine here was prepared by his confrontation with the notion of flux in the *Cratylus* and *Theaetetus*. The initial attitude towards flux was one of rejection. The doctrine of unrestricted change was shown to be not only false but incoherent and unintelligible. Plato's argument shows that some element of stability is required both for the existence of changing things and also for their cognition and description. The refutation of absolute flux in the *Cratylus* and *Theaetetus* can be seen as the beginning of an implicit argument in favor of the ontology of Forms, as Plato's proposed source for the needed stability over time. (This connection between the denial of flux and the assertion of Forms is implied in the *Cratylus*, but not spelled out there by any argument.) Plato's challenge in the *Timaeus* is to integrate the doctrine of flux into his own scheme: to take it over as an incomplete account of Becoming, and then to show how it will be completed by the theory of Forms.

The critique of flux in the *Cratylus* and *Theaetetus* had established two closely connected points: some stability in the object is required, first, for successful reference (saying or thinking "this," *touto* or *tode*); and, second, for successful description or predication (saying or thinking "such," *toiouto*).[17] (This duality corresponds to Plato's analysis of propositional structure into subject (noun) and predicate (verb) in the *Sophist*.) What the *Timaeus* has to offer is an ontology designed to provide the objective basis for this semantic analysis into reference and description, subjects and predicates. In the new account of flux in the *Timaeus* the basis for reference is provided by the Receptacle, as the only fully stable object in the realm of Becoming and hence the only true reference for the indexical "this." (50a) On the other hand, description (as represented here by the adjectival "such," *toiouto*) relies on the dual role of the Forms as the source for objective structure and hence also as the basis for descriptive speech. Phenomena can be identified or picked out by reference to portions of the "this," that is to say, as locations in the Receptacle. On the other hand, phenomena will be structured and described as images and homonyms of the Forms, images that appear in, and disappear from, the corresponding portions of the Receptacle, and that will be named after the Forms they imitate (*ta de eisionta kai exionta tōn ontōn aei mimēmata*, 50c4). (For the moment I leave the notion of imitation unanalyzed; we treat it in the next section, as the relation between phenomena and the corresponding Form.) The phenomena of Becoming all depend for their existence on the three-dimensional space of the Receptacle, within which they occur and "take place." But they depend for their nature and their specific properties on the Form whose name they bear. Since the image "always appears as the moving semblance of something else (namely, the Form), it is fitting that it should come to be in something else (namely, the Receptacle), clinging somehow to Being on pain of being nothing at all" (52c3, trans. after Cornford). (The notion of "clinging somehow to Being" invokes the new mixed notion of "Being-that-has-become" presented in the *Philebus*.) These homonyms of the Forms are "perceptible, generated, always in motion, coming-to-be in some place and again passing-away from it" (52a5). Timaeus describes this

---

[17] See above, p. 56, referring to *Cratylus* 439d and *Theaetetus* 182c–d.

process for the most fundamental case of Becoming, that of the four elements. But his account applies in principle to every natural kind (and hence also to individual examples, although he does not discuss these). His subject is regularity in nature, Forms as displayed in phenomena, essentially the same thing described in the *Philebus* as "becoming into being" and "being that has come to be." We are thus meant to understand this account of Fire and the other elements as representative for the general phenomena of coming-to-be for natural kinds.

It is an essential feature of the full creation narrative that the analysis of Becoming is given in two stages, before and after the Demiurge goes to work. This serves to distinguish Plato's two types of causation: Necessity as represented in the pre-cosmic state of affairs; and Reason as the work of the Demiurge. The first stage is what (since Ovid) has come to be known as *chaos*: the condition of the Receptacle "when deity is absent" (53b3).[18] This is the topic introduced under the poetic title of "the works of Anankē," the unstructured motion of the pre-cosmic elements, to be tamed and shaped by the persuasive action of Nous (47e–48b). More specifically, we are given a picture of the nature of the elements and the condition of things generally "before the genesis of heaven" (48b3), that is, before the creation of an ordered universe. But this second narrative of creation will be preceded by an elaborate introduction.

6.5 The Receptacle and the new introduction to creation (48e–53b)

Plato's undertaking here is complex, and to some extent contradictory. On the one hand, he will paint a picture of his new principle, the "nurse and receptacle of all Becoming," as a spatial framework with no properties of its own but capable of receiving them all from other sources, namely, from the Forms. This part of the picture is essentially negative: the denial of definite properties to the Receptacle. On the other hand, Plato must also give an account of "the wandering cause," all the material and mechanical factors that are independent of the Demiurge but will condition his work. (These factors will include an account of elemental flux, a revised version of the flux doctrine from the *Cratylus* and *Theaetetus*.) Now, this aspect of the pre-cosmic state, conceived as the wandering cause and the works of Necessity, will have to

---

[18] Ovid, in *Metamorphoses* I.vii, seems to be the first extant author to apply Hesiod's term for a pre-cosmic chasm or "gap" to Plato's account of the initial stage in the movement from *ataxia* to *taxis*. But the term *chaos* may have been used earlier for this notion in lost works of Stoic cosmogony.

be more positive in content, since its task is to explain features of the world that are not the work of constructive Reason. This positive aspect of the Receptacle, as representative of Necessity, comes fully into play only at the end of the introduction, in Timaeus' description of the pre-cosmos: the body of the world before creation (52d–53b). The narrative of creation will then begin again with the intervention of the Demiurge at 53b4. But this new narrative is preceded by a long exposition, consisting of four unequal sections:
(1) the preliminary *aporia* about what to call "this" (49b–50a);
(2) an account of the Receptacle as the place for images (50a–51b6);
(3) proof that there are Forms for the four elements (51b6–52a4), with a final statement of the distinction between the three principles (52a–d1);
(4) the state of the Receptacle before creation (52d–53b).
I take these four sections in order.

6.5.1   The preliminary aporia *and the new account of flux (49b–50a)*

The preliminary difficulty takes as its starting point the phenomena of flux, illustrated here by the apparent transformation of the four elements into one another. This passage echoes a familiar theme from Presocratic philosophy.[19] Plato's own treatment of this theme is prepared by his account of flux in the *Cratylus* and *Theaetetus*. From these earlier discussions he now derives the negative conclusion that the flux of appearance, even in the case of the elemental bodies, does not provide a reliable object for deictic reference, a "this" that will remain the same over time. What is new here is the positive consequence. The only element of permanence in these apparent transformations, and hence the only reliable object for reference, is the universal place or Receptacle, "that in which they each (fire, etc.) always appear as coming to be and from which again they pass away" (49e7). In the phenomenal world it is only this universal space or framework, but neither opposite qualities nor elemental forms, that provides us with an entity stable enough to be called a "this." What we see always becoming different at different moments, like fire or water or hot or cold, is to be called not "this" (*touto*) but "such" or "of this sort" (*toiouto*). What we describe as fire or water is not a definite object but a recurrent kind of thing, not a *res* but a *quale*, adjectival rather than substantival, "a suchlike, which always returns as similar" (*toiouton aei peripheromenon homoion*), not an enduring entity but a definite phase in the cycle of qualitative flux.[20]

---

[19]   See Anaximenes A.7, 3, Heraclitus B.31 and 36; Melissus B.8, 3. Cf. Anaxagoras B.16.
[20]   49e5. My reading of the disputed passage 49c–50a largely coincides with that of Zeyl (1975). For fuller discussion see my "Flux and Forms in the *Timaeus*", Kahn (2002b).

The adjectival "such" is to be explained by reference to the corresponding Form, whose image and homonym appears in the Receptacle. The Receptacle itself is thus recognized as the only enduring, self-identical subject of change, the only true substance in the natural world, "providing a seat to all things that possess coming-to-be, a thing difficult to believe in, grasped without sense perception by a kind of bastard reasoning, <a thing> towards which we look in a kind of dream and assert that everything that exists (*to on hapan*) must be somewhere, in some place and occupying some space (*chōra*), but that what is neither on earth nor anywhere in heaven must be nothing at all" (52b1–5). (Note that this negative conclusion is not asserted by Timaeus but ascribed to our dream-like perspective on reality.) Implicitly, then, the text recognizes three kinds of being (*on*): the Forms, their images, and the Receptacle in which the images appear. The four elements as perceived, the traditional building blocks of the world, turn out to be not entities in their own right but only modifications of the Receptacle, adjectival rather than substantival. The correct account presents this new principle as the only true subject of change: "its ignited parts appear as fire, its moistened parts as water, <and other parts appear as> earth and air, to the extent that it receives imitations of these Forms" (51b4).

The focus of this text is on the notion of appearance. We are dealing with the phenomenal aspect of the elemental images as given in perception. Their physical basis is simply assumed here as modified parts of the Receptacle, that is, as perceptually qualified portions of a spatial continuum. The physical structures corresponding to these perceived images will be described later, in geometrical terms.

6.5.2 *The Receptacle as the place for images (50a–52d1)*

Underlying phenomenal flux, then, is this universal matrix, Plato's substitute for the infinite void of atomic theory, but which functions also as the source of raw material for the physical world. How are we to conceive this spatial entity, with no intrinsic properties except extension in three dimensions (and, presumably, spherical shape), but with the capacity to acquire all the attributes of the phenomenal world? In effect, Plato is exploring a concept that Aristotle will develop in his theory of potentiality. The Receptacle can be described as potentially the subject of all phenomenal properties but intrinsically the subject of none, before contact with the Forms. On the other hand, such contact begins automatically, already in the pre-cosmic state. The narrative form requires Timaeus to give an account of the Receptacle before creation (that is, before the beginning of time!); and he will describe it as already occupied by confused and indistinct images of the Forms. First, however, he sketches an account of its intrinsic nature, independent of any influence from the Forms.

This sketch offers a series of examples of raw material that must be neutral in regard to the features it will acquire, in order to receive them faithfully. The first example is gold to be shaped into different patterns (*ideai*); the next is a neutral base for different perfumes; the third is molding different shapes (*schēmata*) from a soft material like clay. In each case the subject must be initially devoid of the properties it will acquire, and also neutral with regard to any property and its opposite. (In the context of a theory of flux, this neutrality implies that in the pre-cosmic state any phenomenal property will fluctuate back and forth between opposites, to avoid the prejudice of a stable condition.) The properties immediately in question are the four elemental qualities: the hot and the cold, the wet and the dry. But in principle this reasoning applies not only to elements but also to compounds, and so on to higher levels of composition. As a receptacle for form, the matrix of Becoming must be neutral not only between wet and dry but also between blood and bone, between human and canine, and between male and female.

Devoid of intrinsic properties, the Receptacle will nevertheless be modified in appearance by all the qualities and kinds of things that occur in it as images of the Forms, even before creation. And here we must recognize different levels or stages that are not always clearly distinguished in Plato's account of creation.

There is, first of all, (i) the intrinsic nature of the Receptacle before receiving any image of the Forms; (ii) its initial properties, due to the automatic influence of the Forms before creation; and (iii) its supervenient properties, due to the intelligent work of the Demiurge in the act of creation. Sensory qualities proper, such as perceived hot or perceived wet, might seem to belong to this latest stage, since they depend upon a contact with the psyche; but the psyche has not been mentioned in stages (i) and (ii). On the other hand, the Receptacle is described as qualified from the start, before the intervention of the Demiurge. Furthermore, in the preceding account of creation, before the introduction of the Receptacle, it was assumed from the beginning that the realm of becoming would be "bodily, visible, and tangible (*hapton*)" (30b4).

There is a problem here, and on this point our commentary is obliged to be more precise than Plato's text. Perceiving the actual qualities of vision and touch will require reception by a sensory psyche, and this is not given in Plato's pre-cosmos. The primeval psyche, which (as Timaeus insists) is "prior to body and more venerable in birth and virtue, <designed> to be the body's mistress and ruler" (34c, trans. after Cornford), turns out to be reason alone; this is the "immortal principle of psyche," the only part created by the Demiurge himself. The mortal elements of soul, including the power of sense perception, will be added later by the lesser gods, his offspring, at the moment when the soul is installed in the body (69c). Strictly speaking, then, there can be no sensations of color, heat, or wet in the pre-cosmos, before the creation of psychic life. To give Timaeus a consistent view we must draw a distinction that Plato does not provide. Strictly speaking, in the primitive Receptacle before creation there are only chaotic motions that are *potentially* hot or wet. But these will not be actually hot or wet until they are perceived by an incarnate psyche. Plato does not have the concept or term for potentiality. (Even Aristotle, who has the relevant terminology, is not always careful to make this distinction.) Such a distinction between possible and actual sense qualities is less important for Plato than the objective status of such qualities (even if only potential) as part of the pre-cosmic world. The essential point, for both Plato and Aristotle, is that qualities such as hot and wet are not created but only revealed, or fully realized, in the act of perception.[21]

Continuing with the description of the Receptacle, we learn that in itself it is "invisible and formless (*amorphon*), all-receiving, hard to grasp, sharing in a most obscure way in what is intelligible" (51a7). This phrase, "sharing (*metalambanein*) in the intelligible," identifies the Receptacle as an object of rational but obscure cognition, one that is "barely credible," that depends upon a kind of bastard reasoning to the effect that whatever comes to be must have a place where it is located (52b). Thus, the Receptacle is required as the framework for any rational account of the phenomena of change.

Looking ahead, we may ask: What is the Receptacle designed to receive? What exactly are those images that appear in, and disappear from, the Receptacle *after* creation? (This is the positive aspect of the doctrine of flux.) Plato is primarily referring here to kinds of things, to generic types that disappear and recur. But examples of flux must also include individual instances that disappear but do *not* recur, like a momentary cloud or a pool of water.[22]

When the pool dries up, water is replaced by air or earth. When it rains the same spot may fill up again, but not with the same water. Plato's first point about flux is the Heraclitean insight that the water in the river is

---

[21] For more on this point, see the Supplementary Note at the end of this chapter.
[22] See discussion in Chapter Five of this ambiguity in Plato's conception of a γένος (p. 172).

always new, even when it appears to be the same. The novel point here is to recognize stability in the relevant portion of the Receptacle, and hence to identify the latter as the subject of change. It is this particular location, this part of the Receptacle that is permanent and in this sense intelligible. But there is one further point to be made here: the modifications of the Receptacle are also regular. It is their recurrent type-identity that makes a new pool of water similar to its predecessor after some previous rain. It is this feature of regularity *within* the flow of transient images that was captured in the *Philebus* by the principle of *peras*, and by the concept of a nature as a "being that has come to be," an element of stability within flux. This principle of stability or immanent form was identified in the *Philebus* in terms of number and ratio; in the *Timaeus* it will appear in the form of geometric solids. This is the new role for mathematics in Plato's late work.

In Plato's earlier discussions of Becoming it was the principle of flux that was emphasized. In the *Philebus*, however, he directs attention to this second aspect of change: the pattern of regularity within flux, the presence of *peras* within *apeiria*. Plato is here developing what will become for Aristotle the notion of a nature, a form embedded in matter, what accounts for the persistence of the species or kind (*eidos*) while individual specimens come and go. This is what the *Philebus* means by "being that has come to be": the species-form as goal and outcome of becoming.[23] In the *Timaeus* it is again the species-form that appears as a recurrent image, "entering" and "departing" and also returning as recognizably similar, but not identical. It is by this pattern of regular recurrence that the phenomena of Becoming are linked to the changeless Being of the Forms. Many pools of water have the same nature because they are "imitations" of the same Form of Water. The kind, as a similarity relation between pools of water (or between birds or fishes) exists only in virtue of this fixed dependence of transient images on a common, unchanging Form. There is no persistent entity that remains identical over time, no image that exists before it "enters" the Receptacle or after it leaves. Talk of entering and departing is only a picturesque way of saying that an image of a specific type appears in and disappears from the place in question. The earlier notion of immanent Forms – the small and large "in us" of the *Phaedo* – is now replaced by talk of images appearing in, and disappearing from, specific locations.

---

[23] Aristotle in his biological works repeatedly echoes this principle from the *Philebus*, without citing that dialogue: "generation is for the sake of being; being is not for the sake of generation" (*Parts of Animals* I.1, 640a18; cited again at *Generation of Animals* V.1, 778b2). I owe to James Lennox the recognition of this implicit quotation from *Philebus* 54b–c.

What Plato means by imitation will be discussed below. What the notion of image implies, however, both in the *Timaeus* and in the classical theory, is that these recurrent features of the phenomenal world will be derived from, and recognized on the basis of, their connection with one or more unchanging Forms.[24] In metaphysical terms the image itself – the phenomenal appearance of water in the pool – is nothing more than a local, temporary modification of the Receptacle, a modification that is identified here in perceptual (visual or tactile) terms. A physical explanation, however, must refer to the mathematical structure of the elemental components. It is in the geometry of the elements that Timaeus will provide a physical account of what is here described as a phenomenal image.

6.5.3 *Argument for the Forms and final summary of the three principles (51b6–52d1)*

The proof of the existence of Forms at 51b–e responds to a question asked specifically about Fire and its peers: are they only what we see? But the question also refers generally to "whatever else we perceive through the body" (51c2), and the argument itself is quite general. If intellection (*nous*) is different from true opinion, then there will be these Forms in themselves, not known to us by sense perception but only as objects of intellect (*nooumena*). Since the argument then shows that these two cognitive capacities are in fact distinct, it is immediately inferred that each one must have its own proper object. (We recognize here Plato's characteristic realism: how could two cognitive faculties be distinct if they did not have distinct objects?) The object of *nous* will "keep its form unchangingly, not having come into being and not perishing, neither receiving anything into itself from elsewhere nor itself going to anything else, neither visible nor perceived by other senses." On the other hand, the homonym and simulacrum (*homoion*) of the Form, the image which is in continuous motion and becoming, will be grasped by opinion with sense perception (52a). Thus, we have a restatement and justification of the realm of Forms that was introduced at the beginning of Timaeus' exposition (27d–28a). I think we may assume that the noetic Forms established by this argument will be co-extensive, or even identical, with the full system of concepts recognized as the object of dialectic in the *Sophist*.

---

[24] As we have noted, in the *Phaedrus* this recognition is understood as recollection, as a move "from many sensations to a unity gathered together by reason," a unity recognized as a result of pre-natal familiarity with the Forms (249b7).

This final summary of the three principles tells us nothing new about the realm of images that constitutes the phenomenal world. Timaeus simply emphasizes the double dependence of this common child on its two parents: the Forms as father, the Receptacle as mother:

> Since the very condition for its generation does not belong to it [the image], but it is always moved as an appearance of something else [sc. the corresponding Form], for this reason it is appropriate for it to come to be *in* something else [sc. in the Receptacle], clinging somehow or other to being on pain of being nothing at all. (52c)

For a fuller account of images we must look ahead, and first of all to the pre-cosmic picture of the Receptacle that closes this introduction.

6.5.4   State of the Receptacle before the Demiurge intervenes (52d–53b)

The first narrative of creation was interrupted at 47e with the reference to Anankē and the call for a new beginning to take into account the principle so far omitted, namely, the Receptacle. The second creation begins at 52d with a description of the pre-cosmic state of this Receptacle, followed by the intervention of the Demiurge at 53b.[25] These two narratives are separated by a long introduction, beginning with the *aporia* about what to call "this" that we have discussed above (in section 5.1). The description of elemental flux in this *aporia* (49b–e), like the rest of the introduction, refers to the present state of the world, to the elements as experienced today, and not to some pre-cosmic state of affairs.[26]

It is easy to confuse this passage on flux with the later account of the Receptacle "before the heavens came into being" (at 52d), because there again the description is given from the point of view of an observer: "it appeared as variegated to see" (*pantodapēn idein phainesthai*, 52e1). In both passages Plato is concerned with what he calls appearance – what we (following Sellars) may describe as the manifest image of the world, the phenomena as we experience them in sense perception. But this phenomenal perspective is the only thing these two passages have in common. The first text (49b–e) refers to our present experience in an orderly world,

---

[25] The resumption of the creation narrative is marked by the return of the past tense at 53a8 (εἶχεν) and 53b1 (ἐπεχειρεῖτο); cf. τότε at 53a2, b4. The intervening introduction was in the present tense. (See below, n. 26.) As Zeyl points out (2000) 42 n. 58, the non-finite verb forms in present stem also serve to make the description of chaos more vivid in 52d–e.

[26] The contemporary reference of the flux passage is signalled by the use of the present tense. See ὡς δοκοῦμεν ... ὁρῶμεν at 49b8, c1; ὡς φαίνεται at c7; φεύγει at e2, etc. There is, of course, a partial similarity here with the rejected flux of the *Theaetetus*.

whereas the second describes the experience of an imaginary observer of the Receptacle in its chaotic condition before creation. It is the latter passage (52d–53b) that concerns us now. This is the only text in the *Timaeus* that seeks to describe the Receptacle in its pre-cosmic state (the state anticipated at 30a and 48b and recalled at 69b).[27]

The narrative form serves here to divide the account of creation into two stages, before and after the Demiurge goes to work. The first stage describes those aspects of the world that are independent of the rational, benevolent action of the creator. This specifies the raw material that must be available in advance to make creation possible, and that sets limits to what the creator can do. (The Receptacle is initially in the natural state of "anything from which deity is absent.") This is the stage referred to poetically as Anankē – the Necessity that even the gods cannot escape – and more prosaically as the wandering cause. This primeval condition is characterized by both disorderly motion and qualitative diversity (for an imaginary observer); and these two features are thought of as essentially connected. Thus, the phenomenal character of the world is given from the start: "it appeared as variegated to see" (52e1).

It is an essential feature of Plato's account that the perceived qualities of the world, including the qualities associated with the elements, are given independently of the activity of the Demiurge (and independent, also, of their actual perception by sensory observers). These are part of the pre-cosmic state of the Receptacle, together with random motion. When Timaeus later comes to give an account of sense perception, he will add (as the work of the Demiurge) the geometric properties of the elements and their compounds, on the one hand, and the physiology of vision, on the other. But that the pyramids of fire feel hot to us and the icosahedrons of water feel wet is not explained by demiurgic action. These qualitative features are taken for granted, inherited from the pre-cosmic state of the world, as tendencies to act on the perceptual capacities of the psyche – even before such a psyche is available.

Where does this phenomenal diversity come from? Since the Receptacle itself has no properties, these qualities must represent "traces" of the elements in the pre-cosmic Receptacle. Thus, it is the nature of elemental water to feel wet and the nature of fire to feel hot, even if these feelings cannot be realized until the appropriate psychic capacity is available. In principle, then, perceptual qualities are given in the Receptacle before

---

[27] There is a partial, microcosmic parallel to the pre-cosmos in the confused state of the psyche as newly incarnate in an infant body, described earlier at 43a–44a.

creation – given potentially, as Aristotle will say. By contrast, its cosmic structure comes later, from the action of the Demiurge. This distinction is marked by a division in Timaeus' narrative between what we might call the manifest image and the scientific account. Democritus had already drawn a similar distinction but from a different point of view, independent of the narrative framework. "By custom (*nomos*) there is sweet, by custom bitter, by custom hot, by custom cold, by custom color; in truth there are atoms and void" (fr. 9). For Democritus, as for Sellars, it is only the scientific account that corresponds to reality. But for Plato both accounts are true, as accounts of Becoming. In the *Theaetetus*, as we recall, Plato had presented an account of perception from the point of view of perceived qualities.[28] In the *Timaeus* he is, like Democritus, taking this manifest image for granted, but reversing the logical order. In the *Timaeus* the subjective, perceptual account is taken as primitive and unquestioned. The scientific account is introduced as new and explanatory. Plato's project now is to offer an alternative to Democritus for the explanatory account, a new and improved version of geometric atomism.

It follows that the Forms will function twice in Plato's narrative, both before and after the intervention of the Demiurge. The pre-cosmic Receptacle is already filled with disorderly "traces" of the four elements, unstable forms (*morphai*) of fire and water with their perceptual qualities as hot and wet. The Receptacle serves as a kind of screen on which these properties are mechanically projected, like shadows on the wall of the Cave. Thus, the Receptacle before creation will already possess the qualitative diversity of the manifest image, in unstable and distorted form. (Strictly speaking, these disorderly motions are only *potentially* hot or wet, waiting to be perceived by a sensory psyche.) But the geometric structures that constitute the true images of fire and water (according to the "likely account" that is Plato's alternative theory) will not take shape until the Demiurge goes to work.

The pre-cosmic state of the Receptacle is, however, already complex. We recall that the Receptacle has no intrinsic properties but only the material capacity for taking on various forms, like the clay made ready for modeling. But before the Demiurge intervenes, the Receptacle is already undergoing the influence of the Forms; it would otherwise have no character at all. It is marked not only by phenomenal "traces" of the elements but also by disorderly motion. These phenomenal and kinetic properties are scarcely distinguished from one another, just as they were not separated in earlier Greek physics. On the contrary: heat rises and expands, cold shrinks and

---

[28] See Appendix Three to Chapter Two.

solidifies. (This is true generally: in the *Timaeus*, in Aristotle, and in later physics.) It would be a mistake to introduce here a Lockean distinction between primary and secondary qualities. Qualities such as hot and wet are not conceived as derivative or detachable from physical motion, as they are in post-Cartesian dualism. Just as in the cosmos the world soul is physically extended to wrap around the body of the world, so in the pre-cosmos the secondary qualities like perceivable hot and perceivable wet are not distinct in principle from random motions of the Receptacle.[29]

Before creation, the Receptacle seems to possess not only spatial extension but also something like material substance capable of being moved around. Here again, Plato's account of the pre-cosmic Receptacle may be less than fully consistent. For example, the automatic influence of the Forms before creation must distinguish portions of the Receptacle from one another, not only phenomenally but also physically, if such local disparity is to explain the imbalance and motion of the pre-cosmos. But how can the parts of the Receptacle be so different from one another that some parts become hot and others cold, some fiery and others wet? What accounts for such a distribution of different traces to different places? Symmetry would suggest that all four elemental Forms must be reflected in every location. (Or if not, why not?) But if so, why don't they cancel one another, instead of producing the swinging movement back and forth assigned by Timaeus to the pre-cosmic Receptacle?[30]

There is another, perhaps even more intractable problem in this depiction of chaos. How can the Receptacle have enough physical structure to be shaken? This chaotic motion implies a conception of the Receptacle as a storehouse of raw material, rather than as a purely geometric framework for movement and change.

It may be that a more ingenious reading of Plato's account can demonstrate its consistency here.[31] My own impression is that Plato's desire to

[29] The intimate link between kinetic and perceptual properties is not limited to the pre-cosmos, as we will see. Compare Barker's comments on the fusion between physical and sensory elements in the account of hearing in *Timaeus* 67b–c: "Timaeus does not say that the movement between head and liver is the object of hearing ... or that it is responsible for hearing; he says that this movement is hearing." (Barker (2000) 88, on *Timaeus* 67b–c.)

[30] Furthermore, since the non-rational soul has not yet been created, is this pre-cosmic motion compatible with Plato's own conception of the soul as the *archē kinēseōs*, the source of motion? Or is the soul the source only for the rational, orderly motion that will appear after the Demiurge intervenes?

[31] For example, one might try to explain the imbalance and swaying of the Receptacle in terms of a principle of qualitative neutrality, the logical refusal of any portion to be determined by a given quality rather than by its opposite. The physical result of this logical incompatibility could then be a fluctuating movement back and forth between opposite qualities.

incorporate as much as possible of Presocratic physics into his picture of Anankē has led him to give an account of the pre-cosmos that is not entirely compatible with his own conception of the Receptacle as qualitatively neutral. In order for the like-to-like principle to account for pre-cosmic motion, there must be pre-existing differences between positions and powers in the Receptacle. But that seems to contradict the principle of pre-cosmic neutrality between opposites, the principle so vividly depicted in Timaeus' similes of molding gold or clay and preparing a neutral base for perfumes. The initial imbalance and heterogeneity implied in the shaking of the Receptacle (52e) might present no problem for the cosmic scheme of Anaxagoras or Democritus. But it is hard to square this asymmetry with the intrinsically formless character of Plato's principle – which is admitted in any case to be difficult and obscure (49a3).

6.6 Images and imitation: the *Timaeus* solution to the problem of participation

At 53b the Demiurge takes the chaotic state of the Receptacle in hand and begins to impose a system of natural order, in imitation of the structure of the Forms. But how is it possible for the changing phenomena of sense perception to imitate the eternal reality of the Forms? It is at this point in the narrative of creation that Plato is obliged to confront the problem of participation.

As presented in the *Parmenides* and restated in the *Philebus*, the challenge of participation is the following. How can a given Form – the Form of Beauty or the Form of Human Being – remain forever one and the same and yet be present in, or shared by, a multitude of sensible, perishable individuals?

As stated, this problem is insoluble. The *Timaeus* strongly reasserts the immutability and "separateness" of the Form: it cannot be present in its participants, nor can the participants make contact with the Form, since "it does not allow anything other into itself from elsewhere nor does it go itself anywhere to something else" (52a2). This represents an unequivocal denial of immanence for the Forms. But in any case there would be little clarification to be achieved from the notion of an immanent form, as suggested in earlier texts where an image of the Form of Beauty is described as "the beauty present in us" (in the terminology of the *Phaedo*) or "the beauty that we have" (in the equally problematic language of *Parmenides* 130b4). For either such immanent forms will make the transcendent Form superfluous (as in Aristotle's critique of the theory, and already in the "greatest aporia" of

Parmenides 133b), or else we will be left with the problem of relating many immanent forms (my humanity and your humanity) to the unique Form itself. Hence, this apparent solution in terms of immanent forms, or images of the Form, turns out to be equivalent to the problem we were seeking to solve: namely, how is a plurality of distinct images (for example, my humanity and yours) related to the single, unchanging model, Humanity itself?

If now, having given up talk of participation, Plato will claim that these sensible images *imitate* or *resemble* the Form, we are left with the problem of interpreting the relevant notion of similarity. What can it mean for a sensible fire to resemble the Form of Fire, which is not hot at all? The concept of similarity must point here to some formal relation, in virtue of which the Form and its homonym will have the same structure. Such a structure can provide a middle term, a link between the eternal (intelligible) Idea and the perishable (sensible) instance. In order to connect the one Form with its many homonyms, there must be something in between that is both one and many, itself intelligible but capable of providing structure for the sensible correlate.

It is precisely this missing link between Form and homonym that Plato will now provide in terms of mathematical structures, including numerical ratios as well as geometric forms for the four elements. The first example will be the complex pyramid that Timaeus describes for the construction of elemental fire. It is by instantiating this geometric structure that the fire burning on the hearth will imitate the Form of Fire. Furthermore, it is by the same kind of structural similarity that two sensible fires will resemble one another, in virtue of this elemental composition which they share. The visible or tactile resemblance between two fires – sensible similarity – will be derived from, and dependent on, this more fundamental notion of similarity that connects each sensible image to its intelligible model. As the literal meaning of participation in or imitation of an eternal Form, we now have this similarity relation between visible pyramids and their common model in Euclidian geometry.

To illustrate this participation relation in the simplest case, take two equilateral triangles drawn on paper or in sand. These visible triangles resemble one another because they both exemplify the pattern of the equilateral triangle as defined in plain geometry. These two visible triangles represent the same image or species-type because they are both equilateral, that is, they both satisfy the conditions specified in the Euclidian definition. The existence of such visible triangles depends upon their location in the appropriate receptacle – in paper or in sand. But their identity as triangles depends upon their relation to the form of (equilateral) triangle as specified in Euclidian geometry.

The species-type of the *Timaeus*, a form such as man or ox, will correspond to a mathematical structure like the equilateral triangle only vastly more complex – a structure in solid geometry that is at the same time one, as uniquely defined, and also many, as indefinitely repeatable. (We might imagine as a parallel the mathematical formula for a DNA molecule.) In this intermediate role between the intelligible and the perceptual, between the eternal and the changing, mathematics provides the instrument by which the one becomes many, as an invariant form is repeatedly instantiated in regular modifications of the Receptacle.[32]

This is, I suggest, the reasoning that lies behind Plato's solution to the problem of participation. For a fuller picture, we return to the pre-cosmic stage of the narrative, before the moment at which the Demiurge intervenes. As we have seen, the qualitative diversity of Becoming is present in this pre-cosmos, where it is represented by the "powers" of the elements as hot and cold, dry and wet. As passive field or "mother," the Receptacle itself provides only the space within which such powers appear and in which they move. All structure and diversity, including all phenomenal qualities, must derive from the Forms, the "father" of Becoming. But in the pre-cosmic Receptacle these traces of the Forms constitute only a chaotic and agitated soup of qualities, recalling the fluctuation between opposites in the account of *apeiria* in the *Philebus*. In this stage we have only the crude raw material for qualitative diversity and physical motion. Despite the tendency of like to move to like, there is nothing here definite or stable enough to constitute an image.

Systematic imitation of the Forms (as distinct from these random traces) begins with the action of the Demiurge. His first task is to organize this qualitative mess into definite kinds of things, into types of phenomena whose appearance, disappearance, and reappearance in different parts of the Receptacle will be perceived as distinct moments of Becoming. On the one hand, these recurrent items exist only as local modifications of the Receptacle: the fiery part appears as fire, the watery part as water. On the other hand, these same items can be identified as images of the corresponding Form. These phenomenal types constitute the recurrent natures that are

---

[32] Compare *Timaeus* 52c on the nature of an image: "Since the very condition for its generation does not belong to it [the image], but it is always moved as an appearance of something else [sc. the corresponding Form], for this reason it is appropriate for it to come to be in something else [sc. the Receptacle], clinging somehow or other to Being on pain of being nothing at all" (52c).

described in the *Philebus* as *gegenēmenē ousia*, "being that has come to be." Now, it is just this mixture of Becoming with Being that corresponds to what was described in earlier dialogues as participation in a Form. In the mythical language of the *Timaeus*, it is this blend of Being with Becoming that constitutes the activity of the Demiurge in imposing order on chaos.

Our task now is to recognize such demiurgic action as an explanatory substitute for the earlier notion of participation. What exactly does it mean for the Demiurge to produce an image of the Forms? The answer comes at a critical point in the mythic narrative, at the very moment when the Demiurge intervenes: "He differentiated the shape of things with figures and numbers" (*dieschēmatisato eidesi te kai arithmois*, 53b4).

It is by imposing mathematical structure on the disorderly movement of phenomena in the pre-cosmic Receptacle – by imposing *peras* on *apeiria* – that the Demiurge produced the body and the psyche of an orderly world as images of the Forms. In particular, for the bodily creation he transformed the random traces of the four elements into regular, law-like images by combination and multiplication of two elementary triangles (or, in the case of earth, by the multiplication of a single triangle). His imitation of the Forms consists in giving geometric structure to these bodily elements, and imposing numerical ratios on the psyche. Thus he made use of mathematical principles to organize the phenomena and motions of the Receptacle in the best way available, making them resemble as far as possible the system of eternal Forms that served as his model.

It is by way of mathematics, then, that Plato specifies his answer to the question how sensibles imitate Forms. They do so by instantiating the appropriate mathematical structures, beginning with the formation of the four elements. Thus, mathematics is not only the device by which the Demiurge imposes order on chaos. It is at the same time, and by the same token, the instrument by which Plato resolves the paradox of participation by making the image resemble the Form.

6.7 Textual support for this interpretation

I submit that this mathematical construction of the bodily elements and the world soul is Plato's ultimate exegesis for his claim that the world of nature is an imitation of the Forms. As textual support for this interpretation, I refer now to the passage where Timaeus promises to offer just such an explanation.

In summarizing his account of the Receptacle, Timaeus describes it as a natural matrix (*ekmageion*) for Becoming:

> Changed and altered in shape (*diaschēmatizomenon*) by the things that enter it, the Receptacle appears (*phainetai*) different at different times; but the things that enter and depart are imitations (*mimēmata*) of the eternal beings, imprints (*tupōthenta*) taken from them in a manner that is marvelous and difficult to explain (*dusphraston*), which we will pursue later on (*eis authis*). (50c2–6).

This is Timaeus' only explicit reference to the manner by which sensible phenomena imitate Forms, and it is not entirely clear whether this promise is said to be fulfilled in any later passage of the dialogue. Cornford (followed by many others) translates *eis authis* here as "on another occasion" and implies that the promise is left unfulfilled. But it is equally possible to take this phrase as referring to a later passage in the *Timaeus*.[33] In that case the relevant passage will be our central text at 53b4, 3 Stephanus pages later, where the Demiurge is said to have taken things in disorder and "differentiated their shape (*dieschēmatisato*) with figures and numbers." The construction of the verb *dieschēmatisato* is slightly different in these two contexts (since the Demiurge is mentioned as agent in the second passage but not in the first). But these seem to be the only two occurrences in Plato of this extremely rare verb.

If 53b is an echo of the preceding passage, the promise of a marvelous and difficult explanation is in fact fulfilled by the geometric construction of the elements. The latter is introduced as an "unfamiliar account" (*aēthēs logos*, 53c1), but one which the interlocutors will be able to follow, "because they have been educated in the methods needed for these explanations," namely, the methods of advanced geometry. The difficult account of imitating the Forms is thus provided by the construction of the elements as perfect solids.

This intra-textual reading of *eis authis* at 50c (which seems to have escaped the notice of most commentators) may not be regarded by every everyone as beyond dispute. Furthermore, even if this reading is accepted, Timaeus has not explained exactly *how* these mathematical structures serve as likenesses or imprints of the Forms. (If that was ever to be explained, it can only have been in Plato's oral teaching.) But that they do so serve is clearly implied by the conjunction of these two texts, or indeed by either text alone.

6.8   Final thoughts on the relation of mathematics to the Forms

The mathematical constructions produced by the Demiurge must, of course, be distinguished from his model, the Forms themselves. This

---

[33] For *authis* in this sense as a forward reference, compare *Tim.* 61d4 where the reference is to 69a ff.

ultimate paradigm, which is described in the *Timaeus* as a noetic Animal, must somehow correspond to the network of Forms sketched in the *Sophist* as the object of dialectic. The mathematical structures of the *Timaeus* can be seen as providing a middle term between these intelligible Forms and the phenomena of sense perception. The mathematical structures constitute just that blend of Being and Becoming in the natural world that is presented in the *Philebus* as the combination of *peras* and *apeiron*. The constructions of the Demiurge will thus correspond to what Aristotle calls "the mathe-maticals" in his report of Plato's oral teaching. According to Aristotle's account, Plato's mathematicals play an intermediate role between Forms and sensible particulars: "differing from the sensibles by being eternal and unchanging, differing from the Forms by being many and similar, whereas each Form itself is only one."[34] Thus, the ratios and constructions described in the *Timaeus* represent not Forms but images of Forms. As images, they permit us to imagine what the models must be like. But what these ratios and constructions define is not a Form but a species-type, something intermediate between the transcendental Form and its perishable instances. This is a temporary and regular modification of the Receptacle that can disappear and reappear, as a given portion of space is altered by the influence of different Forms.

This Platonic conception of a natural type or species-form clearly antici-pates the Aristotelian notion of form-in-matter. However, it differs funda-mentally from the latter in at least two respects. First of all, this species-form is purely mathematical in structure: "a relation of number to number or measure to measure" (*Philebus* 25a). As Galileo put it, the book of nature is written in the letters of mathematics. This is what has made the Platonic view so attractive to mathematicians and physicists through the centuries, from Kepler and Leibniz to Whitehead and Heisenberg. And secondly, there are no natural individuals – no true "this" – except for the Receptacle as a whole. The Receptacle does not have enough intrinsic structure to perform the individuating role that matter plays for Aristotle. Individual images in the *Timaeus* will be identified only by their location in the Receptacle, or by the continuity of their movement from place to place.[35] Plato's conception of mathematics as the link between Forms and their sensible images suggests that the Forms themselves will have something like

---

[34] *Met.* A.6, 987b14–18.
[35] Living beings like us will presumably be individuated by their enduring psyche. The issue of personal identity seems to be envisaged by Plato (if at all) only for psyches, and only within the framework of myth.

mathematical structure. But how exactly Plato understood this quasi-mathematical character of the Forms we can scarcely guess. Our written sources do not allow us to recover the line of reasoning that Plato presented in his public lecture on the Good, or in his private discussions in the Academy.

What the later dialogues do confirm is a principle presented earlier as a basis for the education of the guardians in the *Republic*, namely, that the study of mathematics will prepare the mind for an understanding of the Forms. As Socrates reminds us at the conclusion of the *Philebus*, it is by such a study of harmony and proportion – of the *metrion* and the *summetron* – that we can arrive at the threshold of the Good. Hence it is in these late works that Plato appears most Pythagorean. But, of course, the explanatory principles of the *Timaeus* still bear familiar marks of the classical theory. Since the Demiurge, the maker of the world, was good (*agathos*), he wanted to make everything as good as possible (*Tim.* 29e–30a). The cosmology begins with this unmistakable echo of the central theme of the *Republic*. Although many things in the *Timaeus* have changed, one thing that has not changed is this radical primacy of the normative principle.

However, in these late works even more than in the classical theory, the normative and the mathematical conceptions tend to merge. This probably explains why, in his famous lecture on the Good, Plato is reported to have disappointed his audience by speaking not about the usual notion of good things, such as health or pleasure, but about mathematics, number, and unity. Normative concerns remain fundamental, of course; but the concept of the good seems no longer distinct in principle from the formal structures of mathematics. That is why in the enumeration of ingredients for the good life at the conclusion of the *Philebus*, it is measure, symmetry, and proportion that head the list of what makes a life good. Echoing an old theme from the *Gorgias* (508a), but with new detail and precision in natural philosophy, the *Philebus* and *Timaeus* present the mathematical structure of the cosmos as the divine pattern for a good human life.

6.9   Supplementary note on sense qualities in the *Timaeus*

In his implicit competition with Democritus in the *Timaeus*, Plato offers an account of sense perception in terms of the atomic structure of the objects perceived. For Plato, however, this is only one part of the story. Despite the mechanistic detail of Plato's explanation, it would be a mistake to assume that he follows Democritus in drawing a radical distinction between this scientific account and the more qualitative dimension of sensory experience;

namely, that aspect of perception that has come to be regarded as mental or subjective in post-Cartesian dualism. Plato is a dualist of a different streak. Thus, he never suggests that feelings of hot and cold exist only in the mind of the perceiver. On the contrary, such qualitative experience belongs to the organism as a whole. On the side of the object also things are more complex: colors and sounds belong to the things perceived and not only to our perception of them. Feelings such as heat and wetness are conceived as objective "powers," acting upon our sense organs to produce the corresponding sensations in us. And when a feeling of heat occurs, it occurs in the relevant part of the body, not in some mental correlate or separate psychological faculty. In all these respects, Plato's view of perception differs fundamentally from the tradition that has been dominant since Descartes.

The complexity of Plato's view will become clear if we look more closely at the texts in which sense perception is explained, beginning at *Timaeus* 61c. We will find that his mechanistic account is everywhere combined with an assumption of objective reality for the corresponding quality – a quality that belongs both to the corporeal event and to its external cause. Thus, in answering the question "how we call fire 'hot,'" Timaeus begins by claiming that "we all perceive that this affect (*pathos*) is something sharp (*oxu*)." The explanation of heat is systematically mechanical: it is the fineness of the edges, the sharpness of the angles, the smallness of the parts, and the swiftness of the motion of the microscopic pyramids (61e), "all of which makes fire severely piercing, so that it makes sharp cuts in whatever it encounters . . . It is this nature (*phusis*), more than any other, that divides our bodies throughout . . ., thereby giving us both the affect (*pathēma*) and the name that we naturally [*eikotōs*, i.e. "by likeness"] call 'hot'" (62a, trans. after Zeyl).

Notice that in this passage the *pathēma* to be explained includes both the physical effect on the body (being cut) and the corresponding sensation (feeling heat). No distinction is drawn between the bodily and the sensory impact. What is being explained is the corporeal fact of feeling hot, not a separate mental sensation of heat. And the external property of fire is characterized by a similar duality. The fire is assumed to be qualitatively hot, even though it is the geometric shape that is invoked to account for the transmission of a hot sensation to the observer. The qualitative bond between subject and object in perception is so close that the same term "hot" is reasonably (*eikotōs*) ascribed to both (62a4). This double use of the name, for both the passive affect (*pathēma*) and its active cause, is repeatedly emphasized in this text. This linguistic duality points to the fundamental fact of perception, namely, that the quality perceived is automatically assigned to its external cause. There is no suggestion that this name is applied to the sensation and its cause in error, or in some restricted sense. The fire and the feeling are both properly called "hot."

The same point is made in the account of cold that follows. The affect of cold is explained mechanically, by the trembling and shaking of the body in response to the pressure exerted by the intrusion of the larger particles of moisture. Nevertheless, "both this entire affect (*pathos*) and its causal agent (*to drōn auto*) received the name 'cold'" (62b5). The point is generalized in the summary at 65b: "Some account has now been given of the common *pathēmata* of the body as a whole and of the shared names (*epōnumiai*) bestowed on the agents that produce them." It is taken for granted, then, that both the sensation and its external cause are called "cold" in the same qualitative sense, even though the causal link between them is described in purely mechanical terms. As a parallel, we might compare the telegraphic transmission of an important verbal message by means of electronic dots and dashes. The cognitive-emotional content is meaningful at both ends, although the connection between sender and receiver is strictly mechanical. Similarly, Timaeus assumes that both the fire and the feeling are really hot, even though the causal link between them is to be explained in mechanical terms.

As we will see, these secondary qualities of hot and cold, wet and dry, play an even more fundamental role in the explanation of pre-cosmic motion. It is the primeval movement of like-to-like between these qualities that brings bodies together in an initial sorting, even before such elemental kinds receive their geometric structure from the creative action of the Demiurge. The objective reality of sensory qualities is thus presupposed as cause of physical motion in the pre-cosmos, before the involvement of any psychic power of perception. In this context, the sensory aspect of these qualities seems as it were secondary; it is their kinetic role that appears as primary.

In historical terms, we might say that Plato's dynamic conception of secondary qualities in the cosmogony is pre-atomist, whereas his mechanistic account of sensory perception is post-atomist. (For a more unified view, I refer to Chapter 2, Appendix 3, on sense perception as a system of motions in the *Theaetetus*.) What seems clear in any case is the fundamental difference here from any post-Cartesian view. Just as the qualities of hot and cold play a fundamental role in Plato's account of pre-cosmic motions, so also in the created world the objective reality of these qualities is taken for granted – despite the fact that the detailed account of their perception can be purely mechanistic.

We are so accustomed to the modern notion of the mental that we do not easily recognize it as an innovation, introduced for the first time by Descartes in his Second Meditation. Descartes created this notion by his skeptical stratagem of imagining the entire realm of thought and sense experience available to a subject whose body might not exist. It is this Cartesian fantasy of a percipient ego without a body that opened up the perspective of a purely psychological or mental realm for sensory experience.[36] Where we (following Descartes and the atomists) are inclined to draw a sharp line between the physiological changes produced in the body by sense perception and the qualitative content of such perception, Plato will systematically identify the two. He regularly locates the sensory feeling in a corresponding bodily event in the subject, while assuming that this qualitative content is derived from, and hence properly attributed to, an external cause.

Although this attitude may sound plausible to us, the results can be surprising. Thus, in his careful study of *Timaeus* 67b on hearing, Andrew Barker points out that the sensation of hearing (*akoē*) is identified with – not caused by – a movement (*kinēsis*) internal to the body, passing from the head to the liver. The mechanical cause of hearing, on the other hand, is a movement that begins *outside* the body, a movement of the air reaching through the ears to the brain.[37] Thus perception for Plato is a bodily event, but an event whose essential nature it is to reflect the quality of its external source – the quality whose name it shares. In order to see how deeply this bodily conception penetrates the ancient view of sensory cognition, it will be useful to glance at some earlier accounts that provide the historical context for Plato's view.

The fullest statement of what we may call Presocratic panpsychism is found in the fragments of Empedocles. We might suppose that Empedocles was only speaking metaphorically when he refers to "the impulse of persuasion flowing into the mind (*epi phrena*)."[38] But in fact Empedocles has a

---

[36] See my "Aristotle versus Descartes" article in the Sorabji Festschrift (Kahn 2005). There were, of course, some ancient antecedents for mind-body dualism of the Cartesian type, above all in the Neoplatonic-Augustinian tradition. The beginnings go back as far as Plotinus, who was probably the first major thinker to conceive the human body as an alien object, separable in principle from the subject of perception. We may find an occasional hint of such an attitude earlier, for example in Socrates' indifference to the future burial of his body in the *Phaedo*. But this conception of the physical body as alien to the human subject plays no role whatsoever in Plato's account of sense perception.

[37] Barker (2000) 85–99.

[38] Empedocles fr. 114. Cf. fr. 133, where "the highway of persuasion" is described as descending into the φρήν.

very concrete physical conception of the mental event in question, namely, being persuaded by what one hears. It is by means of their bodily elements that all things think (*phroneousi*) and feel pleasure and pain (fr. 107). Human thought (*noēma*) is most fully located in the blood around the heart (fr. 105), because it is in this part of the body that the elements are most successfully blended.[39]

The central role of the blood in human thinking is the most striking example of Empedocles' general view that "all things have some intelligence (*phronēsis*) and a share in thought (*noēma*)." This wider thesis is announced by Empedocles as part of the warning that his teachings may soon abandon an inattentive auditor, because of their desire "to return to their own dear kind" (fr. 110). This notion of a like-to-like desire on the part of Empedocles' doctrines may sound like a bold figure of speech, but it seems to be intended literally. The mechanical principle of like-to-like motion is applied here to the cognitive content of human speech, in exactly the same way as to the bodily elements.

We may recognize a view of the embodied mental not unlike that of Empedocles in the Hippocratic treatise *On the Sacred Disease*. (Since this is a major treatise with some claim to be recognized as the work of Hippocrates himself, I will refer to the author as Hippocrates.) This author denies that the heart can be the seat of thought or intelligence (*phronēsis*), for that is the function of the brain. The heart, together with the diaphragm (*phrenes*), can be the center only of feeling and perception (*aisthēsis*) (ch. 20). The brain is the master organ of the body, for its role is to receive intelligence (*phronēsis*) from the air and transmit it to the body. The limbs and organs of the body perform their role in accordance with this cognitive action (*ginōskein*) of the brain. The brain is the messenger that transmits intelligence from the air to the understanding (*sunesis*). "For when a man draws breath into himself, it comes first to the brain; and when the air is dispersed to the rest of the body, it leaves behind in the brain its best part (*akmē*) and what has intelligence (*phronēsis*) and cognition (*gnōmē*)."[40] The author's psychological vocabulary is not entirely transparent, and perhaps not consistent. (Thus, in chapter 10 to lose one's senses is *ouden phronein*; to regain consciousness is *phronēsai*.

---

[39] See Theophrastus *De Sensibus* 10.

[40] *The Sacred Disease* ch. 19. Because of textual difficulties I have omitted the intriguing sentence that W.H.S. Jones translates as "the whole body participates in intelligence in proportion to its participation in air." For this connection between breathing and receiving cognition from the air, compare the doctrine reported by Aristotle (from the "so-called Orphic poems") that the psyche is "breathed in from the universe and carried by the winds" (*DA* I.5, 410b28). This archaic view, deriving life and intelligence from the air, is portrayed at length in Aristophanes' *Clouds*.

Aisthanesthai may mean "to take notice of" as well as to perceive by the senses.) My goal here is not to reconstruct the cognitive terminology of this archaic text but only to establish its radical distance from any mind-body dualism of the Cartesian type. What is clear is that, according to Hippocrates, cognition comes to human beings from the air, and it is distributed by the brain to the rest of the body.

Between Empedocles and Hippocrates, on the one hand, and Plato on the other, stands the revolutionary figure of Democritus. By his clear distinction between sense perception and rational thought (fragments 11 and 125), and above all by his denial of physical reality to sensory qualities (fr. 9), Democritus initiates a radical break from the archaic tendency to panpsychism. The world of atoms and the void is conceived in strictly mechanical terms, leaving no place for sense qualities, so that even the basis for cognition becomes problematic. (As the senses say to rational thought: "our overthrow is your fall!") Besides their geometric properties, atoms have only solidity and (apparently) weight. In the *Timaeus* Plato will go a step further, deriving even weight from the mechanical tendency of bodies to move from like to like.

As the fundamental principle of attraction between bodies, this movement of like-to-like plays the role in Presocratic thought that is taken over by gravitation in Newtonian mechanics. As employed by Plato in the *Timaeus*, this principle presupposes the existence of sensory qualities in the pre-cosmos; and the same will be true for the physics of Anaxagoras and Empedocles. For the atomists, on the other hand, although the same principle remains fundamental, basic likeness will no longer depend on sense qualities but only on factors such as weight and geometric form. Aside from this difference, Leucippus could follow his predecessors in explaining the origin of the world by a cosmic whirl (*dinē*) in which things are separated out by the movement of similars to similars (*ta homoia pros ta homoia*): "Light things move to the outer void, as if they were sifted out (*diattōmena*)." On the other hand, heavy things drift to the center and form the earth.[41]

Leucippus is the first we know to have introduced this comparison to the harvest seive, an image that will recur in the cosmogony of Democritus and again in the *Timaeus*. Democritus presented this as a universal law:

> Animals flock together with animals of the same kind (*homogeneis*), dove to dove and cranes to cranes, and similarly in the case of other beasts. And so

---

[41] DK 67.1, 31–32: Diogenes Laertius on Leucippus, following Theophrastus.

also for lifeless things (*apsucha*), as may be seen in the case of seeds being sifted and pebbles borne by the waves. For in the whirling of the sieve lentils are arranged separately with lentils, barley with barley, and wheat with wheat; while in the movement of the wave the long pebbles are pushed to the same place as the long ones, and the round pebbles with the round, as if the similarity in things had some power of attraction (*sunagōgon ti*). (Democritus fr. 164)

Thus, for the atomists, shape and weight play the attractive role that mass will play in modern mechanics.

Plato is echoing such doctrines in his image of the winnowing-basket, which separates grains not by shape but (more realistically) by size and weight (*Timaeus* 52e–53a). For Plato, as for his predecessors, the principle of like-to-like is thus invoked to explain the primitive cosmic layering of the elements into something like concentric rings, with the earth at the center. Initially, of course, the Receptacle was in total confusion: "becoming moist and fiery and receiving the forms of earth and air . . . appearing diversified to see," as it is filled with powers (*dunameis*) that are neither similar nor balanced (52d–e). The first signs of order then appear: "at that time the four kinds were being shaken by the receiver . . . separating the kinds most unlike each other furthest apart and pushing those most like each other closest together into the same region" (53a, trans. Zeyl). The kinds in question are identified as sensory qualities, making the Receptacle appear "moist and fiery and diversified to see." But these same qualities are also forces, pushing fiery traces to the periphery and heavier traces to the center. Thus Plato's *dunameis* are at the same time sensory qualities, like the hot and bright, and also kinetic powers responsible for, and responsive to, the disorderly motion that tends to separate them into distinct regions.

There is a fundamental discrepancy here between Plato and the atomists, for whom the principle of like-to-like operates only on physical factors (shape, size, and weight), not on sense qualities. For Plato, on the other hand, such geometric properties come later, as the expression of reason, and they make no appearance until the Demiurge goes to work. In comparison to Democritus, Plato's pre-cosmos is more qualitative, less rationally structured. Hence in this account it is the manifest image that comes first, although in chaotic form. Plato is thus able to avoid the modern paradox of recognizing a rich manifest image of the world created, as it were, in and by the act of human perception, with only a mechanical link to the underlying scientific account. In Plato's account the scientific-mathematical image comes last, as the rational work of the Demiurge; but it can take for granted the qualitative diversity of nature that was given in the pre-cosmos.

Note that the distinction between possible and actual sense qualities plays no role in Plato's account of the pre-cosmos, since sense qualities cannot be actualized before the creation of sense organs, which comes later in the course of the cosmic development. Strictly speaking, then, in the pre-cosmos all sensory qualities will be only potential. But this is not a factor in Plato's theory, according to which the elemental constituents of the pre-cosmos will be sorted on the basis of their sensory qualities (cold to the center, hot to the extremes).

It remains to be seen whether the potential-actual distinction would suffice here to give Plato an entirely consistent account. This is one of the points where his initial disclaimer of consistency (29b–c) may well be appropriate.

Epilogue. *Plato as a political philosopher*

This study has been devoted to Plato's work in theoretical philosophy, beginning with the critique of the Forms and accounts of knowledge and Being, surveying then the method of dialectic and concluding with Plato's theory of the natural world. We have referred in passing to the digression on ethics in the *Theaetetus*, and to the relation between the philosopher and the politician in the *Statesman*. But I have said nothing about the political philosophy of these dialogues, nor anything about the role of pleasure in the good life as discussed in the *Philebus*. Above all, I have ignored Plato's last and longest dialogue, the *Laws*, which is entirely devoted to organizing the life of citizens in a good society.

There is a danger, then, that this study might misrepresent Plato's own conception of philosophy, in which the Aristotelian distinction between theory and practice plays no role. Plato in the Seventh Epistle tells us that, as a young man (perhaps until the age of 40!), he had expected to engage in a political career, like many members of his family. It is no accident that his three longest dialogues – the *Gorgias*, *Republic*, and *Laws* – are primarily concerned with ethics and politics. The dialogues discussed here were written in a period of Plato's life when his philosophical activity in Athens was interrupted twice by long and dangerous journeys to Sicily, undertaken in the hope of influencing the political situation there.

To do any justice to this practical dimension of Plato's philosophy in his later years would require another volume. In partial compensation for this lack, I append here two essays that point in this direction: an account of the argument against atheism in *Laws* X, and a revised version of my earlier article on political topics in the *Statesman* and the *Laws*.

1   Cosmology in *Laws* X

Since the *Laws* was apparently left unfinished at Plato's death, the cosmological passage in *Laws* X may be Plato's last word on the subject. But the doctrine presented here is surprisingly different both from the full cosmology of the *Timaeus* and from the briefer theory of the *Philebus*. There is no trace here of eternal Forms, no cosmic Demiurge or Receptacle – not even a dualism of Limit and Unlimited. Hence, some interpreters have supposed this contrast to reflect a profound change of mind on Plato's part in his last years, regarding both the nature of the physical world and the place of physics within philosophy.

I think such an interpretation is mistaken. The *Laws* is in many ways a special case. Even from a formal point of view it is unique, as the only dialogue in which Socrates does not appear, and where Plato himself presides as chief interlocutor, thinly disguised as an elderly Athenian. The Spartan and Cretan interlocutors have no background in philosophy, and little knowledge of the world outside their Dorian traditions. With regard to content, the *Laws* is equally aberrant. The Athenian Stranger displays a systematic reluctance to engage in the deeper questions of philosophical theory. The interlocutors are so unfamiliar with such topics that the Athenian must occasionally apologize for guiding them through elaborate stretches of argument (for example, at 892d–893a). What is generally characteristic of the *Laws* is the relative absence of philosophical theory and the systematic focus on practical, this-wordly concerns.

It would be a mistake, then, to see the striking philosophical contrast between the doctrine of the *Laws*, on the one hand, and that of the *Republic* or the *Timaeus* on the other hand, as reflecting a fundamental change in Plato's views in his old age – as if he had, for example, abandoned the doctrine of Forms and the tripartite conception of the psyche. The twelve books of the *Laws* must have been several years in preparation, and some of these books may have been composed at roughly the same time as the *Philebus* and *Timaeus*. I suggest that the peculiarities of doctrine in the *Laws* are to be explained not by any supposed change of mind in Plato's old age but rather by his designing this work for an entirely different, less philosophically informed audience.

The passage to be discussed here from Book X of the *Laws* is a special case, since it deals with technical matters of cosmological theory. Apart from the general silence of the *Laws* in regard to such theoretical questions, there are particular circumstances determined by the context in *Laws* X. The discussion here aims to demonstrate the existence of gods and the falsity of atheism. Our text is part of the proem for the law against impiety, a proem designed to prove "that the gods exist, and are concerned with human affairs" (907b). More specifically, the argument aims to establish the reality of the gods as rational souls responsible for the cyclical movement of the heavenly bodies. This is the least metaphysical and most accessible chapter in Plato's theology, the assertion of divine powers directly revealed in the visible phenomena of the sky.[1]

By referring only to entities and principles that serve as direct cause of visible motion, the argument of *Laws* X avoids any mention of transcendental principles such as the Demiurge or the immutable Forms, just as it avoids such theoretical topics as the Receptacle and the tripartite concept of the soul. This conversation with a Spartan and a Cretan, both innocent of philosophy, is not an occasion for Plato to revisit or revise his deeper thoughts on these complex topics of philosophical exegesis. He is concerned here to provide only a minimal theoretical basis for the legislation against atheism.

The argument for the existence of gods falls into two parts. The first section (from 892a to 896c) is concerned to demonstrate the priority of psychic causality over bodily-mechanical factors. The psyche is understood here as the principle of self-motion and hence as the primary causal source, whereas bodily motions are shown to be secondary and derivative. The priority of soul defended here is thus a matter not only of chronology but also of control: "by nature the soul rules (*archousa*), the body is ruled" (896c2). The argument relies on a biological conception of the psyche as principle of life, defined here as *archē kinēseōs*, the source of motion and change. This definition of the psyche in terms of motion rather than cognition had been introduced once by Plato much earlier, in his argument for immortality in the archaic style at *Phaedrus* 245c–e. But this conception of the psyche in terms of self-motion was largely ignored in the *Timaeus* and *Philebus*.[2]

In dialogues such as the *Phaedo* Plato's treatment of the soul is ambivalent, referring sometimes to the biological function of psyche as principle of life, but more often to its cognitive role as faculty of knowledge and perception. (The distinction so sharply drawn by Aristotle, between the biological and the cognitive functions of the psyche, is generally left implicit in Plato.) The argument of *Laws* X relies on this older, biological conception of psyche as the motive power of life, as in the popular view that the magnet is alive because it causes motion. The argument of *Laws* X assigns this vital

---

[1] A similar conception of the gods as direct cause of visible phenomena is also presented in the astral religion of the *Epinomis*, the book apparently added to the *Laws* by Plato's literary secretary Philip of Opus.

[2] The only reference to self-motion in the *Timaeus* is the problematic passage on plants at 77b–c, where a plant is said to be deprived of external motions that are self-caused, but allowed only to rotate "in itself around itself" (b7). This seems to imply that external self-motion is distinctive of animal *psuchai*.

role to the great organism of the heavens, and thus develops at length the notion of a world soul that Plato had introduced in the *Philebus* and *Timaeus*.

In effect, the argument here for the causal priority of psyche serves as a simplified replacement for the central theme of the *Timaeus*: the victory of rational explanations (*aitia*) over mechanical necessities (*sunaitia*), in which reason prevails by persuasion and by incorporating necessity into its projects (48a). The cognitive and emotional activities of soul – that is to say, thoughts and feelings – are counted in *Laws* X as primary actions (*prōtourgoi*). These psychic causes act to provoke the mechanical motions of the body, which follow as secondary actions (*deuterourgoi*) such as growth and decrease, separation and combination. These bodily motions have in turn as their consequence the secondary qualities of heating, cooling, heaviness, lightness, hard and soft, white and black, bitter and sweet (897a). In this brief passage, the Athenian Stranger thus offers a thumbnail sketch of the physical theory of the *Timaeus*, invoking rational causation as the primary form of explanation, but including bodily motions and qualitative changes as successive levels of consequences.

This quick summary of Platonic physics is followed now in section two by a new, less mathematically developed substitute for the teleological activity of the Demiurge. The pattern of cosmic motions aiming at the good is said to be guided here by a principle of wisdom (*to phronimon*) "full of virtue," that is, by the benevolent activity of a "best psyche" accompanied by *nous*, "who takes in charge the whole cosmos and leads it on its way" (897c). This teleological function is recalled later, in the conclusion to the *Laws* at the end of Book XII, by the description of Reason (*nous*) as "setting the universe in order by its power over the path of the astral bodies" (966e3). It is as if the all-pervasing cosmic action of the Demiurge in the *Timaeus* were reduced in this account to the visible revolution of the heavenly bodies.

As in the *Timaeus*, such cosmic guidance aims to make the world as good as possible.[3] In *Laws* X these good consequences are concretely expressed in the eternal revolution of celestial lights, as a visible image of the motion of Reason (*nous*) itself. We are moving in the direction of Aristotle's own conception of the cosmic god, whose activity will be displayed in the unending cycle of the heavenly bodies. This conception of a noetic soul

---

[3] Cf. *Laws* XII, 967a: the study of astronomy should lead us to understand how the phenomena are explained by "thoughts of a rational desire for achieving good things (διανοίαις βουλήσεως ἀγαθῶν πέρι τελουμένων)."

for the cosmos represents the highest mode of divinity recognized by Plato in the *Laws*. But how does this divine principle cause bodily motion? The answer is left open, but one possibility is that the movement of the world comes "from outside, in a marvelous way, since <the god> is incorporeal" (899a). We see here how the doctrine of cosmic *erōs*, by which the Unmoved Mover moves the world (*Met.* Lambda 1072b3) serves as Aristotle's answer to Plato's question.

In *Laws* X the world soul of the *Timaeus* has been reshaped as the highest mode of divinity, omitting all mathematical and astronomical detail, and excluding all metaphysical factors such as the Forms or the Demiurge. Thus, according to the general method of the *Laws*, esoteric theory has been eliminated and Plato's theology has been fully naturalized, situated within the sensible world as defined by change (*kinēsis*). The deity of the *Laws* is simply a cosmic soul (or souls) that is self-moved and that, as *archē kinēseōs*, has become the life-principle of the world, revealed in the eternal revolution of the celestial bodies. Plato's refutation of atheism thus consists in recognizing the astral cycles as the visible expression of divine life, and at the same time as the physical manifestation of a rational control of the world by *nous*. Hence, rather than risk blindness by attempting a direct vision of *nous*, we are urged to look instead at its likeness in the eternal and invariant symmetry of the celestial revolutions (897d–e). In particular, the motion of the sun is offered (at 898d–899a) as visible image for the divine activity of *nous*. The cosmological argument of *Laws* X thus ends with a subtle echo of *Republic* VI, where the sun served as image for the supreme role of the Good, both as source of motion and as object of knowledge.[4] This repeated reference to the conception of astral cycles as an image of *nous* may represent the clearest hint in the *Laws* of a concept of reality and divinity that would lie outside the realm of motion and change.

In conclusion, we can recognize both the parallels and the contrasts between *Laws* X and *Timaeus*. The opponent to be addressed is the same, a conception of nature relying on corporeal principles alone, with elements and opposites as basic factors, governed by chance and necessity. On this view, inanimate nature is primary and fundamental; art and reason are secondary and derivative. In both *Timaeus* and *Laws* X Plato will reverse this claim by his reinterpretation of nature. But instead of presenting nature as a work of art (as in the *Timaeus*), *Laws* X redefines *phusis* in terms of the motive power of psyche, with the additional claim that the decisive cosmic mover is a *good* psyche, whose causal agency is guided by *nous*.

---

[4] The term for image (εἰκών) appears three times in this context: *Laws* 897e 1, e5, and 898b3.

Despite these general parallels, we must recognize how remote the cosmology of *Laws* X is from the full doctrine of the *Timaeus*, or even from the briefer version of the *Philebus*. We have here a minimalist version of Plato's physical theory, adapted to the non-philosophical interlocutors of the *Laws*, and strictly limited to the task of refuting atheism by a naturalistic conception of the divine. The discussion of cosmology in the *Laws* does not aim to replace the accounts of Democritus and the naturalists with a better theory covering the same field, as was the case in the *Timaeus*. The goal of this project is more narrowly focused: to reject the materialist and atheist tendencies of the naturalist tradition by a reinterpretation of the notion of *phusis* on which this tradition is based. The audience in view is not the professional philosophers addressed in Plato's other late dialogues but a much wider class of readers.[5]

These will include members of the younger generation, who have been impressed by the popular success of the naturalist tradition. Plato's argument is addressed above all to those who have been influenced by the skeptical critique of traditional piety and morality – the critique represented in earlier dialogues by Callicles and Thrasymachus. The goal here is to defend the principle of divine governance on strictly rational grounds.

Thus, the aim of the argument in *Laws* X is not to offer a new philosophical theory to replace the cosmology of the *Timaeus*, but rather to define a simpler anti-materialist conception of nature, one in which the principles of psyche and reason will be recognized as more fundamental and more explanatory than any doctrine of mechanical necessity. But precisely because it was designed for a broader, less technical audience, the cosmology of *Laws* X was destined to have a deep influence on the future of ancient thought and religion. After providing the immediate model for Aristotle's conception of the Prime Mover, the deity of *Laws* X will become a principal source for the doctrine of the cosmic god that tends to dominate Hellenistic theology. From the point of view of the history of western thought, the theology of the *Laws* has been extraordinarily influential. However, seen in the context of Plato's own philosophy, what this naturalized conception of divinity represents is essentially a compromise with popular conceptions and, to this extent, not a theoretical advance.

---

[5] Thus, the arguments are addressed even to those who are slow learners, the *dusmatheis*, who will need to study them repeatedly (891a).

2 The myth of the *Statesman*[6]

Among Platonic myths, the myth of the *Statesman* is a special case. Unlike the myths of judgment, which come at the end of the dialogue as a kind of postscript to the argument proper, the *Statesman* myth comes close to the beginning of the dialogue and it seems to provide a premise for the following argument. In this respect, it is like the prenatal vision of the chariot souls in the *Phaedrus*, which is also centrally located in the dialogue and serves as basis for the account of recollection that follows. Furthermore, both the *Statesman* and the *Phaedrus* passages are genuine myths. They not only include supernatural elements but also require a certain suspension of disbelief, since the fantastic story they tell makes a doctrinal contribution to the theory that follows. In this respect they differ from the story of the Cave in the *Republic*, which is sometimes called a myth but is better described as an allegory. By contrast with a genuine myth, the Cave narrative is basically naturalistic, involving no supernatural elements, and making no claim on belief. The Cave story is a powerful illustration of progress up the Divided Line, but the epistemological theory of the *Republic* does not depend at all on this illustration. And there is no sense in which we are invited to believe that there were once prisoners strapped facing these shadows on the wall. In the *Phaedrus*, on the other hand, the prenatal vision of the Forms is required by the theory of love presented in that dialogue. Similarly, some aspect of the myth of the *Statesman* seems to be decisive for the correct definition of the *politikos*, as we shall see. In this case, however, it is not clear exactly how the myth is supposed to contribute to the following discussion of constitutional theory. That is the question I attempt to answer here.

The myth is introduced in response to a problem raised by the initial definition of the art of the Statesman at 267b–d, where this was specified as the knowledge of the nurture or rearing (*trophē*) of the two-footed flock of humans. The problem is that, unlike shepherds and cowherds who are unrivaled in their ability to care for their flocks, the Statesman is surrounded by a horde of competitors – from bakers to doctors – who claim to contribute to the nurture and maintenance of the human herd (267e–268b). Our definition will not be satisfactory until it separates the Statesman from these competitors. (These turn out to be only the first of a series of rivals who will be progressively eliminated in later stages of the definition.) The problem of the competitors is not directly solved by anything in the myth. On the contrary, when after completing the myth at 274e

---

[6] An earlier version of this essay was published in Kahn (2009) 148–56.

the Eleatic Stranger draws the moral from his long narrative, he scarcely mentions the problem of competitors that was supposed to be addressed. (He does mention it, but only in passing at 275b2–3.) Instead, he says that the myth will be useful by calling attention to two errors: a major error in offering a definition of the divine shepherd of the Age of Kronos instead of the human ruler of our own era; and a minor error in defining the Statesman as the ruler of the city without specifying the form of his rule (*ho tropos tēs archēs*, 275a8). The myth has apparently nothing to do with the second, strictly political error, which is mentioned again in the distinction between voluntary and coercive rule (at 276d11–e13). This defect in the initial definition – the failure to distinguish the true statesman from inferior forms of political rule – will be corrected much later, in the discussion of different constitutional forms that occupies the central section of the dialogue.

There is thus a curious discrepancy here, both before and after the myth, between what the Eleatic Stranger says about the function of the myth and what actually follows in the dialogue. It seems that these two secondary problems, the existence of competitors and the question of constitutional form, are mentioned here only as warnings that the definition reached so far is incomplete and will be discussed more fully in the sequel. The myth is directly concerned only with what is described as "the much greater and nobler mistake" of the original definition (274e7), namely, that it applies to the divine shepherd instead of the human ruler. It turns out that this mistake results from the error of taking the shepherd as the model (*paradeigma*) for the Statesman (275b–4).

But why did the Eleatic Stranger propose such a misleading definition in the first place? And why did he introduce such an extravagant cosmic myth in order to rectify this error? Is the error of taking the ruler as divine shepherd designed solely to motivate the myth, or is it of some independent interest? It will turn out that, in the case of the *Statesman*, an interpretation of the myth is inseparable from an interpretation of the dialogue as a whole.

Before attacking these larger questions let us look more closely at the myth and at the initial definition that it is supposed to correct.

2.1   The myth

The myth of the *Statesman* is an elaborate composition. Its ingredients include (1) stories from traditional mythology; (2) themes from Empedocles, in particular from his account of cosmic cycles; (3) parallels to the doctrine of reincarnation; (4) items from Plato's own cosmology as more fully expounded in the *Timaeus*; and (5) a brief account of the origins of civilization. There are also (6) fantastic examples of Plato's comic imagination, the most memorable of which is an account of the human life cycle going backwards, with grey hairs growing black and bearded cheeks becoming smooth again, while adolescents return to infancy. Leaving aside for the moment these comic elements, I briefly list the first five components of Plato's own cosmic cycle.

1. Plato establishes a mythical atmosphere for his story by beginning with a mention of three episodes from the poetic tradition: the temporary reversal of sun and stars in response to Thyestes' crime against Atreus, the Golden Age under Kronos as recounted by Hesiod, and the legend of men born from the earth. All three play an important role in Plato's own myth, but each has been given an entirely new meaning. In particular, Plato has transformed the temporary celestial reversal from the story of Atreus into a complete cosmic epoch, following Empedocles.

2. The Empedoclean parallel determines the general form of the myth. This parallel is obscured by a recent interpretation of the myth in terms of "a three-stage cycle, with the period of reversal sandwiched between the age of Kronos and that of Zeus."[7] The parallels to Empedocles point to a simpler, two-stage cycle, with a symmetrical movement back and forth between diametrically opposed situations. Thus, Empedocles fr. 17, verses 7–8: *allote men . . . allote de . . .* (repeated in fr. 20, 2–4) is twice echoed by Plato as *tote men . . . tote de . . .*, at *Statesman* 269c4–5 and again at 270a3–5. This strict symmetry rules out any distinction between the period of reversal and the age of Kronos. Notice that the modern controversy over the interpretation of Empedocles' cosmic cycle does not affect this dispute over Plato's cosmic periods. Scholars dispute whether or not there is more than one cosmogony in Empedocles, but all agree that (within cosmogony) there are two opposite cosmic movements back and forth between the poles of unity and plurality. This is precisely what Plato borrows from Empedocles, who was cited in the preceding dialogue as the Sicilian Muse, where his doctrine is reported in just this form: *tote men . . . tote de . . .* (*Sophist* 242e5–243a1).

---

[7] See Rowe (1995) 13, 188–97, with references there to a similar interpretation by Brisson (1995). As Grube noticed (1935: 278 n.), there is a slight incoherence in the mythic account of the godless period, between "two images, one of all life going into reverse, the other of a *gradual* departure from the ideal," as the world slowly forgets the instructions of the god (273b–c). The incoherence is real, but the attempt to remove it by a three-stage cycle introduces a remedy worse than the complaint.

There are other Empedoclean echoes in the myth, the most important of which is the description of the previous period as one of harmony between humans and beasts, without warfare or discord (271e1–2; compare Empedocles frs. 128 and 130).

3. Hints of the doctrine of reincarnation (as when the earthborn are said to "return to life" at 271b5–7) can be thought of as Empedoclean, but they also recall Plato's own presentation of similar doctrines, for example in the *Phaedrus*. Thus, the fixed period for rebirths at 272d6–e3 parallels the thousand-year cycles of transmigration in the *Phaedrus*; and both have their antecedent in the period of punishment for the *daimōn* in Empedocles fr. 115, 6. Presumably there is an older tradition, Pythagorean or Orphic, on which Empedocles and Plato are both drawing. This archaic tradition may also be the source for the idea that exceptional individuals may be liberated from the cycle of rebirth (271c2).

4. Even more systematic than the echoes of Empedocles are the myth's borrowing from Plato's own cosmology, to be more fully formulated in the *Timaeus*. Thus, we recognize at least half a dozen points in common between the *Statesman* myth and the *Timaeus*: the notion of the cosmos as an intelligent living creature constructed by a craftsman god (*dēmiourgos*), with innate circular movement as its best approximation to the unchanging stability of divine beings (269d–5); also a period of disorder preceding the creation of the cosmos (273b–5). These points shared with the *Timaeus* suggest that, at the moment of composing the *Sophist-Statesman*, Plato was already planning the outlines of his own cosmological scheme.[8]

There is another passage in the *Statesman* myth with a parallel in the *Timaeus*, namely, the great destruction caused by the cosmic reversals (270c11). In this case, however, the corresponding passage in the *Timaeus* belongs not to the cosmology proper but to the frame narrative, which describes cycles of destruction of mankind by fire and water (*Timaeus* 22c, echoed in *Critias* 112a and *Laws* 677a). Plato uses this same mythic theme for different purposes in different dialogues.

5. The myth concludes with a very brief and traditional account of *Kulturentstehungsgeschichte*: the gift of fire by Prometheus, the *technai* from Hephaistos and Athena, and so on (274c–d).

---

[8] Compare Rowe's commentary (1995: 188–90).

The richness of the *Statesman* myth derives from its drawing on so many diverse sources. But the central, most original idea is Plato's adaptation of Empedoclean cosmic reversals to paint a picture of the age of Kronos in which the conditions of human life are radically reversed. This reversal is represented symbolically in the picturesque account of old men melting back into the condition of babies. But the key philosophical point is that, since in the Golden Age the gods as caretakers were directly in charge of human life, human beings could live at ease in peace and natural abundance, with no need for the arts or *technai*, and also without families or political organizations – no *politeiai* (271e8). In this pre-political age, there was of course no need for *politikē*, the art of the statesman. It is thus ironical that the Eleatic Visitor's initial attempt to define the Statesman should turn out to be a mistake, because it described the divine shepherd of mankind in an earlier cosmic era, thus identifying "a god instead of a mortal" (275a2). The source of the mistake, as it turns out, was to look for the Statesman according to the model of a shepherd. On the other hand, the notion that the true statesman is more divine than human will turn out to play a positive role in later sections of the dialogue.

Clearly, then, the central point of the myth is the contrast drawn between the human statesman and the divine shepherd of the previous cycle, "so that we may see more plainly that person who alone, according to the *paradeigma* of shepherds and cowherds, having charge of human rearing, is the only one who deserves to be called by that title" (275b6, trans. after Rowe). The title in question is apparently "shepherd of the human herd," and the only person who deserves this title is the divine herdsman of the preceding era. Since our aim was to define the human statesman of the society we live in, this definition clearly led us in the wrong direction. It was precisely because of this error that the myth was needed as a corrective. The formal correction is made at 276d5 by the distinction drawn between the human caretaker and the divine shepherd. The Stranger insists that both types are to be investigated (275c6), but in fact the protective god of the age of Kronos is apparently ignored for the rest of the dialogue.

Why, then, was the initial definition formulated in such a way as to introduce this divine figure, and thus to require the correction of the cosmic myth? This was obviously a deliberate choice on Plato's part. But the question of his motivation cannot be answered from the text of the dialogue alone. Before attempting a meta-textual response, let us look at what the dialogue has to tell us about the human *politikos*. We will return later to the question of the divine shepherd. We begin with the initial definition of the Statesman that precedes the myth.

2.2 Definition of the Statesman

The dialogue opens with an attempt to define the Statesman by a set of divisions, according to the method analyzed in our earlier chapter.[9]

The art of the ruler is provisionally defined as the knowledge of giving orders on one's own authority (260e). This is a general definition of ruling, which applies to rule over a household or over slaves, as well as to political rule. (The political case will later be specified as "ruling over the whole city," 275a3). It is emphasized from the beginning, and repeated later, that this knowledge for giving political commands may be possessed by someone who does not serve as ruler, and that such a person is properly regarded as possessing *politikē* even if he does not exercise political rule (259a6, recalled at 292e10). It is natural to see here, in the claim of political expertise for someone not actually in power, Plato's reference to his own case.

Thus far, the initial definition does not involve a mistake. Trouble begins at 261b1, when the Stranger asks "Won't we find that all rulers who make use of commands will give orders *for the sake of something coming into being* (*geneseōs tinos heneka*)?" A few lines later this is reformulated as *genesis kai trophē* (at 261d2): the Statesman-King exercises his power of command for the "birth and rearing" of living things and, more precisely, for beings living in groups or herds. The ruler has now been classified with the shepherd, and the divisions that follow are all required in order to distinguish the human community ruled by the Statesman from the various animal herds. We end up with both a longer and a shorter definition of the King's herd: among land animals traveling by foot, he is responsible for the hornless, non-interbreeding bipeds, or (in the simpler version) for the featherless bipeds. Both formulations specify Statesmanship as *anthrōponomikē* "the art of herding humans" (266e8, 267c1).[10]

All of the Stranger's methodological ingenuity (from 261 to 267) has been expended on zoological classification, that is, on separating human beings from other animal herds. It is in this biological context that an important distinction is drawn between an arbitrary "part" or class (*morion*) marked off by any term and a natural kind or form (*genos, eidos*). It is essential to recognize that not every word in the language serves to cut nature at the joints. The problems that the myth picks up, however, relate not to this methodological point but to the discussion that precedes it.

---

[9] See above, Chapter Four, section 4b.   [10] For comic elements in this definition see above, p. 144.

The attempt to define the Statesman began with two assumptions. The first is that the Statesman and King (who are here treated as equivalent) are both defined by a certain form of knowledge, the art or science of ruling: that is, knowing how to give orders with authority. This epistemic assumption is never challenged, and it governs the entire dialogue. The second assumption is that this political art is to be understood by a parallel to the shepherd's skill in caring for his flock. It is this assumption, and more generally the use of the shepherd as paradigm, that will be challenged by the myth.

In drawing a lesson from the myth, the Stranger says that it will be useful for indicating two mistakes in the preceding definition. As we have seen, the much greater and nobler mistake was that "when asked for the king and statesman from the present rotation and generation, we described the shepherd of the human herd from the previous cycle, a god instead of a mortal!" This fundamental mistake is a consequence of seeking the Statesman after the wrong *paradeigma*, the shepherd (278b5); and later in the dialogue we will find a better model in the weaver. The shepherd is, after all, "a more divine creature, superior to the flocks he cares for" (271e6). Just as the human shepherd is superior to his sheep, so our rulers in the age of Kronos were superior to their human herd. (This is the lesson from the myth.) Hence, the divine herdsman of the previous cosmic cycle is "a greater figure than a king, while the statesmen of our present era are much more like their subjects in nature and have shared in a similar education and nurture" (275c1, trans. after Rowe). So when we return to a definition by division, the decisive cut will be to distinguish the divine herdsman from the human caretaker (276d5, echoing the distinction between divine and human *poiētikē* at *Sophist* 265b6). This cut requires us to replace the term "nurture" (*trophē*) with a more neutral term for "taking care of" (*epimeleia*) in order to identify a genus of social caretakers of which both divine shepherds and human rulers can be species (276d1). This change in terminology is a technical consequence of correcting the fundamental error, which consisted in taking the shepherd as paradigm for our definition of a political ruler.

Ultimately we will return to the meta-textual question, why Plato chose to begin his discussion of the Statesman with such a basic error, to be corrected by such an extravagent myth. Since the divine shepherd seems to disappear after this cut between divine and human rulers, why was he introduced in the first place? But first we must see what the text can tell us about the other half of the dichotomy, the human *politikos*.

2.3   The "politikos" and the "politeiai"

The Stranger mentioned as a secondary error of the initial definition the failure to specify the form of rule (*ho tropos tēs archēs*) by which the Statesman governs the city. As we have seen, he began to remedy this omission by a dichotomy between voluntary and enforced rule that permits him to distinguish between the king and the tyrant (276d–e). But this discussion of political institutions is immediately cut short, when the Young Socrates expresses his premature satisfaction for what he takes to be a completed definition (277a–1). The Stranger responds that the portrait of the Statesman has only been sketched in outline, and the details still need to be filled in. But instead of continuing with the political discussion, he initiates a new methodological account of the function of models (*paradeigmata*), illustrated in detail for the example of weaving. From now on, the weaver will replace the shepherd as paradigm for the eventual definition of the Statesman. In the meantime, however, the pursuit of this definition is left in suspense, while the digression continues with an extended discussion first of paradigms and then of measurement, including a distinction between two kinds of measurement.

The Stranger finally returns to the definition of the Statesman at 287b1, and promises to apply the model of the weaver (as he does in fact, only much later). Instead of returning to the analysis of constitutional structures, however, he first addresses the problem (mentioned before the myth, but confronted only now) of excluding competitors and resemblances from our account of the Statesman. The Stranger reports that we have already separated the Statesman from those who take care of other herds (287b). We now return to definition by division, distinguishing the Statesman from other factors concerned with the city, both as responsible causes (*aitia*) and as contributory causes or necessary conditions (*sunaitia*). It is only after clearing away both *sunaitia* and subordinates that we return to the political theme proper at 291a, with the recognition of another "very large crowd of people . . . a mixed tribe . . . some resembling lions and centaurs . . . and satyrs . . . [who] quickly change their shapes and capacity into one another." These strange creatures are, it turns out, the ordinary politicians of contemporary cities, the last set of rivals to be excluded from the definition of the Statesman.[11]

---

[11] There is one later set of potential rivals: the educators, generals, orators, and judges to be mentioned at 303d–305d. But these roles turn out to be not rivals but rather subordinate functions of the true statesman.

It is in this stage of the definition, where the usual competitors for the title of Statesman or King are to be be eliminated, that we reach the fundamental discussion of different political constitutions (*politeiai*). That discussion is concluded at 303d2, where (with the verbal repetition that marks ring composition) we say goodbye to "the band of centaurs and satyrs" who represent contemporary politicians and rulers.

This long discussion of constitutions or "forms of rule" "(*tropoi tēs archēs*), stretching from 291b to 303d, has as its centerpiece the argument for the superiority of rule by knowledge over rule by law. Plato first takes up the classification of *politeiai* into monarchy, aristocracy, and democracy (traditional since Herodotus) and crosses this with a new division between lawless and lawful constitutions. Of the six constitutional forms that result from this two-fold classification, a law-abiding monarchy is the best but tyranny or lawless monarchy is the worst. (Plato's judgment on tyranny has not changed since the *Republic*.) Democracy is the weakest of the three lawful forms, but it is the least bad of the lawless alternatives. All six of them are imperfect, however, and scarcely to be described as *politeiai* at all. In fact, their politicians are not so much statesmen (*politikoi*) as party hacks or "experts in faction" (*stasiastikoi*, 303c1). The only true constitution is one ruled by expert knowledge; the only true king or statesman is the one who possesses the relevant wisdom, which is the art or science of ruling over human beings (292d3).

The dialogue does not specify the content of this art of ruling. But since the wise ruler will pursue justice and make the city and the citizens better (297b1), he must know what justice is and he must know what is the good.[12] Only the city ruled by such wisdom has a true *politeia*; other cities possess only imitations of the genuine constitution, some better copies and some worse (293e, 297c–d, 300c4, 301b2). The better constitutions are all law-abiding. But despite the importance of legality as a criterion for judging constitutions, in the final analysis written laws cannot prevail over a wise ruler. Nothing in the human world deserves to prevail over knowledge.

The Eleatic Stranger expounds this thesis at length, in the most fully developed philosophical argument of the dialogue (293e–299e). Useful and even indispensable as written laws may be, they cannot have the right to restrain the action of a ruler equipped with genuine knowledge. Thus the rule of law is recognized as only a second best (297e–4, 300c–2). But

---

[12] Nothing is said here about Forms. As we have seen, the *Sophist-Statesman* generally avoid transcendental metaphysics. But this dialogue does once refer to incorporeal, divine entities that are not accessible to the senses (at 285e4–286a7).

arbitrary rule without knowledge is far worse (300a–b). Therefore a constitution without a wise ruler must preserve itself by imitating the true constitution (293e, 297c).

The notion of imitation serves here to connect the six types of empirical constitutions with the one true form, by recognizing the principle of legality (obedience to the laws, whatever they may be) as a second best. But this notion of imitation is applied here in several different ways that are not entirely consistent with one another. At one point it is suggested that imperfect constitutions "should use the written laws of the one correct constitution" (297d–6). But this is scarcely a practical suggestion, since we have no written copy of these laws. (Or could this be a forward reference to the future composition of the *Laws*?) In general, however, law-abiding constitutions will be better imitations (293e). Hence, it may be necessary to agree on a written law code in order to "follow on the tracks of the truest constitution" (301e–3). Established laws are based on experience and on the advice of persuasive counselors. When written as far as possible by those who have knowledge, these laws will be "imitations of the truth" (300b–c).

The notion here of imitating the best constitution by using its written law code may represent Plato's conception of his own legislative work in the *Laws*, as a (second best) imitation of the ideal form sketched in the *Republic*. The *Laws* would thus constitute the creation of a law code by a *politikos* with the necessary knowledge – namely, Plato himself. We recall that the Eleatic Stranger has insisted all along that someone with the appropriate form of knowledge is a true *basilikos*, whether he rules or not (292e9).[13] But in the absence of a true statesman, the second best solution will be the principle of legality: accepting the laws of the city as inviolable (297e1–5; 300c2–3).

Suppose, now, that the written laws are very bad. Does the second best solution allow for a city to improve its established laws? The Stranger mentions the possibility of persuasion here (296a). But, instead of developing the notion of imitation into a theory of political reform, he argues, first, that benevolent action by the rulers will be justified, even if it is done coercively without persuasion (296b–297b); and secondly, that the only alternative to rule by knowledge is obedience to the laws, whatever they are. The possibility of legal reform seems to be ignored, or identified with action contrary to law. Thus, the Stranger considers the case where an individual or a majority undertakes to act contrary to law "on the grounds that an alternative is better"; he describes them as attempting to imitate the true constitution. "If they do this without knowledge, they will imitate it very

[13] Compare Rowe (2000) 257 on the author of the *Laws* as an expert in legislation.

badly; but if they do so with knowledge, this is no longer imitation but the very truth itself" (300d4–e2). There seems to be no space here between the utopian rule of an expert and blind obedience to whatever laws are in force – no room in this dialogue (as there will be in the *Laws*) for a legal procedure of legal reform. Existing political institutions are described only with contempt, and anyone who participates in such rule is said to deserve whatever punishment he gets (299a7). The *Statesman* seems to have been written at a moment of complete political pessimism on Plato's part, reflecting, perhaps, his disastrous experience in Syracuse in 367 BC.

But can any human being possess the knowledge required for the true *politeia*? Or is every actual system a second best, while the preferred constitution is only a "model laid up in heaven," as Plato suggested in the *Republic*? Our dialogue is not unambiguous on this point. On the one hand, it insists that if political rulers are equipped with knowledge (*entechnoi*), what they do is not an imitation at all but "the very truth itself" (300e1). Hence, if a person with genuine knowledge rules alone, he is a true king and his city has the only true *politeia* (301b5–8). But the ordinary king will have at most true *doxa* (301b2). Furthermore, "human beings complain of this one ruler, and they doubt whether anyone will ever be able to rule with virtue and knowledge, so as to distribute justice and pious respect (*hosia*) to all" (301c–d). They fear, in fact, that a ruler with unchecked power will abuse and exploit his subjects as a tyrant does:

> But if there were to come to be someone of the kind we are describing, he would be accepted with affection and would govern in happiness the only strictly correct constitution . . . But as things stand, when, as we say, it is not the case that a king is born in the cities as a queen bee is born in the hive, immediately superior in body and psyche, it seems to be necessary for people to come together and write things down, pursuing the traces of the truest constitution. (301d4–e4, trans. after Rowe)

I take it that the contrast drawn here between the preferred constitution and "things as they stand" (*nun de*) means that, in the human world as we know it, there is no true *politeia*, but that we must be satisfied with imitations, some better and some worse, and the better ones will all include the rule of law. Hence, accepting the principle of legality is a necessary condition for the second best constitution.

Ever since the divine shepherd disappeared with the introduction of the myth, we have been pursuing an account of the human ruler, distinguishing him by successive divisions from the various rivals and pretenders, so as to isolate and define the true Statesman. The last set of pretenders, described as a crowd of centaurs and satyrs, turned out to be the dominant figures in the six actual constitutions. The only true constitution, and hence the only true Statesman and King, was the seventh case: the city ruled by genuine knowledge. But once the six ordinary constitutions and their leaders are rejected, the true Statesman disappears from the historical world of the polis, which is peopled only by its imitations. In the end, the true Statesman turns out to be not of this world. The seventh form is "separated from all the other constitutions, like a god separated from human beings" (303b4). This seems to be Plato's final theme in the *Statesman*, to be echoed by Aristotle in the *Politics*: the natural king, whose excellence is not comparable to that of all others, is "like a god among humans" (Aristotle *Pol.* 1284a10).

2.4   The meaning of the myth

Thus, there is a certain parallel, after all, between the true Statesman and the divine shepherd of the myth. Both are godlike rulers over mankind, but neither is present in the ordinary human world, the world of the polis. Of course, these two figures are not identical. In principle, at least, the Statesman rules over a city, and his rule is a model to be imitated in the *politeiai* of actual cities. The divine shepherd, on the other hand, is the caretaker for humans in a Golden Age, without a *polis* and hence without *politeiai*. But if we allow for a meaningful parallel between these two ideal rulers, we can understand a deeper motivation in the myth, and in the initial error that provoked the myth, by leading us to a divine ruler rather than to a human statesman. For now we can recognize the myth as a device for removing the ideal Statesman from the human world and relocating him in the mythical space of an alternative cosmic cycle. But to the extent that the divine ruler of the myth parallels the true Statesman, he remains relevant to the constitutions of our world. These constitutions must imitate the wisdom of his rule as best they can. These human institutions can only be second best, since no actual ruler has the wisdom of true *politikē*. Hence, the best compromise will be the rule of law. Law is the second sailing, the *deuteros plous* (300c2; cf. 297e4).

On this point the political philosophy of the *Statesman* prefigures that of the *Laws*. The city of the *Laws*, in which the rulers must be servants of the law, is repeatedly described as second best (*Laws* 739a, e, 807b, 875d). Thus, the *Laws* remains faithful to the central thesis of the *Statesman*. If a human being with appropriate knowledge could be trusted with absolute power there would be no reason to limit his power by law. Nothing deserves to be supreme over knowledge (*Laws* 874e–875d).

If the rule of law is only a second best, what is the first best? In the *Statesman* the preferred model is rule by knowledge, personified in the true Statesman or King. When we come to the *Laws*, the unavailable first choice would be the city of the *Republic*, the rule of philosopher-kings.[14] Since the second best is the same in each case, it is natural to assume some identity also between the two first choices: the wise Statesman and the philosopher-king. Of course the text of the *Statesman* will not directly support this identification. Since it avoids all metaphysical doctrine, our dialogue does not specify the cognitive content of Statesmanship beyond the knowledge required for giving commands to the city. But as we have seen, the Statesman must know something about justice and the good, if he is to "use justice to make the city better" (293d8; cf. 297b1–3). More specifically, his knowledge must cover the normative trio: the good, the just, and the noble (*agatha, dikaia, kala*, 295e, 296c). But nothing is said about training in mathematics or dialectical access to transcendent Forms. So we cannot simply identify the expertise of the *Statesman* with the epistemology and metaphysics of the *Republic*.[15] Leaving the question of content aside, however, and regarding only the practical application of philosophic knowledge, there is no reason to distinguish in principle between the cognitive competence of the true statesman and that of the philosopher-king.

Assuming some degree of equivalence between these two figures, we can see the *Statesman* and the *Laws* as representing essentially the same position in political theory. Despite their differences in other respects, both dialogues hold that the rule of a wise King, with a commitment to justice and a knowledge of what is good, is the best possible political solution. Furthermore, both agree that, since such a ruler is not actually available, the best compromise is a city rigorously ruled by law.

But although in this respect the two dialogues expound the same political philosophy, they do so from radically different points of view. In the *Statesman*, which is earlier, Plato apparently feels obliged to reassert the primacy of knowledge in the strongest possible terms, before embracing the second best, which is the rule of law. Written later, from a viewpoint that accepts without question the principle of legality, the *Laws* can express Plato's deep preference for the rule of philosophy only indirectly, as it were with nostalgia. The *Laws* is fully committed to the principle that it is laws

[14] That is the usual view, which I accept. See below for a discussion of Bobonich's rejection of this view.
[15] There is, however, a hint of this identity at *States.* 286a, in the reference to the Statesman's dialectical pursuit of the "greatest and most valuable things" that do not have sensible images.

rather than men that should rule, and that the supreme rulers should be servants of the law (715d). The whole constitution is designed to restrict the power of the magistrates. But it is only because of the weakness of human nature and the demoralizing influence of absolute power, that the principle of the philosopher-king must be abandoned (875a–d). In this regard the *Statesman* and the *Laws* are mirror images of one another. The former argues fiercely for the supremacy of knowledge, and accepts legality only as a compromise. The latter trumpets the rule of law and mentions the deep preference for knowledge only as an aside.

The *Statesman* is rightly seen as a transitional dialogue, in which Plato is moving from the position of the *Republic* to the position of the *Laws*. For Plato this move was of monumental importance, and he has symbolized it in the cosmic myth. If we see the myth as locating the ideal ruler in a mythical age of Kronos, we can answer our original question: why does this dialogue begin with a "mistake" that would identify the Statesman with this divine figure in a mythic Golden Age? We can now answer: because that is where the philosopher-king of the *Republic* has been relocated.

My interpretation of the myth implies that, at some level of meaning, the divine shepherd of the Golden Age stands both for the true Statesman and also for the philosopher-king. This reading is confirmed by the application that Plato himself gives of this myth in *Laws* IV, where he establishes the principle of legality on the basis of a lesson from the age of Kronos:

> It is said that in the time of Kronos there was a very happy rule (*archē*), of which the best of present governments possesses an imitation (*mimēma*) . . . This was a blessed life, with a spontaneous abundance of everything. The cause is said to be the following. Since Kronos recognized that no human nature was adequate to govern human affairs with unlimited authority (*autokratōr*) without becoming filled with injustice and crime, he established as rulers of our cities not human beings but members of a better and more godlike race of divinities (*daimones*) . . . And even now this tale says truly that for cities ruled not by a god but by a mortal there is no escape from evils and suffering. It holds that we must by all means imitate the life that is called the age of Kronos, ruling our households and our cities in obedience to what we possess of immortality, giving the name of law (*nomos*) to the dispensation of reason (*hē tou nou dianomē*). (*Laws* IV, 713b–714a)

This text from the *Laws* is remarkable in that the best human constitution is here said to imitate not the rule of the ideal Statesman, as in our dialogue, but that of the divine shepherd of the Age of Kronos, in a myth recalling the myth of the *Statesman* (but without cosmic reversals and the absence of *politeiai*). Plato thus confirms the interpretation I have suggested, according to which the myth of the *Statesman* serves to relocate the perfect ruler as a divine figure in an ideal space.

In the myth of the *Laws*, as in the doctrine of the *Statesman*, the ideal ruler serves as a model for human imitation, and in both cases the best imitation is a city ruled by law. What is new in this passage from *Laws* IV is the conception of law as the rule of reason (*nous*). This is Plato's way of resolving the tension between law and knowledge that was the focus of his concern in the *Statesman*. The rule of law is still second best, but it is now seen as an expression of the rule of reason, and hence of knowledge. There is also a hint here of the messianic politics of the *Republic*. The "escape from evils and suffering," which calls for divine rule according to the passage just cited from the *Laws*, echoes the "cessation of evils (*kakōn paula*) for the cities of mankind" that had been promised for the reign of philosopher-kings (*Rep.* V, 473d5). But in the *Laws* it is only the second best, the rule of law, that is actually proposed as the necessary condition for a happy public life.

The concern for the rule of law, which is so prominent in these two late dialogues, is not a new theme in Plato's work. Socrates' refusal to escape from prison was explained in the *Crito* by an appeal to the principle of legality, the fundamental law which ordains that judgments of the law courts must be carried out (50b); and Socrates' argument in the *Crito* is put in the mouth of the personified Laws. The *Republic* as a whole is conceived as a work of legislation, where the laws of education, marriage, and property form the backbone of the system. Nevertheless, such laws are ultimately an instrument in the hands of the philosopher-king, whose claim to authority (as Sabine noted) lies not in any legal provision but in "the fact that he alone knows what is good for men and states."[16]

The argument of the *Statesman* makes clear how difficult it was for Plato to propose subjecting such a sovereign to any system of written rules. However, at some point in his life, perhaps as a result of bitter experience in Sicily but also out of his desire to have a practical effect on Greek legislation, Plato's theoretic concern began to shift from messianic politics to a project of legislative reform. This change is reflected in the gigantic undertaking that produced the detailed law code of the *Laws*. In the *Statesman* we see Plato still wrestling with the fundamental commitment to the rule of law that will be required as philosophical justification for his final project of legislation. The myth of our dialogue, with the ideal Statesman located "by mistake" in a mythical past, can be seen as a mark

---

[16] Sabine (1961) 68.

of this struggle. When he writes the *Laws*, Plato has made his peace with the second best solution, and he can regard this compromise as the decision of wisdom. Shortly after the passage quoted from *Laws* IV, the Athenian Stranger restates his view that a city will prosper only when "the law is master of the rulers, and the rulers are slaves of the law." The interlocutor remarks that the Stranger's vision is acute; and the latter responds: "Everyone sees these matters more dimly in youth, but more keenly in old age" (715e1). This seems to be Plato's own comment on the shift in his political philosophy, from the *Republic* to the *Laws*.[17]

I have argued here for a reading of the myth that is not new, but one that has not always been fully appreciated. The central point was recognized, for example, by Grube: "the philosopher-king of the *Republic*, endowed with perfect knowledge . . . is now relegated to a mythical past and an equally mythical future."[18] The parallel between the divine shepherd of the *Statesman* and the rule of the Guardians in the *Republic* has often been drawn.[19] The fullest discussion of the theoretical issues is by Sabine, who correctly saw that, in the *Statesman*, the state of the *Republic* is "definitely relegated to its place as a 'model fixed in the Heavens' for human imitation but not for attainment."[20]

Plato's preference for the city ruled by law has become more uncon-ditional. But the notion of imitation serves, both in the *Statesman* and in the *Laws*, to bind this second best solution to the original vision of the *Republic*. The wisdom of old age has brought Plato to a more acute sense of the dangers of unchecked power, and hence to a more profound appreciation of the rule of law, but not to the point of abandoning his philosophic principles! If the law deserves to reign supreme, it can only do so as the embodiment of reason.

3   On the first best constitution in the *Laws*

On three occasions in the *Laws* the Athenian Stranger refers to the legis-lative project he is developing as a second best.

---

[17] Compare *Laws* 691b where a similar insight is said to be not difficult to recognize now, with the hindsight of history, "but if anyone could have foreseen it then [in prehistoric Dorian times] he would have been wiser than us."
[18] Grube (1935) 279.   [19] See e.g. Ostwald (1992) xvii.
[20] Sabine (1961) 74. Sabine's account is mistaken in only one respect. What is missing from the *Republic* is not law as such but the principle of legal supremacy over the action of the rulers. Sabine's error was corrected by his student, Glenn Morrow, discussing Plato's "later view that no human being can be trusted with irresponsible power . . . It is here, rather than in a belated recognition of the importance of law, that the difference between the *Laws* and the *Republic* is to be found." See Morrow (1960) 583.

1. The first such reference comes in Book V, 739a, at the very beginning of the legislation, after the long initial prelude on religion and moral character. In giving advice to a legislator, says the Stranger, one should describe the best constitution and the second and the third, and allow the law-maker to choose between them. He proceeds then to declare that "the first city and constitution and the best laws" is one in which the whole city is organized according to the old proverb *koina ta philōn*, "friends have everything in common": common wives, common children, common property. This should remain the model constitution (*paradeigma*), whether it exists or ever will, inhabited either by gods or by children of gods (739c–d). "The constitution we are engaged in will, if it occurs, be very near to immortality and second in honor" (739e). What follows is the distribution of land and houses according to a principle of equality.

2. In Book VII, 807b, we have what is in effect a reminder of this preference for universal sharing. After a description of the extent to which women will share the activities of men, including access to their own common messes, the Stranger adds that the way of life he is describing will probably not be fully achieved as long as wives and children and houses remain private. "But if we could have the second arrangement after this, which we are now describing, that would be quite satisfactory (*mala metriōs*)" (807c1).

3. In Book IX, 875d, the current legislation is described as second best for an entirely different reason. The issue here is not private versus communal possession in family and economic matters, but rather the central political question debated in the *Statesman*, namely, the supremacy of law over the ruler with knowledge. And the respect in which the constitution of the *Laws* is inferior here is in fact identical with the reason why the *Statesman* describes the principle of legality as second best (297e4, 300c2): because, for both dialogues, the ideal constitution would be a ruler with complete knowledge.[21]

It has generally been assumed that these passages in the *Laws* are referring to the city of the *Republic* as the best constitution. For example, Wilamowitz comments on the first passage (739a–b) as follows: "Plato describes the constitution that he previously outlined as the unique, enduring model, which one should approximate as far as possible. The

---

[21] Rowe (2000) 256 would distinguish the second best in the *Statesman* from that in the *Laws*, since the former refers simply to "the principle of strict adherence to law." But this principle also applies in the *Laws*, and in both cases the contrast is to unrestricted rule by a monarch with expertise.

constitution that he outlines in the *Laws* does this, and is thus the one true constitution in a second way. But it is also only an outline, and its realization will require more compromise. The resulting state will thus be the third."[22]

It would be easy to cite other scholars who assume that these references in the *Laws* to a second best constitution presuppose the constitution of the *Republic* as the unconditionally best.[23] This way of understanding these references has recently been challenged by Christopher Bobonich. He discusses only the first of these passages, and claims that it "presents as the first best city, not that of the *Republic*, but one in which there is, throughout the entire city, a community of property and of women and children."[24]

It is true that the text of the *Laws* at 739c1, in applying the principle of communal ownership to all the city (*kata pasa tēn polin*), ignores the class structure of the *Republic* and the limitation of this principle to the two upper classes. And the tripartite class structure is precisely one of the features of the model that the constitution of the *Laws* does not attempt to imitate. But this is scarcely a reason to suppose that Plato has some quite different, classless paradigm in mind as first best. On the contrary, the rationale given here for communal property and communal families, with the emphasis on unity as the supreme criterion (*horos*) for excellence in the city (739d5), is exactly the same as in *Republic* V, 462–64.

Passages (1) and (2) above refer to the first two waves of paradox in *Republic* V: the equality of women and the community of property and children. Passage (3) implies a reference to the third wave, the rule of philosopher-kings, which is reasserted here in the principle that "neither law nor any order is superior to knowledge, nor is it allowed for reason (*nous*) to be subject or slave to anything, but it must rule over all" (875c6).

The constitution of the *Laws* is second best, precisely because it must compromise on all three waves of paradox, that is to say, on the three strongest, most controversial theses of the *Republic*. Thus in relation to the three passages where a second best is mentioned in the *Laws*, and to the two similar passages in the *Statesman*, the *Republic* is in every case the natural point of comparison. Why is there any reason to doubt, then, what Plato had in mind as the model for his first best constitution?

---

[22] Wilamowitz-Moellendorff (1948) 521 n. 1.   [23] See e.g. Laks (2000) 269.   [24] Bobonich (2002) 11.

Bibliography

Allen, R.E. (ed.) (1965) *Studies in Plato's Metaphysics*, London
    (1997) *Plato's "Parmenides,"* revised edn., New Haven
Annas, J. and Rowe, C. (2002) *New Perspectives on Plato, Modern and Ancient*,
    Harvard University Press
Barker, A. (2000) "Timaeus on Music and the Liver" in M.R. Wright (ed.), *Reason*
    and Necessity: Essays on Plato's 'Timaeus', Duckworth, 85–99
Bobonich, C. (2002) *Plato's Utopia Recast*, Oxford
Brisson, L. (1995) "Interpretation du mythe du Politique," in Rowe and Schofield
    (2000)
    (2002) "'Is the World One?' A New Interpretation of Plato's *Parmenides*,"
    Oxford Studies in Ancient Philosophy 22, 1–20
Burnet, J. (1900–7) *Platonis Opera*, 5 vols., Oxford
Burnyeat, M. (1976) "Plato on the Grammar of Perceiving," *Classical Quarterly* 26,
    29–51
    (1982) "Idealism and Greek Philosophy," *Philosophical Review* 91, 3–40
    (1990) *The "Theaetetus" of Plato*, Indianapolis, Hackett
    (2002) "Plato on How Not to Speak of What is Not: *Euthydemus* 283a–288a" in
    Canto-Sperber and Pellegrin (2002) 40–66
Caizzi-Decleva, F. (1966) *Antisthenis Fragmenta*, Milan
Canto-Sperber, M. and Pellegrin, P. (eds.) (2002) *Le Style de la Pensée. Recueil de*
    texts en hommage à Jacques Brunschwig, Paris, Les Belles Lettres
Cherniss, H. (1932) "Parmenides and the *Parmenides* of Plato," *American Journal of*
    Philology 53, 122–38
    (1944) *Aristotle's Criticism of Plato and the Academy*, Baltimore
Cooper, J. (1970) "Plato on Sense-Perception and Knowledge (*Theaetetus*
    184–186)," *Phronesis* 15, 123–46
    (1999) *Reason and Emotion: Essays on Ancient Moral Psychology and Ethical*
    Theory, Princeton University Press
Cornford, F.M. (1934/1957) *Plato's Theory of Knowledge*, Indianapolis, Bobbs-
    Merrill
    (1937) *Plato's Cosmology*, Routledge and Kegan Paul, London
    (1939) *Plato and Parmenides*, London
Diels, H. and Kranz, W. (1952) *Die Fragmente der Vorsokratiker*, 3 vols., 6th edn.,
    Berlin

Fine, G. (1993) *On Ideas: Aristotle's Criticism of Plato's Theory of Forms*, Oxford
Frede, D. (1993) *Plato. "Philebus,"* Indianapolis/Cambridge, Hackett
Frede, M. (1967) "Prädikation und Existenzaussage," *Hypomnemata* 18, Göttingen
    (1992) "Plato's *Sophist* on False Statements" in *Kraut* (1992) 397–424
Gill, M.L. (1996) "Introduction" in Gill and Ryan (1996) 1–109
Gill, M.L. and Ryan, P. (1996) *Plato. "Parmenides,"* Indianapolis
Grube, G.M.A. (1935) *Plato's Thought*, London, Methuen
Harte, V. (2002) *Plato on Parts and Wholes: The Metaphysics of Structure*, Oxford
Heath, T.L. (1921) *A History of Greek Mathematics*, Oxford, Clarendon
Heinamen, R. (1997) "Plato: Metaphysics and Epistemology" in Taylor (1997)
    356–93
Henry, P. and Schwyzer, H. (1973) *Plotini Opera*, 3 vols., Leiden
Huffman, C.A. (1993) *Philolaus of Croton: Pythagorean and Presocratic*, Cambridge
Johansen, T.K. (2004) *Plato's Natural Philosophy*, Cambridge
Kahn, C.H. (1960) *Anaximander and the Origins of Greek Cosmology*, Columbia
    (1981) "Some Philosophical Uses of 'To Be' in Plato," *Phronesis* 26, 105–34
    (1985) "Democritus and the Origins of Moral Psychology," *American Journal of*
    Philology 106, 1–31
    (1996) *Plato and the Socratic Dialogue*, Cambridge
    (2002a) "On Platonic Chronology" in Annas and Rowe (2002) 93–128
    (2002b) "Flux and Forms in the *Timaeus*" in Canto-Sperber and Pellegrin
    (2002) 113–31
    (2003) *The Verb "Be" in Ancient Greek*, Indianapolis, Hackett (reprint of 1973 edn)
    (2004) "A Return to the Theory of the Verb 'Be' and the Concept of Being,"
    Ancient Philosophy 24, 381–405
    (2005) "Aristotle versus Descartes on the Concept of the Mental," in R. Salles
    (ed.), *Metaphysics, Soul, and Ethics in Ancient Thought. Themes from the Work*
    of Richard Sorabji, Oxford University Press
    (2007) "Why is the *Sophist* a Sequel to the *Theaetetus*?," *Phronesis* 52, 33–57
    (2009) *Essays on Being*, Oxford
Keyt, D. (1971) "The Mad Craftsman of the *Timaeus*," *Philosophical Review* 80,
    230–35
Kirk, G.S., Raven, J.E., and Schofield, M. (1983) *The Presocratic Philosophers: A*
    Critical History with a Selection of Texts, Cambridge
Kock, T. (1884) *Comicorum Atticorum fragmenta* vol. 2, Leipzig, Teubner
Kraut, R. (ed.) (1992) *The Cambridge Companion to Plato*, Cambridge
Laks, A. (2000) "The *Laws*" in C. Rowe and M. Schofield (eds.), *The Cambridge*
    History of Greek and Roman Political Thought, Cambridge
Lennox, J.G. (2001) "Plato's Unnatural Teleology" in *Studies in the Origins of Life*
    Science, Cambridge University Press
McDowell, J. (1973) *Plato "Theaetetus,"* Oxford
Meinwald, C. (1991) *Plato's "Parmenides,"* Oxford
    (1992) "Good-bye to the Third Man" in Kraut (1992) 365–96
Menn, S. (1995) *Plato on God as Nous*, Carbondale, Southern Illinois University
    Press

Morrow, G.R. (1960) *Plato's Cretan City*, Princeton University Press
    (1970) "Plato and the Mathematicians: An Interpretation of Socrates' Dream in
    the *Theaetetus*," *Philosophical Review* 79, 309–33
Mueller, I. (1983) "*Parmenides* 133a–134e: Some Suggestions," *Ancient Philosophy* 3,
    3–7
Nehamas, A. (1979) "Self-Predication and Plato's Theory of Forms," *American
    Philosophical Quarterly* 16, reprinted in Nehamas (1999) 176–95
    (1982) "Participation and Predication in Plato's Later Thought," *Review of
    Metaphysics* 36, reprinted in Nehamas (1999) 196–223
    (1999) *Virtues of Authenticity*, Princeton University Press
Ostwald, M. (1992) *Plato: Statesman*, J.B. Skemp (trans.), Indianapolis, Hackett
Owen, G.E.L. (1957) "A Proof in the ΠΕΡΙ ΙΔΕШΝ," *Journal of Hellenic Studies* 77,
    103–11
    (1970) "Notes on Ryle's Plato" in Wood and Pitcher (1970) 341–72
Palmer, J. (1999) *Plato's Reception of Parmenides*, Oxford
Patterson, R. (1985) *Image and Reality in Plato's "Metaphysics,"* Indianapolis
Peterson, S. (1973) "A Reasonable Self-Predication Premise for the Third Man
    Argument," *Philosophical Review* 82, 451–70
    (1981) "The Greatest Difficulty for Plato's Theory of Forms: The Unknowability
    Argument of *Parmenides* 133c–134c," *Archiv für Geschichte der Philosophie* 63,
    1–16
    (1996) "Plato's *Parmenides*: A Principle of Interpretation and Seven Arguments,"
    Journal of the History of Philosophy 34, 167–92
Rickless, S.C. (2007) *Plato's Forms in Transition. A Reading of the "Parmenides,"*
    Cambridge University Press
Robinson, R. (1953) *Plato's Earlier Dialectic*, 2nd edn., Oxford
Ross, W.D. (1924) *Aristotle's "Metaphysics,"* 2 vols., Oxford
Rowe, C.J. (trans.) (1995) *Plato. "Statesman,"* Aris & Phillips
Rowe, C.J. in Rowe, C.J. and Schofield, M. (eds.) (2000) *The Cambridge History of
    Greek and Roman Political Thought*, Cambridge University Press
Ruijgh, C.J. (1979) "A Review of: C.H. Kahn, *The Verb 'Be' in Ancient Greek*,"
    Lingua 48, 43–83
Sabine, G.H. (1961) *A History of Political Theory*, 3rd edn., New York
Sayre, K. (1996) *Parmenides' Lesson*, Notre Dame
Sedley, D. (1998) "Platonic Causes," *Phronesis* 43, 114–32
    (2004) *The Midwife of Platonism: Text and Subtext in Plato's "Theaetetus,"*
    Oxford, Clarendon Press
    (2007) *Creationism and its Critics in Antiquity*, University of California Press
Strang, C. (1963) "Plato and the Third Man," *Proceedings of the Aristotelian Society,
    Supplementary* vol. no. 37, reprinted in Vlastos (1971) 184–200
Striker, G. (1970) *Peras und Apeiron: Das Problem der Formen in Platons Philebos*,
    Vandehoeck & Ruprecht
Taylor, A.E. (1934) *The "Parmenides" of Plato*, Oxford
Taylor, C.C.W. (ed.) (1997) *Routledge History of Philosophy*, vol. I, *From the
    Beginning to Plato*, London

Vlastos, G. (1954) "The Third Man Argument in the *Parmenides*," reprinted in
    Allen (1965) 231–63
    (1996) "Creation in the *Timaeus*: Is it a Fiction?" in *Studies in Greek Philosophy*,
    vol. II, 265–79
Vlastos, G. (ed.) (1971) *Plato: A Collection of Critical Essays*, vol. I, New York
Wilamowitz-Moellendorff, U. von (1948) *Platon*, Berlin/Frankfurt, Weidmannsche
    Verlag
Wood, O. and Pitcher, G. (eds.) (1970) *Ryle: A Collection of Critical Essays*, Garden
    City
Zeyl, D.J. (1975) "Plato and Talk of a World in Flux," *Harvard Studies in Classical
    Philology* 79, 125–48
    (2000) *Plato "Timaeus,"* Hackett

Index

Aeschines 55
Allen, R. E. 19
alphabet, as exemplar of Forms theory 78–82, 85,
    113–14, 153–56, 173
    invention 153–54
    relationship with naming 133
    see also "vowel forms"
ananke see Necessity
Anaxagoras 7, 98, 138, 158, 161, 162, 166, 167, 179,
    200, 211
Anaximander 161–62, 165
angler, definitions of 140
animals, humans distinguished from 225
Antisthenes 77, 109, 110, 160–61
apeiron, concept of 151–52, 154–55
Apology 84
appearance(s)
    focus on 37–38
    of plurality 38
Aristophanes, *Clouds* 210
Aristotle 5, 10, 11, 15, 17, 35, 42, 74, 80, 96, 193, 210,
    214, 216
    Categories 72
    De Anima 63
    De Interpretatione 71, 125
    Metaphysics 54, 218
    Physics 18, 82, 186
    Politics 231
    Posterior Analytics 82
    Rhetoric 55
    commentary on Plato 164, 173, 200, 205
    cosmology 167, 186, 199
    prefiguration by Plato 109, 169–70, 191, 194,
        198, 205, 219
    treatment of cognition 61–62, 63, 142
    treatment of plurality 26, 28
    works on zoology 139, 194
artifacts, place in Forms theory 175
astronomy 217–18
atheism, arguments against *see* God(s), proofs of
    existence

Athenian Stranger, figure of 215, 235–37
atomism 179, 208–09, 211–12
    contrasted with Platonism 212–13
Augustine of Hippo, St. 178

Barker, Andrew 199, 209
Beauty/the Beautiful, conceptions of 9–10, 137,
    148, 187, 200–1
Becoming
    and creation narrative 178, 185–89
    pre-cosmic 202
    relationship with Being *see* Being
    role in Forms theory 106
    role in Platonic cosmology 164, 174–75
    two stages of 189
Being 66–68, 98–99, 103–12, 147
    as attribute of the One 40
    attributes of 23, 25
    contradictory aspects 118–19
    distinguished from Different 116–17
    grammatical basis 97
    linguistic/grammatical basis 97, 102
    non-ascription to the One 32, 34–35
    place in hierarchy of Forms 113, 114–19
    positive conclusions 107
    pre-Platonic theories, survey of 103–7
    presence on list of *koina* 64, 66–67
    relationship with Becoming 50–51, 74, 169,
        175, 180
    relationship with Motion/Rest 107–8,
        110–11, 116
    relationship with truth/falsehood 127–28
    role in Platonic cosmology 174
    three kinds of 191
    see also einai; Not-Being
"bird-cage" model (of mind) 74–76
blood, (perceived) role in thought
    processes 210
Bobonich, Christopher 237
bodily organs, role in mental perception 199,
    209–11

242

Printed in the United States
By Bookmasters